Reflections of the Badlands:

A HISTORY OF IT'S PEOPLE

by
Philip S. Hall

With a foreword by
Paul Higbee

Reflections of the Badlands
Revised and Expanded Edition
© 2008 by Philip S. Hall

All Rights Reserved

This work may not be used in any form,
or reproduced by any means,
in whole or in part,
without written permission
from the publisher.

ISBN: 978-1-57579-384-9

Library of Congress Control Number: 2008935663

Cover Photo by Author

Index Prepared by Gilbert French

Book price: $ 19.95

First Printing 1993
Second Printing 1994
Third Printing (Revised Edition) 1997
Fourth Printing (Revised and Expanded) 2008

Printed on Acid-free paper

Printed in the United States of America

PINE HILL PRESS
4000 West 57th Street
Sioux Falls, SD 57106

To

Monte & Martha

Two of the finest people
to call the Badlands home.

Table of Contents

Preface vii
Acknowledgments ix
Foreword xi

    Chapter 1:   Vast, Mysterious and Unknown 1
    Chapter 2:   The Bone Diggers 13
    Chapter 3:   The Promoters' Trail 27
    Chapter 4:   In Quest of Gold 49
    Chapter 5:   The Last Cowboy and Indian War 59
    Chapter 6:   The First Family of the Badlands 79
    Chapter 7:   Missouri John Massengale and the 15 Ranch 91
    Chapter 8:   George Porch 123
    Chapter 9:   Denizens of the Badlands: 1890–1896 153
    Chapter 10:   The Last Years of the Open Range 187
    Chapter 11:   Starvation Claims 201
    Chapter 12:   Big Leases, Big Celebrations, and Big Busts 227

Epilogue 241
Chapter Notes 243
Bibliography 259
Index 266

List of Photos

1876 map of western South Dakota xiv
South Dakota Badlands, c. 1895. 1
South Dakota Badlands – Showing School of Mines Canyon 5
South Dakota Badlands 9
South Dakota Badlands 12
De Girardin's sketch of the Evans party in the Badlands 13
De Girardin's drawing of Badlands 17
Wagon Train... 27
Map of Chamberlain-Rapid City freight trail 28
Charley Collins... 30
The Town of Chamberlain about 1881 37
Rapid City around 1883 39
John Brennan 40
Fred Evans 42
Bull train 43
Steamboat landing at Fort Pierre 45
South Dakota Badlands 49
Soldiers and government officials at Pine Ridge, 1890............... 63
Brook's Camp on the Pine Ridge Reservation 62
Richard F. Pettigrew 61
Short Bull 64
Wounded Knee Battlefield, December 30, 1890...................... 77
Indian Chiefs and officials at Pine Ridge, 1891...................... 78
The Ludvig and Margaret Johnson family.............................. 79
Oliver and Mary Johnson... 82
Wallace Wells and Emma Johnson Wells 83
Guy Trimble 84
Guy Trimble ranch, 1894... 85
Interior around 1890 87
Hauling wool to Gordon, Nebraska...................................... 88
Miller – sheepherder for Oliver Johnson 89
John Massengale 91
The 15 Ranch in 1894 99
Getting ready to ride: 15 Ranch... 108
Dude Rounds and Ranch Hand 109

Pontoon bridge at Chamberlain	110
Gray Wolf in Badlands in 1917	112
Charley Thompson 1894	114
Portrait of George Porch	123
Turner family	154
Ab and Rose Porch	158
The Warren Young Ranch	162
John and Ellen Farnham	163
John and Ellen Farnham and grandchildren	164
Bessie Farnham Trimble	166
Guy Trimble and family	166
Nellie Farnham Gallagher	167
Charley Gallagher	167
Ben Tibbetts	168
Emily Janis Tibbetts	170
Lunch at the 6L Ranch	171
Henry and Annie Lange	172
The Bale family	176
Map of settlers in the east half of Badlands: 1890–1896	182
Map of settlers in the west half of the Badlands: 1890–1896	183
Frank Turner	187
Corb Morse	190
Craven's Open Buckle Ranch	193
Branding a calf on spring roundup	194
Roundup scene on the Cheyenne River	196
"Farm" in the Badlands	201
Recluse	205
First school in Kadoka	208
Pettyjohn railroad track crew	209
First train penetrating the Badlands	210
Johnson brother's store	214
James Smalley general store	214
Main Street, Conata, 1910	217
Bud Dalrymple	220
Hynes mansion	222
Hynes family	224
Mowing hay on Sheep Table	229
Hay slide off of Sheep Table	230
Traveling the Badlands by car	231
Frank Hart	234
Interior in 1920	239

Preface

This book was written for the traveler who wanders into these mysterious lands and, where others see only bleak barrenness, finds spellbinding beauty. I welcome these kindred spirits and pay them homage by sharing the understanding and knowledge of this land that time and heritage have graciously afforded me.

However, the book belongs to the people who call the Badlands home. Almost without exception, they are the progeny of individuals who tamed this tough region. I am proud to have cast their history into words and flattered that they shared with me their time, hospitality, and heritage.

Philip S. Hall
Vermillion, South Dakota
1993

Preface to the 4th Edition

When I told someone that I was writing a fourth edition to correct some inaccuracies about some of the people in the book, he replied, "Why bother? They're dead and gone. No one will know the difference."

To a historian it matters. We spend thousands of hours squinting at blurry microfilm, searching historical archives, and turning over every rock that might reveal even the smallest tidbit. When we finally put words on paper, we want to "get it right." But far too often there is unknown or undiscovered information that would appreciably enhance or even alter the story. This fourth edition is a case in point.

When I was researching the book in 1975, I was told that there existed an unpublished manuscript about George Porch, a legendary if not down right infamous Badland character. But every effort I made to find the manuscript came to a dead end. Well, the manuscript surfaced in 2001. It was George Porch's 586 page autobiography as dictated to Nora Steele, the editor and publisher of the Kadoka Index in the 1930s. Stanley Porch and his niece Peggy (Porch) Schoon alerted me of the find and graciously shared it with me. I also drove to Macon, Missouri to visit with direct descendants of Jefferson Morrow. They welcomed me into their home and shared their extensively documented family history. Nancy Anderson, curator of the Hanna Basin Historical Society, and Dan Kinnaman, preeminent Rawlins historian, provided key information about Massengale's life in Wyoming. Finally, Penny and Jerry Thompson shared results of the considerable historical research they had done on Charley Thompson, Jerry's great-grandfather. Without this new information the history of the Badlands would not be complete.

Philip S. Hall
Spearfish, South Dakota
June 15, 2008

Acknowledgments

This book was inspired by the "old-timers" of the Badlands. Over the past two decades, I interviewed such Badland denizens as Bill Norman, Otto Prokop, Mary Porch Borberly, Hallie Young, Eloise Brown, Bryon Bradfield, A.E. "Doll" Johnson, Fern Johnson, George Carlbom, Mrs. Henry Thompson, Tony Kudrna, Clarence Jurisch, "Goldie" Jurisch, Mrs. Frank Stangle, Peg "Dakota" Jurisch, Harvey Bell, Arnold "Buzz" Benson, Virgil Post, Louie Blummer, Lloyd Thompson, and Robert Yoast. The stories and information that each of these people shared significantly enriched this book. To a person they said, "I sure want to read your book when it is finished." Well, the book is finally done. Unfortunately, all of these old-timers are now part of the Badlands. I regret being unable to share this book with so many who contributed so much to its spirit and its substance.

I want to thank David Kemp for information about material in various archives around the state, Arnold "Buzz" Benson for loaning me several rare books about local history, Jim Scribbins and Dr. Paul Woekman for their assistance in accessing archival material about the Milwaukee Railroad that was in the Milwaukee Public Library, Dr. Willis Stanage for doing some primary source research about Captain John Daugherty, Dr. Herbert T. Hoover for general historical advice, Professor Don Hofsomer for assistance with locating archival material, Joe Zarki and Val Naylor for assistance in reviewing the archival material at the Badlands National Park, Leonel Jensen for providing resource material and proofing one chapter for historical accuracy, Ted Hamilton for assistance with reviewing the archival information at Oglala Community College, Sister Celine Erk for assistance with reviewing archival material at the Catholic Diocese for Rapid City, Muriel Kjos for assistance with the collection of primary resource material, the late Mary Peterson for sharing unpublished material about the Ludvig Johnson family, Marvin Bale for sharing unpublished material about the Bale family, Peg Hynes Jurisch for an unpublished history of Sheep Table and the Mary Hynes family, and Ann Zeitzig for providing information about the history of Conata and the E.B. Yoast family.

Finally and especially, I thank my wife Nancy for her unwavering moral and financial support of this unconscionably long project. Who else has a wife who only smiled when, with the regularity of spring, her husband came home from work to announce that he had quit his job that day because the crocus had bloomed and it was time to go wandering in the Badlands, get lost in libraries, and go looking for old-timers who had stories to tell. Obviously, without her support this book would not have been written.

Foreword

My boots don't make a mark on the grey hardpan as I hike off Castle Trail looking for a spot I remember above Cedar Pass. I haven't seen another person all day. It's May, summertime warm in the Badlands, and I'm alert for snakes as I pass through a clump of buffalo grass. But the eyes in the grass belong to a young jackrabbit, more curious than startled.

Late in the afternoon I find my spot, a ring of small, saw-tooth buttes. The place seems like it should have the acoustics of a natural amphitheater, but when I clap my hands and whistle and shout, but the sound dies. Maybe the hardpan absorbs noise, or maybe this ring, looking to be a couple hundred yards across, is bigger. It's hard to calculate distance here. It feels like the silence is fighting back against violation.

It's a mysterious spot and I like it. I think of the people I've sent into the Badlands over the years. Half came back searching for new words to describe desolate beauty. The others returned convinced I'd pulled a practical joke, sending them into a mostly treeless, waterless desert. I've long wondered about this difference in response. For a while I held a theory about the Badlands appealing to highly visual people, equipped to discern earth hues that change with the movement of sun and clouds, people stimulated by the array of pinnacles, chimneys, gargoyles and impossibly balanced boulders. For the other people, I thought, all this blurs together, becoming a drab muck baked hard by the sun.

There may be something to that theory. But Phil Hall, in this book, reinforced a recent notion I've had about something else at work here. Some people, I think, would rather not meet the breed of folk who are drawn to places like this. Not that these folk are dangerous, but in their own habitat they're bold and inclined to shatter comfortable truisms about a nurturing earth, the charms of progressive convenience and the practicality of formal community. Phil writes of those who came here after most of the West was tamed, people suspicious of law, government and "anyone who might be carrying the seeds of structure and conformity."

Native Americans of the last century used the Badlands as a place for vision quests. The Lakota described the area as the remnants of an Eden – like paradise, destroyed as a divine warning. They called it Mako Sica, land that is bad. Fur traders mostly skirted the Badlands as they journeyed from Missouri to the Rockies.

Starting with the mid-1800s, Badlands history is out of step with the rest of the region. Thirty years before the gold rush in the adjacent Black Hills, the Badlands won attention, but not from prospectors or pilgrims or trappers. Rather, paleontologists and geologists made trips to collect fossils and observe the eroded landscape. White civilization conquered the Black Hills in the 1870s, but experimented for the next six decades with how to claim the Badlands. First were the days of open-range cattle, an era that ended with tens of thousands of cow carcasses buried in snow. Then came the homesteaders. The homesteaders quickly learned that 160 acres of Badlands could not support more than a family of prairie dogs and could be rattlesnakes, and they left in droves. They were followed by ranchers, many of whom failed during the dust bowl years of the 1930s. At that point the federal government stepped in and began buying up land that became today's 244,000-acre national park. The feds labeled the land "sub-marginal," a bureaucratic term meaning Mako Sica.

That's just skimming the historical surface, of course. Phil fills in the details: 115 degree days, 17-foot snowdrifts, one of the West's most tragic massacres, its biggest roundup, a wolfer who climbed into dens after prey, schemers, criminals, inspired immigrants and hearty folk who stuck around even after being told their land was sub-marginal. Phil is a writer equal to these stories. It won't surprise readers to learn he is one of the Badlands breed himself. He began this book 20 years ago while living at Scenic, but the Badlands hold on him runs deeper. His father lived in a cabin and ran cattle here in the 1930s, but Phil's bond is as much inherent as it is inherited. He's Badlands scrappy, a man who needs to drop everything, get on his horse and wander now and then, self-reliant as the old 15 Irons cowboys as he rides off with just a canteen and a few chunks of raisin bread. Of one of his characters Phil writes: "He would, in time, explore the length and breadth of the Badlands, wandering in and out of every gully and wash, passing by nearly every pinnacle and butte..." The same can be said of Phil. I suspect he gathered stories for this book as few other writers could, because Badlands old-timers recognized something of themselves in him.

The sun is sinking fast, turning the hardpan silver as I stand and walk into the glare. Before dark I need to find landmarks pointing to Saddle Pass Trail, my route back down to the Badlands floor. I don't want to spend the night out here.

Once Phil told me about camping by himself in the Badlands, and I wondered if the vast loneliness bothered him. Now I know he never really came to the Badlands alone. He rode in spirit with the Minneconjou, and with Ferdinand Vandereer Hayden, Oliver and Mary Johnson, Dude Rounds, Missouri John and Louie Blummer.

Paul Higbee
Saddle Pass Trailhead
May 1993

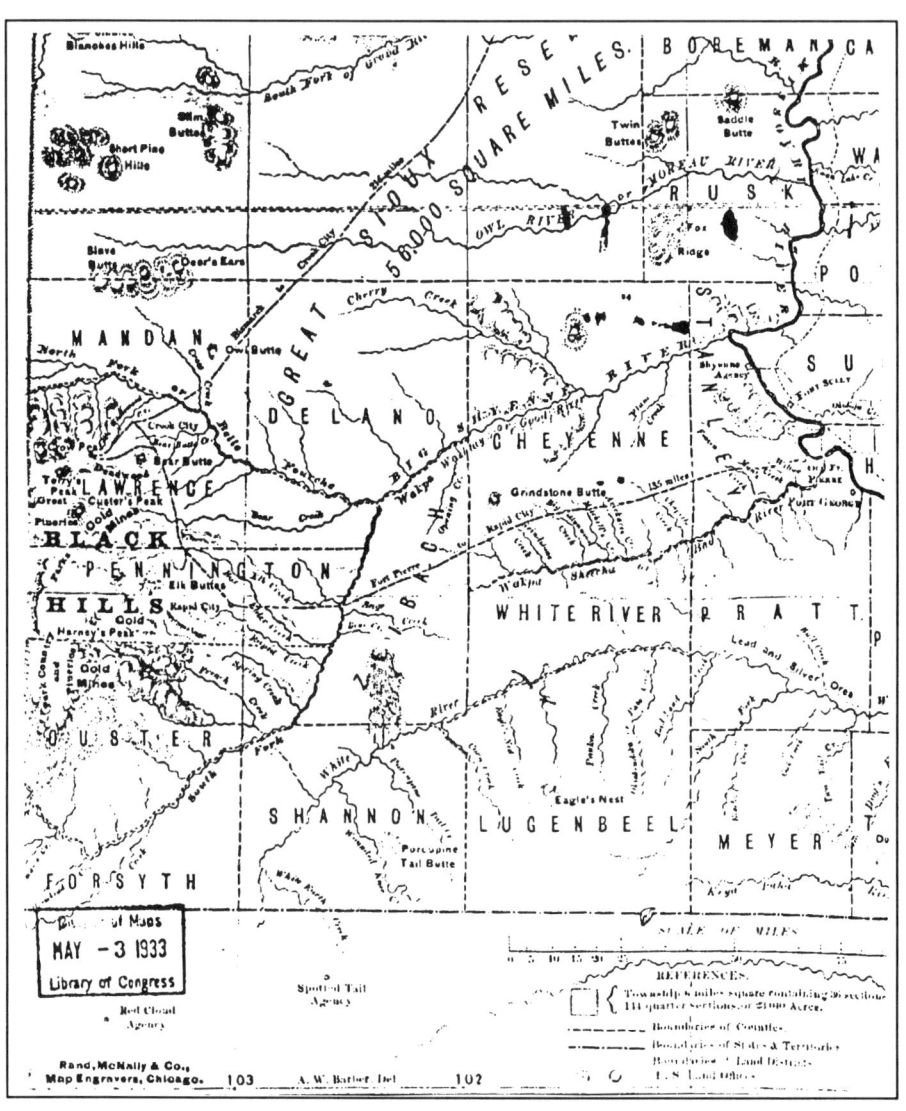

1876 map of southwestern Dakota Territory, including the Badlands.

CHAPTER 1

Vast, Mysterious and Unknown

The present-day explorer who patiently listens can hear the Badland winds whispering across the mesas, along the canyon walls, and down the arroyos. The breeze beckons the inquisitive and the romantic to wander into this strange, seemingly untraveled land. History, which belies most myths, stands softly mute to this beguiling invitation. The Badlands appear today as they looked to the first explorer: vast and mysterious.

South Dakota Badlands, ca 1895.
Photo courtesy of the Department of the Interior, Badlands National Park.

There is an area in southwestern South Dakota of barren pinnacles, twisting canyons, grass-covered mesas, saw-toothed ridges, and dry-wash gullies. The area has variously been described as hell with the fires burned out or, as it looks from a distance, the ruins of an ancient city. This strange, ominous-appearing land was claimed by France in the early 1700s, but it was virtually unknown to anyone but indigenous Indian tribes until the early 1800s.[1]

France was almost constantly at war during the 18th century. On the verge of financial collapse and ripe for internal revolution, the country was ill-prepared to systematically explore its vast holdings in the interior of North America.[2] The Monarchy sanctioned only one expedition into the Louisiana Territory. The party, led by François La Verendrye and Louis Joseph La Verendrye, set out in the spring of 1742 from Fort La Reine, a fur trading post near present-day Winnipeg, Canada, in search of a waterway to the Pacific. They reached the Mandan Indians near present-day Bismarck, North Dakota on May 19th

After a rest, they headed southwest across the plains. They broke their astrolabe the first day and thereafter were unable to determine their position; their journal notes are too vague for geographic verification. However, the evidence suggests that the Verendrye party visited the Black Hills in February 1743 and then traveled east down either the Cheyenne River or the Bad River to the site of present-day Fort Pierre, where they buried a lead plate.[3] Their travels brought them close to the Badlands, possibly within 30 miles, but the party did not catch even a glimpse of the breathtaking pinnacles.

In 1763 France ceded the Louisiana Territory to Spain, which sought to strengthen her possession of the area by establishing a settlement in 1764 on the present-day site of St. Louis. But the Spaniards did little to claim or explore the upper Missouri.[4] Thus, the Spaniards were unaware of the historically significant events unfolding on the northern plains.

During the 1700s the Teton Sioux had been driven out of the territory near the headwaters of the Mississippi River by their two enemies: the Cree to the north and the Chippewa to the east. Both tribes had acquired guns from French traders. The Sioux had little previous contact with Europeans and were still armed with lithic (manufactured stone) weapons. Thus, they were relatively defenseless against the inventive combination of European metallurgy and Chinese pyrotechnics-guns.

The Teton did not enter the prairie as conquerors, but as poor people who wandered the vast plains afoot. Dogs and women carried their possessions from one camp site to another. Hunger often stalked them. They reached the Missouri River by 1760 where, between the present-day cities of Chamberlain and

Pierre, they encountered the Arikara Indians. The Arikara had another product of the European incursion—the horse. The Sioux were no match for the mounted Arikara warriors, and their westward migration was blocked.

Soon, the Arikara were swept aside by yet another thing that came from Europe – smallpox. By then, the Teton Sioux (also known as the Lakota) had acquired horses from the Arikara, and they crossed the Missouri and continued west. The Oglalas, one of the seven council fires of the Teton, moved up Bad River (once called the Teton River). According to a winter count, an Oglala war party led by Standing Bull "discovered" the Black Hills in 1776 [A]. The Oglalas were soon followed by the six other council fires of the Teton.[5]

Mounted on the conquistador's horse and armed with the Frenchman's gun, the Sioux brought their culture to its zenith. They quickly dominated the northern plains. By 1810 the Sioux claimed everything east to west from the Minnesota River to the Big Horn Mountains and south to north from the Platte River to the Canadian border. No other Indian tribe was ever able to claim such a vast area and, by prowess, hold it.[6]

The White River Badlands were near the geographical center of the Teton's domain; but the Lakota had little regard for the desolate terrain. The barren land was stiflingly hot in the summer. The sun's reflection off the snow-white hardpan caused temporary blindness. Water was scarce, bitter to the taste, and disagreeable to the stomach. The wasteland was bone-chillingly cold in the winter. The Sioux considered it a land of spirits where men were led astray, never to be seen again. The Lakota called it *Mako Sica*—the land that is bad.[7]

Lakota mythology explains the origin of this strange land. According to the Lakota legend, all of the land east of the Paha Sapa (Black Hills) was once covered with the greenest and richest grasses. There were trees for shade, herbs for medicines, cool springs for drinking, and many animals. Wakantanka (The Great Mystery) decreed that all quarrels between tribes must be set aside when they camped upon this paradise.

This continued for many years. Then, a barbaric group of people from the western mountains swept onto the plains. They were without meat and skins. In their desperation they were not willing to share. They drove off all other tribes. Those who were driven off attempted to regain the paradise; but gifts, peace pipes, prayers or pleading could not persuade the newcomers to share this bountiful land. At last, the displaced tribes gathered together to drive out the mountain tribe.

On the day set for their advance, Wakantanka caused dark clouds to hide the sun. Lightning streaked across the blackness and thunder rumbled over the hills. Fire flamed from the ground. The earth shuddered and rocked. A wide gulf opened, and the contentious mountain tribe and all they possessed sank into it. With them sank all life—all tall waving grass, the clear springs, and the animals.

As suddenly as it came, the storm ceased. The area where the mountain tribe had lived was now a barren wasteland upon which nothing could grow. Wakantanka had taken away the paradise that had caused warring among his children and left, in its place, the Mako Sica to forever remind those he spared that they should not abuse the natural harmony of nature nor gain advantage over each other in sharing nature's benefits.[8]

The Lakota entered the Mako Sica only when it was necessary to go from one place to another. Their crossings were made over the few passes along the sixty-mile wall that forms the north rim of the Badlands. Coming from the south, their primary trail entered the Badlands at the confluence of Wounded Knee Creek and the Mankizita Watpa (River of White Clay). The Indian trail led north past two springs, about ten miles apart, and ascended the Badlands wall just north of Bear Creek. From there, the trail turned northeast, crossed a large flat, and came to a spring above Sage Creek. There, the trail dropped into Sage Creek Valley, crossed the creek, and wound for five miles out of the valley and up to the prairie.

The Lakota had only two uses for the Mako Sica: burial and vision quests. One Lakota burial site in the Badlands was beside Indian Creek – a long valley

South Dakota Badlands.
Photo courtesy of the South Dakota State Historical Society.

that meanders northwest below a large Badland mesa that eclipses the eastern sky. In this timeless valley, so undisturbed the silence can be heard, the Lakota placed their dead and the deceased's personal possessions on scaffolds in the comforting boughs of cottonwood trees. The elements eventually claimed their bodies and released their spirits.[9]

The Lakota also used the Mako Sica for vision quests. The vision quest was a vital part of a Lakota boy's rite of passage. He went alone to a sacred place. There, he went without food, water, sleep, or protection from the elements until he lapsed into unconsciousness. When his mind was free from earthly distractions, the spirits communicated to him in a dream. In the vision quest, the youth learned such things as the important role he would play for his tribe, what fate laid in store for him, or the source of his special, personal power. The Maco Sica offered the Lakota the solace needed for a vision quest. Many vision quests were held on Sheep Mountain Table.[10]

While the Teton were laying claim to the northern plains, no white man ventured into the Badlands. But new links were being forged in the chain of discovery. Spain returned the Louisiana Territory to France in 1802; but Napoleon Bonaparte, needing money to finance his wars, sold it to the United States in 1803 for 15 million dollars-three cents an acre.[11] President Thomas Jefferson promptly commissioned his personal secretary, Meriwether Lewis, to explore the vast wilderness.

Meriwether Lewis, William Clark, and 43 men set off from St. Louis on May 14, 1804 to ascend the Missouri River and to chart a path to the Pacific Ocean. The Lewis and Clark party reached present-day South Dakota by late summer. On October 1, 1804, the explorers came upon three white traders who were living at the mouth of the Cheyenne River.[12] Their presence in this area suggests that at least one of the fur traders might have been the first white man to discover the Badlands.

Jean Vallé and Hugh Heney were two of the traders. They came up-river in 1802 or 1803 as associates of the Missouri Fur Company. Vallé related to Lewis that he had passed the previous winter in the shadow of the Black Hills.[13] In all likelihood Heney was with him. If Vallé and Heney traveled up the south fork of the Cheyenne to winter under the shadow of the Black Hills, they unquestionably would have seen the Badlands. But they did not. Valle' and Heney traveled up the north fork the Cheyenne River (which is now called the Belle Fourche River) to winter with the Oglala Indians, who were then camped at the base of Bear Butte.

It is unlikely that either Jean Vallé or Hugh Heney saw the White River Badlands after 1804. The Missouri Fur Company soon moved their operations farther up the Missouri. Hugh Heney became clerk of the Upper Red River

Division (North Dakota) later in 1804, and by 1810 Jean Vallé was operating out of a trading post on the Jefferson River (Montana).[14,15]

William Garreau was the third trader with Vallé. He first came up-river with D'Eglise in 1793. To avoid arrest on a murder charge waiting for him in St. Louis, Garreau remained with the Arikara Indians.[16] He and his Indian family settled at the mouth of the Cheyenne River in 1796, where they operated a small trading post.[17] Garreau's early presence in the area suggests he might have been the first white man to discover the Badlands; but this, too, is unlikely. Garreau was married to an Arikara woman. Therefore, he and his wife would not have traveled with the Lakota, and they would not have been safe wandering alone into Sioux territory. Thus, it is unlikely that any white man knew of the White River Badlands when Lewis and Clark came up the Missouri River in 1804, less than 200 years ago.

When Lewis and Clark returned to St. Louis in 1806, President Jefferson rewarded each man with a government post. William Clark was named Principal Agent of Indian Affairs for the Louisiana Territory. Among other responsibilities, he licensed fur traders operating in the upper Missouri. Only Americans or men giving their loyalty to the American government were licensed.[18]

William Ashley, a former lieutenant governor of Missouri, realized the monopoly offered him an opportunity to make a fortune. In the spring of 1823, Ashley advertised in the *Missouri Gazette* for enterprising young men to ascend the Missouri River to its source and there work in the fur trade.

The Ashley party proceeded 1,200 miles up the Missouri River, at which point their advance was forcibly blocked by the Arikara. They retreated down-river to Fort Kiowa, a trading post built in 1822 ten miles above present-day Chamberlain. Here, Ashley's men split into three groups. Ashley and a few men returned to St. Louis, Andrew Henry led 13 men back up the Missouri River Valley, and Jedediah Smith led ten men west across the prairie. The ten men in Jedediah Smith's party became the first known white men to see the White River Badlands.19 James Clyman, a member of the party, related the journey. The party left Fort Kiowa in late September 1823. With each man walking and leading a pack horse, they proceeded west-southwest over dry, rolling prairie to White Clay Creek (White River).

> The river was running thick with white sediment and resembling cream in appearance but of a sweetish pungent taste. Our guide said it caused excessive costiveness, which we soon found out.[20]

They proceeded up the White River Valley all of the next and part of the third day. Their guide informed them to take what water they could (probably from a spring-fed creek), as they would not reach water again until noon the next day. They set out in intense summer heat to cut across a wide bend in the river. They expected to obtain water about mid-way across this area, but when they arrived at the water hole, it was dry.

Saying that it was another 15 miles to water, the guide went on ahead and soon disappeared over the horizon. With each man walking at the best pace he could manage and deviating right or left in search of water, the party became so widely scattered that it appeared to Clyman they would never be rejoined. Clyman deviated right of the guide's tracks; and about an hour before sunset, he stumbled upon a water hole. Clyman fired his gun and ran into the pool of water. His horse followed him. By dark, everyone was collected at the water hole except two men who had given out. Jedediah Smith, the only man still able to walk, took some water and rode two miles back to where the exhausted men lay buried up to their necks in the sand to conserve their moisture.

In the morning, the party struck out in the direction the guide had last been seen. After traveling four or five miles, they reached White River. There, they found their guide waiting for them. Here, the river was a beautifully clear stream running over a gravelly bottom (probably near the mouth of Wounded Knee Creek and at a place now known as Rocky Ford). The party was at the southwest edge of the Badlands.

They traveled a few miles up the river valley; and probably at the mouth of White Clay Creek, they came upon an encampment of Brule Sioux. They remained with the Indians several days, resting and trading for 28 horses. Here, the guide then left them and returned to Fort Kiowa with the horses they had borrowed from the Missouri Fur Company.

Smith's party crossed White River and proceeded northwesterly (probably passing south of present-day Cuny Table) over dry, rolling country for several days. They occasionally came across buffalo, which kept them in fresh meat. They also fell in with a band of Oglala Sioux, with whom they traded for better and more horses. The party crossed the Cheyenne River, reached the Black Hills at the point where Beaver Creek issues forth onto the plains, and continued west.[21]

The Jedediah Smith party was the first documented group of white men in the Badlands. Yet, history tantalizingly waves a veiled rebuttal. The group was piloted by an unnamed guide. The guide was knowledgeable of the route, he was aware of the purgative properties of the water in White River, and he knew the principal water holes. The guide had been there before! No one will probably ever know who he was or when he had been there, but sometime prior to 1823 a nameless white man had "discovered" the White River Badlands.

A host of fur traders and trappers followed the Jedediah Smith party into what is now southwestern South Dakota. Fort Tecumseh was built near the mouth of Bad River in 1822. Fort Pierre Chouteau was built in the same vicinity in 1832, and it was hub of an expansive network of small sub-stations located

Badlands of South Dakota.
Photo courtesy of the Department of Interior, Badlands National Park.

at various points along the tributaries flowing into the Missouri River from the west.

The traders set out from Fort Pierre Chouteau each fall for these sub-stations with beads, vermillion, blankets, shirts, calico, hatchets, axes, knives, firearms, gunpowder, traps, and other trading supplies all loaded on a string of pack horses. The traders returned to the fur trading forts in the spring with buffalo hides and beaver pelts.[22]

Seven major wintering houses were located on the two rivers that drained the White River Badlands. Four outposts were on the Cheyenne River. The Cheyenne Post was at the confluence of the Cheyenne and Missouri. A second post was a few miles above the mouth of Cherry Creek.[23] Francis Chadron and William Laidlaw established a wintering house in 1826 at the forks of the Cheyenne[24] where, in 1832, a still was set up for making whiskey. The Oglala Post was built in 1827 near the mouth of Rapid Creek, at the northwest corner of the Badlands. Thomas Sarpy was in charge. Sarpy and two assistants were organizing the storeroom on January 19, 1832 when a candle was knocked into a keg of gun powder. The resulting explosion injured Pierre Hebert and François Broit, and it killed Sarpy.[25] David LaChapelle immediately rebuilt the post. Colin Campbell was placed in charge, and trading went on without interruption.

On White River, one substation was built in 1826 at the forks of White River, just below the Badlands. Pierre D. Papin operated that substation from

1830 to 1834.[26] Another trading post operated for a short time near the mouth of Black Pipe Creek.[27] The third major wintering house on White River was at Butte Cache, just above the mouth of Wounded Knee Creek and at the southwest corner of the Badlands. The fourth trade post was located 40 miles farther up White River on a creek known today as Bordeaux Creek. This post, which was called the Chartran Post, was probably founded by Frederick Laboue (Grey Eyes) in 1830.[28]

The traders at these substations preferred to take their hides to Fort Pierre Chouteau each spring in large, buffalo-hide canoes that could each haul up several tons. For example, Francis Chadron arrived at Fort Pierre on April 9, 1830 with 4,360 buffalo robes and a quantity of furs. The next spring, Chadron brought in 44 packs of robes in 11 skin canoes.[29]

Chartran Post was located too far up White River for the hides to be transported by canoe. Instead, the goods from the Chartran Post were carried by horse-drawn cart to Butte Cache, where they were loaded onto canoes for the trip down White River. A man on horseback followed the canoes. If the water level dropped before the cargo reached the Missouri River, which it often did, the man on horseback rode to Fort Pierre to get pack horses.[30]

White River did not run enough water every spring to float a canoe. When water levels were low, the traders transported their winter booty overland by horse and cart. From as early as 1826, the traders at the Chartran Post and the Cache Butte Post used the Lakota's' trail through the western edge of the Badlands. The trail saw extensive use from 1845 until 1849 when the American Fur Company used it to supply Fort John (later called Fort Laramie) on the North Platte River. The route came to be known as the Fort Pierre-Fort Laramie Trail.[31]

The fur traders were aware of a second route through the Badlands (probably Cedar Pass), but, even though it was shorter, it was seldom taken. Edwin Denig, an early-day fur trader, described the route:

> The descent [off the north wall] is by a road about five feet broad, winding round and among the hills.... In going over this trail great precaution is necessary for a slip of the foot would precipitate either man or horse into the gulf below.[32]

When Denig made the trip, the mixed-blood interpreter in the party was so terrified by the possibility of going over the edge into the abyss that he had to be blindfolded and led down. Once down on the floor of the Badlands, the party had to contend with ravines from five to 20 feet deep that ran in almost every direction. The terrain was so difficult to traverse that Denig and his party covered only 15 miles in four days.

Fur traders traveled these trails through the Badlands until about 1850; but by then, beaver hats were no longer the fashion of Europe, having been replaced by those made of felt. Newly invented spinning looms quickly and efficiently made wool blankets that were cheaper and in most ways better than buffalo robes. The fur trade era rapidly drew to a close.

During the early 1800s every watershed and mountain range from St. Louis to San Francisco had been explored and charted. Trails, which hordes of people would soon follow west, had been forged across mountains and deserts. Yet during this time of exploration, the Badlands were merely skirted by a handful of largely unknown French-Canadian trappers who knew only enough about the area to help cartographers sketch the region in on their maps as the *Mauvaise Terres*—the terrible terrain.

Notes

[A] Traditional Sioux and social scientists differ in their view of the origin of the Sioux. Sioux legend describes the Lakota as having emerged from the ground of the Black Hills. Therefore, Traditionals do not consider the Sioux as interlopers on this land, but its native people.

South Dakota Badlands.
Photo courtesy of South Dakota State Historical Society.

CHAPTER 2

The Bone Diggers

Those early visitors to the Badlands must have gazed at the seemingly barren soil of hard-baked clay and wondered: "What good is this land." Little did they realize that scattered across the landscape and buried beneath the layers of colored earth lay some of the best evidence in the scientific world to support a newborn idea that would shake the foundations of civilization. From the bowels of this God-forsaken land came timely confirmation of the theory of evolution.

De Girardin's sketch of the Evans party in the Badlands.
Photo courtesy of South Dakota School of Mines and Technology.

Many adventurers, scientists, and pseudo-scientists were lured to the upper Missouri River drainage area in the early 1800s by tales of the exotic West brought east by traders and travelers. Most who braved the long journey to Dakota stopped at Fort Pierre Chouteau, where they invariably were told about the strange, barren land five-days ride from the fort, where the ground was littered with the bones of long-dead creatures. Unfortunately for them, most of the explorers chose not to visit what must have sounded like an uninhabited, uninteresting wasteland.

Maximilian of Weld, a German prince who spent much time in the eastern reaches of Dakota collecting Indian skeletal materials for "study" and curiosity, was told of the strange bones of the Badlands when he visited Fort Pierre Chouteau in 1834; but he did not go.[1] Joseph Nicollet, a French scientist who mapped much of the upper Missouri in 1839, was also told about the Badlands by American Fur Company employees. But he did not go.[2] John Audubon, the noted naturalist and artist, stopped at Fort Pierre Chouteau in 1843. He, too, was told of the Badlands and its interesting fossil bones. He went up-river instead.[3]

These adventurers did not visit the Badlands because, like most people of their time, they believed that God, in one miraculous act of creation and at one time, had made the world and all of the living things in it. Without giving the matter a great deal of thought, they believed that the animals living in 1830 looked pretty much like the animals that lived ten million or even a hundred million years earlier. So the fossilized bones of animals were of little interest to them. They were more curious about the living things in the upper Missouri region, a land then virtually unknown to the scientific world.

When the scientists would not come to the Badlands, a few fur traders took some of its fossils to the scientists. Alexander Culbertson, an employee of the American Fur Company, collected fossils when he crossed through the Badlands in 1845. He sent some of them to his father, Dr Joseph Culbertson of Chambersburg, Pennsylvania. Alexander also gave a fossilized bone (the lower jaw of an extinct animal) to Hiram A. Prout, a St. Louis physician.[4] Prout described the fossil in an article that appeared in 1846 in the *American Journal of Science*.[5] Dr. Culbertson donated his Badlands fossils to Joseph Leidy, the curator of the Academy of Natural Sciences. Dr. Leidy described the skull and leg-bone fragments from an extinct, cud-chewing mammal, in the Academy's *Proceedings* in 1847.[6] Later, it was learned that the skull and bone fragments were from an extinct species of camel.

These two publications increased the awareness within the scientific community that animals that lived in the past were distinctly different from extant animals. Highly curious about these differences, scientists suddenly became anxious to collect and examine past forms of life.

The first scientist to become interested in exploring the White River Badlands for fossils was David Dale Owen, then the U.S. Geologist. Unable to go to the Badlands himself, Dale sent his assistant, Dr. John Evans.[7] Evans' party left St. Louis in the spring of 1849 aboard the *Iowa*, a three-story steamboat leased to the American Fur Company. At Fort Pierre Chouteau, Evans rented three light carts and hired five French-Canadian voyageurs as muleteers and cooks. One of them, Joseph La Violette, served as their guide. E. De Girardin, a French adventurer who served as Dr. Evans' artist, described Violette as being a short, thick-set man who was as quick and active as a monkey, tireless, superstitious, boastful, untruthful, quarrelsome, and a drunkard. Possibly because of the flaws in Violette's character, Evans employed a Sioux Indian named Elk Horn as a second guide.

The Lakota Indians temporarily camped outside the gates of Fort Pierre watched the Dr. Evans' party prepare for their departure with suspicion; and the Indians tried to discourage them. Evans and his entourage disregarded the Indian's remonstrations, and they left for the Badlands. The third day out the party traveled for ten hours under a scorching sun and camped that evening near a spring (probably Pino Springs). Their mules and horses grouped themselves in a circle around a hastily built smudge fire, vainly seeking relief from a cloud of mosquitoes.

They woke in the morning to see Elk Horn, totally naked, atop a nearby hill executing a dance of weird gestures and strange contortions while chanting a monotonous refrain that sounded like the barking of a coyote. The apparent purpose of the ceremony was to attract buffalo. Elk Horn's performance abruptly concluded when he saw a cloud of dust about a mile away. Instantly, the voyageurs grouped the animals inside a ring formed by the carts and each man grabbed a gun. Elk Horn sprang on a horse and galloped toward the horsemen, who were advancing rapidly. They were Sioux warriors who, while hunting in the Black Hills, had been attacked by Crow Indians. The Crow had killed several Sioux and had taken a number of their horses.

Evans' party reached the Badlands on the evening of the fifth day. The setting sun tinted the strange formations in rose-colored hues. According to Girardin, the Badlands like an immense city in ruins surrounded by walls and bulwarks and filled with palaces crowned with gigantic domes and monuments of the most fantastic and bizarre architecture. Violette triumphantly told of the marvels of this city, the streets of which were strewn with the remains of animals of every kind, including, according to Indian lore, petrified men.

The group camped that night on Sage Creek; and they found that its white, salty water was drinkable only when mixed with strong coffee and sugar. The

Earliest published view of the White River Badlands, sketched by Girardin in the field, 1849.
Photo courtesy South Dakota School of Mines and Technology.

next day, they went to Bear Creek and pitched their tents under cottonwood trees that grew at the base of a spring. To Girardin, the spring was an oasis sprinkled with charming flowers. Evans' party set out the next day to explore the Badlands. Girardin romantically described their passage between two pillars of antediluvian architecture into a large amphitheater surrounded by embattled, jagged hills of rich ocher color. All around them, on soil so hard the horses left no print, were the crumbling remains of brick-red, petrified turtles. After only a little searching, they found several, well-preserved turtles that weighed up to 150 pounds each. They also found a petrified head of a rhinoceros, the jawbone of a wolf, and the bones of oreodons. Girardin expected at any moment to find the petrified remains of mastodons, elephants, or even men—all of which were to be found, he had been told, in the Badlands.

As they wandered deeper into the Badlands, the heat became stifling. The reflection of the burning sun off the snow-white soil began to produce brief but painful blindness. By noon, Girardin's amphitheater had, for him, become a desert that was entirely empty of water, vegetation, or any living being—not even a bird or an insect.[8]

After three days in the Badlands, Evans' party departed for Fort Pierre with a heavy cargo of turtles and petrified bones. Eight days later, they arrived back at Fort Pierre Chouteau.[9]

David Owen was enthusiastic about the fossils Evans brought back from the Badlands; and he raved about them throughout the eastern United States to various learned groups. The scientific community was soon buzzing with talk about the Badland fossils. Geologists and paleontologists became anxious to learn more about this fascinating region.[10]

Thaddeus Culbertson, Alexander Culbertson's younger brother, was the next adventurer to go west in quest of Badlands fossils. He asked Spencer Baird of the Smithsonian Institution to partially finance his trip, but the newly founded organization could afford only $200 to cover the cost of shipping any fossils that Thaddeus collected.[11] Undeterred, Thaddeus and his brother, Alexander, left Chambersburg, Pennsylvania in the spring of 1850 for St. Louis. They went up-river by steamboat to St. Joseph, Missouri, and from there overland by horse and wagon. They arrived at Fort Pierre Chouteau on May 4th.

Thaddeus left for the White River Badlands on May 7th accompanied by two American Fur Company employees—Owen Mackenzie and another man referred to as "Joe," probably Joseph La Violette. The men had three trail-weary mules and provisions for two weeks. They reached Sage Creek in five uneventful days and set out the next morning for Bear Creek. Culbertson, who was not a trained geologist, thought that some of the geological formations gave striking evidence of having experienced violent convulsions and that other areas looked as if they had experienced the action of fire. He concluded that one Badland formation was an ancient volcanic crater.

From the descriptions others had given him, Culbertson expected that the spring at Bear Creek would be a veritable flowing fountain. He was disappointed to find but three small holes of water in the side of the hill. However, he was pleased by the taste of the water, finding it cool and delightful.

Culbertson set out in the morning to collect fossils. He was shown numbers of ugly, dark red, misshapen masses that were, he was told, the remains of petrified turtles whose shells had been destroyed by the sun. Culbertson was again disappointed. He had expected to find many, perfectly-preserved specimens. His spirits did not flag for long. In the next wash he discovered a nearly perfectly preserved turtle. One of the men found an intact head of an animal the size of a large bear.

The sun was boiling hot and the group had little water. Culbertson decided to finish his collecting in one day. By evening, the men had gathered a half bushel of small things, a number of excellent teeth and jaw bones, several good heads, and a fair sampling of fossilized turtles.

They left the next day for Fort Pierre Chouteau. The party had not gone far when they realized that their heavily loaded wagons were about to collapse. They were forced to stash some fossils near Bull Creek and continue with a lightened load. Fortunately, Culbertson met some American Fur Company employees on their way to trade with Cheyenne Indians beyond the Badlands. The fur men promised to pick up the fossils stored at Bull Creek on their return trip.[12]

Culbertson arrived at Fort Pierre on May 18th. A steamboat, the *El Paso*, had just arrived from St. Louis. Culbertson boarded the steamboat and went up-river to Fort Union, where he stayed until August. He then returned to Pennsylvania. Three weeks after arriving home, Thaddeus Culbertson was afflicted with dysentery and died.[13]

In 1853 James Hall, the New York State geologist, sent Fielding Meek and Ferdinand Hayden to the Badlands to prospect for the remains of prehistoric animals.[14] Dr. Ferdinand Vandeveer Hayden, a twenty-three-year-old, nondescript little man of solitary habits, was to become one of the paramount geologists of the West and the pre-eminent paleontologist of the Badlands. He would, in time, explore the length and the breadth of the Badlands, wandering in and out of nearly every gully and wash and passing by nearly every pinnacle and butte as he scurried about collecting fossils. The Sioux called him the "Man-who-picks-up-rocks-running."[15]

When Hayden and Meek arrived in St. Louis, they unexpectedly met Drs. John Evans and Benjamin Shumard, who were also headed for the Badlands. Evans attempted to lay exclusive claim to every fossil in the Badlands, but Hayden and Meek could not be dissuaded from their expedition. The two parties, hardly managing to feign amicability, departed St. Louis on May 21, 1853 aboard the same steamboat. At Fort Pierre Chouteau they learned that some bands of Sioux were currently ill-disposed to whites; and they were told that any small party that ventured from the fort did so at a perceptible risk. Their scientific rivalry was suddenly outweighed by their apprehension of the Sioux, and they decided to travel together to the Badlands.

Meek's party consisted of himself, Hayden and three fur traders: Henry Clermont, Francis Rondell and Isadore Dorison. Evans and Shumard were accompanied by a man named Henrick, an Indian guide named Iron Horn (probably a mistranslation of Elk Horn) and an unnamed artist (possibly Girardin). The two groups, now joined as one, left on June 20th for the Badlands.

Recent rains had swollen the creeks to the point that the horses often became mired in the mud while pulling the carts across the streams. One cart was broken while being pulled out of the gumbo, and the party was temporarily delayed while Dorison and Hayden went back to Fort Pierre for another. At the end of the third day, the group came to a small tributary of the Bad River that had clear, good water (probably Pino Springs). There, they found "a half-breed by the name of Pino and an Indian camped with their squaws" [A].[16]

Pino invited the explorers to his lodge for supper-buffalo meat cooked in milkweed pods. Meek did not think that the food looked clean, but as a matter of courtesy he sampled it. In his opinion, the dish tasted about like it looked.

Pino conversed with the scientists at length. Among other things, he told them that 150 lodges of Sioux were camped near the Badlands. This group was extremely hostile, and they were bent on robbing and driving away any white men who came into their country.

Undeterred, the explorers continued on. At the end of the seventh day out, they arrived at Sage Creek and immediately began a fruitful search of the creek for ammonites, brachiopods, dentatum, and other shellfish – like fossils. Meek lauded Sage Creek as a fine location where two or three men could load a cart of fossils in only a couple of days.

The scientists were happy to be in this fossil hunter's paradise, but their guides were not. Iron Horn frequently advised that they go back before unfriendly Sioux discovered them. When the scientists would not leave, Iron Horn was reluctant to accompany them any farther. "There is," Meek commented, "some dissatisfaction amongst our men almost amounting to mutiny, but we have succeeded in getting them to go on."[17]

The party left the next day, June 28th, for Bear Creek. They spent a week collecting about 700 pounds of fossils amidst a horde of flies and mosquitoes so thick that the men were concerned the insects would kill the horses. They were also pestered by wolves that hung around the edge of camp at night and occasionally came amongst the tents to steal meat.

Iron Horn returned to camp from a hunting trip on July 4th to report that a large party of Indians had recently passed along the Cheyenne River. He advised the party to leave the Badlands at once. Dr. Evans and his companions immediately began packing, and their party left on July 6th for Fort Pierre Chouteau. One of the voyageurs with Meek and Hayden wanted to leave with Evans, but he was prevailed upon to stay. That evening, the men heard a rifle shot from the direction of White River. They loaded their guns and prepared for unwelcome company; but no Indians appeared.

Meek and Hayden stayed at Bear Creek another four days; and they would have remained longer but their guides would not stay another day. The party set out on July 11th for Fort Pierre. However, the eager fossil hunters had overloaded their carts. Even four horses could not pull a cart out of the Bear Creek Valley. Reluctantly, the men discarded 100 pounds of fossils. Then, half the remaining load in each cart was temporarily taken out. With a great deal of whipping and a liberal amount of cursing in English, French and Lakota, they succeeded in getting one, half-full cart to the top. There, they unloaded the cart and returned for the rest of the fossils and baggage. In this manner, everything of importance was hauled up the Badlands wall. Meek and Hayden gladly walked to Fort Pierre Chouteau so their saddle horses could help pull the heavily loaded carts. Despite having overloaded carts and being completed to walk back to Fort Pierre, Meek and Hayden left the Badlands reluctantly. They felt an even more valuable fossil collection could have been obtained if they had been able to induce their voyageurs to remain a few weeks longer.

Meek and Hayden were partway down the trail when, about noon on July 14th, a party of whites, half-breeds, and Indians (about a dozen men) and a cavalcade of Indian women and children caught up with them. They told the scientists that a fight between the Sioux and the soldiers at Fort Laramie had occurred, during which five Indians had been killed. They related that the band swore vengeance against whites and part of the band was now in the Black Hills, about a day's journey away. Hastening their pace, the Meek party reached Fort Pierre Chouteau on the afternoon of July 18th. That evening they learned that a large party of unfriendly Indians had been on the trail only hours behind them.[18]

Ferdinand Hayden returned to the Badlands in 1854 to spend the summer exploring and collecting fossils. He realized that several epochs of geological time were represented in the Badlands strata, and that the epochs of geological time could be read from bottom to top like an open book – each chapter being distinctly marked with a particular shade of pink, yellow, or gray that could be traced for miles along the Badlands wall. The horizontal banding made it possible for Hayden to readily compare the evolutionary development of a fossil found in one place with similar fossilized animal found miles away.

Enthralled, Hayden spent the winter of 1854–1855 at Fort Pierre [B]. On February 11, 1855, he took advantage of a break in the winter weather to strike out for his beloved fossil trove. His party traveled as far as Sage Creek, but they were then hit by a severe snow storm. Hayden sent his men back to Fort Pierre, and he struck out alone from Pino Springs to the Cheyenne Trading House at the mouth of Cherry Creek. Hayden became lost in a ground blizzard and went without food for three days. He wandered through 18 inches of snow and in and out of the deep ravines of the Cheyenne River before he found his destination.

Hayden was soon back at Fort Pierre, planning yet another trip to the Badlands. He and a guide left for the Badlands in April. In route, they met a trader coming in from the Brule Camp on the upper White River. The trader told such rueful tales of Indian unrest that Hayden's guide would not go on. The eager young scientist's despair at yet another foiled attempt to reach the Badlands prompted him to wish that the government would send troops to wipe out two or three hundred Sioux.[19]

On May 7th, Hayden again departed for the Badlands. This time he did not take the Fort Laramie-Fort Pierre Trail. Instead, he struck out to the south accompanied by an Indian guide, a voyageur and a boy. The weather was beautiful. The spring birds had arrived. The ravines were green with fresh grass. The trees were in foliage and flowers were in bloom. At last on his way to his "remarkable cemetery," Hayden was in a personal heaven.

The party passed the head of Medicine Creek and continued southward to the forks of the White River. The next day, May 11th, they proceeded up-river four or five miles before they found a place free enough of quicksand to cross the river. Following an old buffalo trail, they traveled westward along the river's south bank. They passed Eagle Nest Butte and came to a spring-fed stream, which their Indian guide told them was called "The-creek-where-Indians-plant-corn." They rested a day while the Indian planted a patch of corn and potatoes. The Indian probably would not be back that fall to harvest his crop, but someone of his race would pass by and apparently that was good enough for him.

Hayden's party struck White River and, despite nearly miring the horses in quicksand, crossed it on May 22nd in the vicinity of Red Water Creek. They then traveled northwest across the floor of the Badlands toward Bear Creek, where they stayed five days to add to their collection of fossils. Their carts were full, and they departed the Badlands over the Fort Pierre-Fort Laramie Trail. The party reached Fort Pierre on June 26th after an absence of 30 days.[20]

Over a decade would pass before Hayden would return to the Badlands. During the Civil War he took up the duties of a surgeon in the Union Army. At wars end, Hayden became chairperson of the Geology and Mineralogy department at the University of Pennsylvania, with the proviso that the position would not interfere with his western explorations.[21]

Hayden's expeditions resumed in 1866. His first trip west was back to his beloved White River Badlands where:

> ...the summer sun pours its rays on the bare white walls, which only are reflected on the weary traveler with double intensity, not oppressing him with the heat, but so dazzling his eyes that he is affected with temporary blindness. I have spent many days exploring this region when the thermometer was 112...and there was no water...within fifteen miles. It is only to the geologist that this place can have any permanent attractions. He can wind his way through the wonderful canyons among some of the grandest ruins in the world...at the foot of... [which] the curious fossil treasures are found.[22]

The Academy of Natural Sciences of Philadelphia funded Hayden's 1866 expedition to the Badlands; and by order of General Ulysses Grant, the U.S. Army provided its expeditionary needs. Hayden left Fort Randall on August 3, 1866 with a six-mule team pulling the Army's biggest wagon, five soldiers, a guide, an Indian hunter, and his faithful assistant, James Stevenson. They carried rations for 60 days.

The party traveled along the Keha Paha River. Reaching the river's headwaters, the party continued west across the prairie to White Clay Creek, which they then followed to its confluence with the White River. There, they struck the

Fort Laramie-Fort Pierre Trail. Leisurely exploring to the right and to left of the trail, they followed it to Bear Creek and eventually on to Fort Pierre.[23]

On this trip, Hayden collected the first known remains of a fossil insectivore, an ancestral pronghorn about two feet tall, a saber-toothed cat, and a collie-sized, three-toed horse.[24] He often hunted all day in the most rugged areas in the Badlands to obtain less than 50 pounds of fossils, and not a good head or turtle amongst them. Based on that experience, Hayden concluded that the Badlands would not, as some had imagined, furnish the world with a limitless supply of fossils.[25]

Hayden never again returned to the White River Badlands. His success propelled him to bigger vistas. When the 1866–1867 U.S. Congress established and funded the U.S. Geological and Geographic Survey of the Territories, Hayden was appointed geologist in charge. In that position, he played a prominent role in discovering rich fossil beds elsewhere in the West.

The next scientific expedition into the heart of the White River Badlands did not come until 1874. That summer, Professor O.C. Marsh of Yale University had 12 parties of collectors in the field. However, Marsh remained in New Haven to oversee the construction of the Peabody Museum, a showcase his uncle donated to house Marsh's growing fossil collection. In October, Marsh received a letter from his collecting party in western Nebraska explaining that the enclosed fossilized tooth had been brought into camp by an Indian who claimed it was from a big horse that had been struck by lightning. Marsh examined the tooth and immediately realized the animal was new to science. He called it the Brontotherium (thunder beast). Marsh decided he must explore the place of its origin. General E.O.C. Ord, Commander of the Department of the Platte, promised Professor Marsh every assistance.[26]

Marsh and his frontiersman guide, Hank Clifford, arrived at the Red Cloud Agency on November 4, 1874 in the midst of considerable Indian unrest. The Lakota were upset about Lt. Colonel George Custer's summer expedition into the Black Hills, which they regarded as a violation of the Treaty of 1868; and the Indians were angry that Custer had disclosed to the world that the Black Hills contained gold. To add to the Lakota's anger, Agent J.J. Saville was attempting to count them. Guessing that a census would reduce their rations, the Lakota refused to comply. In retaliation, Saville withheld their rations until the Indians agreed to be counted.

In view of the tense situation, Agent Saville advised Marsh to consult the Indians about his expedition into the Badlands. The chiefs and the headmen held a council. Marsh, with Clifford translating, explained that he was going into the Badlands to collect the bones of animals that lived a long time ago. The Indians could not be convinced that a party of white men was going northward, toward the Black Hills, at the beginning of winter to look for anything of such little value as old bones.

To demonstrate the truth of his claim, Marsh offered that a small group of Indians could accompany him, and that he would pay them to help collect bones. Seeing that Marsh was a man of importance, the Indians complained to him about the poor quality of the food, blankets, and other rations they received. Marsh, possibly believing that this ration matter was the last issue standing between him and the sought-after fossils, promised Chief Red Cloud that he would look into it when he got back to Washington. The Indian council then concluded that the expedition could start the next day.

However, a snow storm further delayed the start of the expedition. When the weather improved two days later, Marsh immediately left Fort Robinson with his military escort. He stopped at the Agency to pick up the Indian workers. The sight of solders in marching order excited the Indian workers. Brandishing guns, the Indians surrounded Marsh. Red Cloud informed the Professor that it looked as though the party was going to the Black Hills to search for gold, and they would not allow it. Marsh could do nothing but return to Fort Robinson.

After several more unsuccessful consultations the Indians, the Agent, the military officers, and Marsh decided that the best way to win the Indian's consent was to give the Indians a feast – at Marsh's expense. Every detail of Indian etiquette was observed. Food was served, presents were distributed, and Professor Marsh made another speech. Ultimately, a reluctant consent was given. The expedition was set to depart the next morning; but when the time came to leave, not a single Indian would go!

Exasperated, Marsh decided to give the Indians the slip. The expedition left at midnight and cautiously made its way through the Indian villages that lay between the agency and White River. Although dogs barked furiously, their owners did not wake. The Indians did not discover until morning that Professor Marsh's expedition had left for the Badlands. Soon, Indian sentinels posted on high buttes had the party under surveillance. Fearing a reprisal, the party chose a camp site flanked by Badlands ravines.

The intensely cold weather prompted the party to work quickly as they made a wide-ranging, but thorough, search of the area for fossils. Soon two tons of fossils were stacked in small, widely scattered piles, each marked with a stick in case of snow. But soon messengers came from Red Cloud to warn Marsh that a large band of hostile northern Indians were planning to attack the party. According to the couriers, the attack could come that night. They advised Marsh to return to the agency immediately. Marsh stayed.

The next day, Marsh and his workers picked up each of the numerous piles of fossils and carefully packed each specimen in the wagon. Then, the expedition left the Badlands. The next day a large war party scoured the Badlands in search of the Bone Chief.

The fossils that Marsh brought out of the Badlands were added to his vast holdings housed in the Peabody Museum. It included the best collection in the world of fossil horses,[27] from which Marsh drew his information for his seminal work tracing the evolution of the horse [C].

From 1892 on, hardly a summer has passed without at least one scientific and/or fossil-hunting expedition roaming through the lonesome ravines of the Badlands. Today, almost every paleontology museum in the world has at least one specimen from the Badlands.

Notes

[A] Pino was not a half-breed. He was Balboa Pynaux, a full-blooded Frenchman who, as an employee of the American Fur Company, was at the Oglala Post in 1832. Pynaux either settled near this spring or camped there often enough for it to become known as Pino Springs.

[B] Fort Pierre Chouteau was purchased by the U.S. Army in 1855 and totally abandoned by 1858. The town of Fort Pierre, South Dakota is located a few miles south of the old fort site, which is now listed on the National Register of Historic Places.

[C] The first horse appeared 58 million years ago. It was the size of a jackrabbit, had four toes on its front feet and three toes on its back feet. This early horse had teeth that were suited only for chewing soft, marsh-like vegetation. By the Oligocene Epoch, fossils found in the Badlands showed that the horse had evolved into an animal 18 inches tall (about coyote-size), with three toes on all limbs. It was slender-limbed and well adapted for speed. Progressively, over millions of years, the horse's jaw lengthened, its teeth became more complex and better suited for eating the hard grasses associated with a drier climate, its middle toe thickened, and its limbs lengthened. The well-preserved remains of the earliest one-toed horse were found along the Little White River. The animal resembled a modern pony. For some unknown reason the one-toed horse became extinct on the American continent, but its progeny migrated across the Bering Land Bridge to Eurasia, where it completed its evolution into the modern horse.[28]

CHAPTER 3

The Promoters' Trail

The development of the West is usually attributed to courageous Generals, wealthy entrepreneurs, and visionary politicians who blazed the trail that others followed. However, it could be argued that the people lauded in historical accounts for their accomplishments in the American West simply held the first press conference to announce what common folk on the frontier had known for some time. Such was certainly the case in the opening of the Black Hills and the development of a freight trail through the Badlands – a trail that could aptly be called the Promoters' Trail.

Wagon train.
Photo courtesy South Dakota State Historical Society.

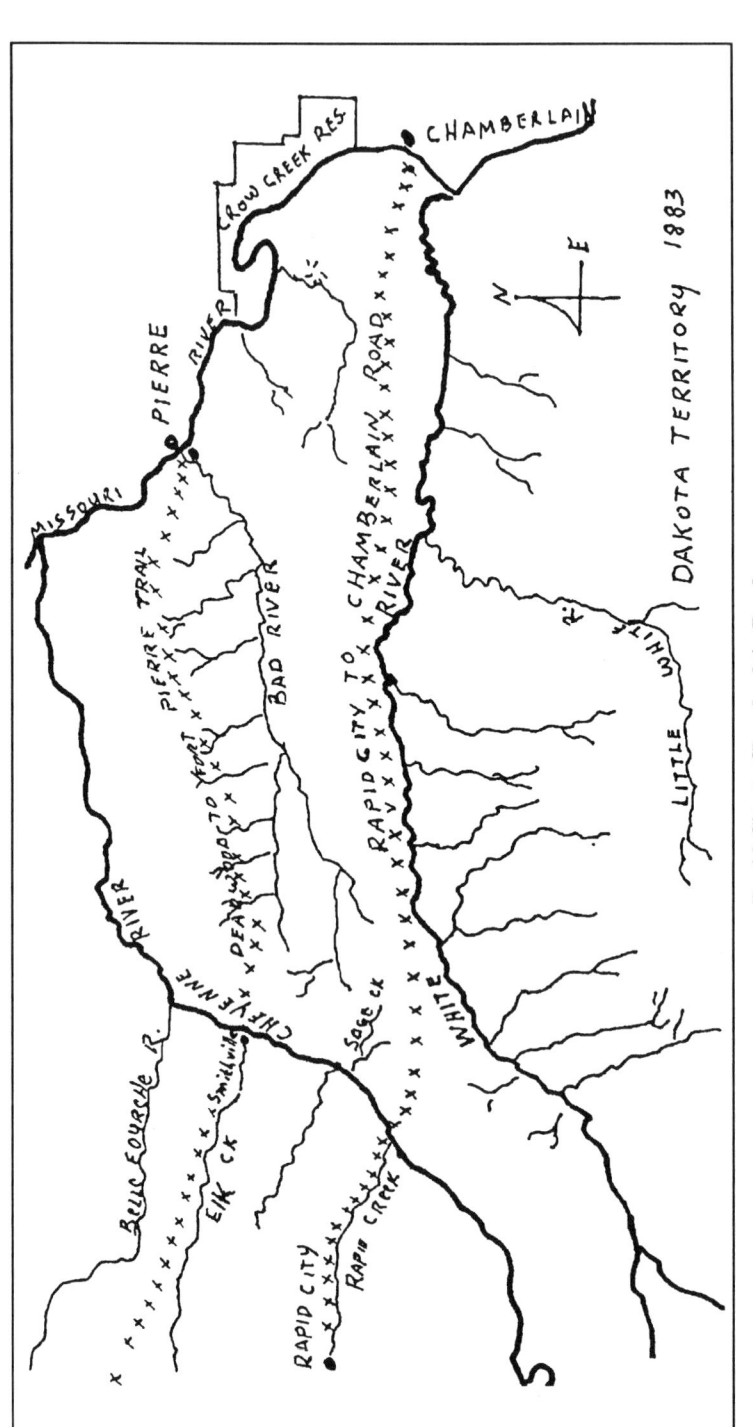

Rapid City to Chamberlain Road.

To set the record straight, Lt. Col. George Armstrong Custer did not "discover" gold in the Black Hills. People living on the edge of the Great Sioux Reservation had known about it long before 1874.[1,2,3,4] Indeed, a group of entrepreneurs in Yankton had formed the Black Hills Exploring and Mining Association in 1861—13 years before the Custer expedition. They were in the audience when Ferdinand Hayden, the same geologist who had explored the Badlands for fossils, announced at a public lecture in October 1866 that grains of gold could be found in almost any little stream in the Black Hills.[5]

No one on the frontier was more stirred by these rumors of gold than Charlie Collins, the owner of the Sioux City (Iowa) *Weekly Times*. During the next decade, Collins hatched numerous schemes to exploit the Black Hills. He launched his first effort in the summer of 1869. His plan was to locate a town on the east bank of the Missouri River, right across from the mouth of the White River.[6] The location had several advantages. First, the site was the "temporary" terminus of Noble's Trail, a trail laid in 1859 that was supposed to run from Minneapolis/St. Paul, Minnesota to California. Second, a large camp of Brule Sioux was located just across the Missouri River at the mouth of White River. It was expected that the Indians would come into the new town to trade and buy supplies. However, the location's most compelling attribute was its location relative to the Black Hills. Brule City would be located at the precise point along the east boundary of the Great Sioux Reservation that was closest to the coveted Black Hills. Collins saw Brule City as the portal through which the courageous and bold would carry tons of gold wrestled from the Indians.[7]

Charley Collins, John Brennan [A], Tom Hodnett, Dan Hodnett, and John P. Hodnett [B] traveled up the Missouri River that summer to the mouth of the White River. As members of the Irish Colonization of America, they intended to secure a location for an Irish settlement. Collins had collected a large amount of cash to buy the location from its purported owner, Jim Somers. However, Dan Hodnett considered himself a skillful sporting man; and he did not believe it was necessary to "purchase" the property. So he challenged Somers to a hand of poker for the site. Hodnett won. But Somers drew a brace of guns, and Hodnett and his party fled down-river.[8]

Undaunted, Charley Collins persisted in his efforts to establish a town across from the mouth of White River. He arranged for a committee of the 1869 Fenian Convention to rendezvous in Sioux City during the summer of 1870. From there, Collins escorted them to Yankton by rail and then overland by wagon to his purposed location for an Irish colony. After a grueling ride across a scorched prairie, the committee was not impressed. They decided against the site. Nonetheless, Collins engineered a favorable minority report.[9]

Collins' next attempt to exploit the Black Hills was more direct. In the spring of 1872, he published a series of highly sensational confabulations in the *Weekly Times* about the gold-ribbed Hills, the riches of which rightfully belonged to those who were courageous and bold enough to pluck them from the Sioux. Collins announced in the *Times* that he was organizing an expedition to the Black Hills.[10]

When Secretary of Interior Columbus Delano learned of the planned expedition onto the Great Sioux Reservation, an area that by treaty was off-limits to whites, he decided that any attempts by whites to enter the Black Hills must be thwarted. Major General Winfield S. Hancock, commander of the Department of Dakota, announced that the leaders of any expedition to the Black Hills would be arrested and thrown in the nearest military prison. The order was the death knell for Collin's expedition.[11]

Charley Collins.
Photo courtesy of the Sioux City Public Library Archives.

Nonetheless, Charlie Collins maniacally continued his crusade to "make it rich" by exploiting and promoting the Black Hills. At Collins' urging, David W. Spaulding, M.F. Coonen, Merritt H. Day, H.M. Leedy, C. McDonald, James Harnett, Dan Harnett, J. McManus, and E.C. Howard, all from Emmetsburg, Iowa, headed to the proposed site for Brule City. They arrived on August 2, 1873.[12] However, Jim Somers still claimed the site, and Jim Somers was a man to disregard. Somers was a giant of a man. He stood six-feet-five, weighed 240 pounds and had the reputation for being the toughest, meanest man in the territory. His escapades were well known throughout the area, and few men were brave enough to cross him [C].

Somehow, Spaulding and his associates reached an accord with Somers. They staked their claims, filed their homesteads with the land office in Springfield, and went back to Iowa. The following spring (1874), they returned and permanently located in Brule City. James McHenry of Vermillion brought a steam-powered saw mill to Brule City by steamboat in May. C.M. Cliff arrived on the same boat with merchandise to start a general store. D. Herman and E.C. Howard laid out an official town site in June.[13] Brule City soon sported two prominently displayed signs:[14]

DANIEL HARNETT & CO.-LAND AGENTS
Town Lots For Sale – Cheap
Timber Lands Located On Short Notice

The other sign read:

HEADQUARTERS FOR THE BLACK HILLS
CORPS OF OBSERVATION
For Particulars Apply To
Charles Collins. Colonel in Command

What the town lacked was people. But Collins was at work on that problem. He contacted Peter Nelson, a Chicago real estate promoter. Nelson convinced 13 Scandinavian families to strike out with him for Brule City. The first installment of the settlers arrived in Yankton on April 30, 1874, consisting of over a dozen men whose families would soon follow. They departed in covered wagons for Brule City. Their families followed, arriving on August 5, 1874.[15]

About this same time Charlie Reynolds, a scout with Lt. Colonel Custer's expedition to the Black Hills, rode into Fort Laramie, Wyoming with exciting news. Reynolds announced that Custer's party had discovered gold in the Black Hills.[16] The news quickly flashed all over the world.

Preparations began immediately in Brule City for the anticipated deluge of miners, freighters, and merchants. The Dakota Territorial Legislature created Brule County and named Brule City as the county seat until an election could be held. A post office opened on October 13, 1874. Dakota Territory Governor William Howard appointed George Trimmer, James Blankerton, and H.M. Leedy as the first county commissioners. They, in turn, appointed M.H. Day the register of deeds and D.W. Spaulding as treasurer. Jim Somers, despite his ongoing horse thieving, was appointed sheriff.[17]

Charlie Collins then devised his penultimate scheme to exploit the Black Hills. He induced 26 men, one woman, and a nine-year-old boy to set out for the Black Hills. The party left Sioux City on October 6, 1874. Under the guise that they were heading for O'Neill's Colony in Nebraska, the Collins party slipped by the military, then turned northwest and illegally entered the Sioux Reservation. After a tough trip through the Badlands, the group reached the site of Custer's gold strike on French Creek on December 23rd. They built a formidable stockade and then looked for gold.[18]

The residents of Brule City waited through the winter for word from the gold seekers. Eph Witcher, a member of the Collins party, reached Yankton on February 28, 1875. John Gordon, whose horse had given out, stumbled in a day later. Their pokes were full of gold. Collins went to Yankton to escort the successful prospectors into Sioux City aboard a Dakota Southern train decked in flags. Collins rode up front in the pilot, waving his arms and howling like a maniac. A crowd of 600 river-front roustabouts waited to carry the conquering heroes on their shoulders from bar to bar. Whiskey flowed freely. Stalwart citizens known to be of normal intelligence soon caught a highly contagious disease – gold fever. Several hundred such afflicted men soon believed they could strike it rich in the Black Hills – if only they could get there.

Two companies were immediately formed in Sioux City to transport would-be prospectors and their supplies to the forbidden gold fields. Fred Evans headed up one transportation company. H.N. Witcher organized the second. John Gordon served as a guide for Evans' outfit. Eph Witcher guided the H.N. Witcher party. Both men recalled the arduous trip of the original Gordon Party through the Badlands, where one man had died; and they both eschewed the Brule City-Badlands route to the Hills. Instead, they guided their parties along the northern edge of Nebraska to a point near the present-day town of Gordon, Nebraska. There, they turned north toward the Black Hills.

An army patrol intercepted the Gordon party almost as soon as it crossed onto the Indian reservation. Gordon was arrested. The wagons, contents and all, were burned. Eph Witcher's party of would-be prospectors did not fair any better. They ran into a large band of Indians, and all but 19 men turned back.

Meanwhile, Charley Collins continued his promotion of the Brule City-Black Hill Trail by organizing the Black Hills Mining Company of Springfield, Dakota Territory. Collins anticipated that 200 to 1,000 men would leave Springfield on May 1, 1875 for Brule City; and from Brule City they would follow the White River Valley west, passing through the Badlands, and continuing on to the Black Hills. Collins announced that he would lead the expedition, personally. However, the ardor of these would-be prospectors dissipated when word reached them about the fate of the Gordon and Witcher parties.[19]

The Army garrison at Fort Randall was significantly strengthened that summer. Patrols were numerous, wide-ranging and led by a skilled scout, William "Wallace" Wells. Many groups tried to slip past the Army patrols guarding the Brule City-Badlands Trail that summer, but only four parties were successful. All of them were led by Philip Faribault Wells, Wallace Wells' younger brother.[20]

The word went out. Organizers in Chicago, Minneapolis, St. Louis, and other points advised would-be prospectors to avoid the Brule City Trail. As a result, hundreds of men left from Sioux City and went to the Black Hills via the southern route. The Sioux City and Black Hills Transportation Company drew a map showing this route to the Black Hills and sent it to the widely-read Chicago paper, the *Inter-Ocean*, for publication. Charlie Collins somehow got his hands on the map, and he re-drew the route so it went from Sioux City to Brule City and then through the Badlands to the Black Hills.[21]

Collins' Machiavellian efforts were to no avail. President Ulysses Grant issued an order in January 1875 that declared that Brule County was still Indian land. Most settlers in Brule City abandoned their claims. By fall, D.W. Spaulding, M.H. Day, A. Peterson, Jim Somers, George Trimmer, and H.M. Leedy were the only settlers left. The post office door swung shut on December 10, 1875.[22]

Brule City received a reprieve in March 1876 when President Grant commanded the removal of all troops guarding the Black Hills. Thereafter, would-be prospectors had to contend only with the Lakota. Charley Collins was in Chicago, where more than a thousand men waited for an expedition to leave for the Black Hills. Collins hit upon yet another scheme to promote the Brule City Trail. He organized a contest to see whether the Sioux City-Nebraska Trail or the Brule City-Badlands Trail was the quickest route to the Hills. Dan Harnett guided the group that took the Brule City-Badlands Trail. They left Chicago on March 15th by rail for Yankton. From there, Harnett's group went by horseback to Brule City and on to the Hills. Harnett's party probably never made it to the Hills. If they did, they did not get there ahead of the group that took the Sioux City-Nebraska Trail because Collins never again made mention of the race.[23]

A rumor circulated about this time that a railroad was headed for Brule City. New settlers arrived in Brule City to take up claims. A school was started, with Mrs. D.E. Spaulding as its teacher.[24] The Brule City post office re-opened.

Dan Harnett announced plans to run a stage between Brule City and the Black Hills, commencing April 1, 1876. Collins looked for a light, draught boat to run between Sioux City and Brule City, and he also entered into an arrangement with Saltiel and Company of St. Louis to operate a steamboat line from St. Louis to Brule City. The first departure was scheduled for June 8, 1876 on the *M. Livingston*. The organizers let it be rumored that Wild Bill Hickok, a name that even then strengthened the faint hearted, would be aboard to guide the group into the Black Hills. Collins negotiated for a ferry to ply back and forth across the Missouri at Brule City. With enthusiasm for Brule City running high, Collins sold a portion of his interest in the town to Charles T. Campbell and John Dillon.[25] Campbell and Dillon had a stage line of four Concord coaches that ran between Yankton and Deadwood via Scotland, Fort Thompson, and Fort Pierre. They intended to shorten their stage route by going through Brule City and then over the Brule City-Badlands Trail to the Hills.[26] Collins then went east, one of many such trips, to present the press with the advantages of the Sioux City-Brule City route to the gold fields.[27]

J.B. Pearson arrived in Sioux City that summer with $20,000 in gold dust taken from Deadwood Gulch. A fresh dose of gold fever broke out. Six such afflicted men from Dubuque, Iowa arrived in Brule City in route to the Hills. Somewhere in the Badlands, the Lakota killed them.[28] Their deaths again closed the Brule City-Badlands Trail.

Despite such setbacks, Brule City and the Brule City-Badlands Trail refused to die. Collins and his associates used each new development to breathe life back into their quest to establish the Brule City-Badlands Trail as the principal route for people and materials bound for the Hills. The next opportunity came in February 1877 when Congress ratified the Black Hills Agreement, appropriating the Black Hills from the Lakota for four-and-a-half million dollars. The Agreement stipulated three routes across the Great Sioux Reservation to the Hills—one of the routes was to begin at Brule City. The Dakota Territory Legislature followed with the Black Hills Wagon Road Act. The Wagon Act appropriated $3,000 to survey the routes and improve each trail. Governor John L. Pennington appointed M.H. Day, a man with credentials as a frontiersman, a contractor, or a surveyor, to survey and to improve the Brule City Trail.[29]

Staggering amounts of freight were hauled into the Black Hills in 1877. The bulk of it was loaded on steamboats at Yankton, brought up-river, and sent overland by oxen or mule trains for delivery in Deadwood. The freight carried up-river that summer kept 36 steamboats busy. But not one steamboat stopped at Brule City to unloaded supplies destined for the Hills. Instead, the steamboats unloaded at Fort Pierre.[30]

Exasperated, Charlie Collins deserted Brule City. He loaded his printing press on a steamboat bound for Fort Pierre, and from he there went to Deadwood. Collins was in Central City by June 1887, where he printed the *Black Hills Champion*.[31] M.H. Day moved to Swan Lake and was elected in 1879 to the Dakota Territory Legislature.[32]

However, Brule City seemed to have nine lives, or at least nine chances for one life. The town was revived yet again when a rumor circulated that the Chicago Milwaukee & St. Paul Railroad was headed for Brule City. H.H. Stout, Jerry Sieck, and F.W. Hemingway settled in Brule City in 1878. Arthur C. Van Metre, a noted frontiersman and reputedly the richest man in Clay County, South Dakota, moved from Vermillion to Brule City to cash in the boom.[33] The town grew to 150 people.

A few miles down-river, E.M. Bond established a ferry across the Missouri River. The county was officially opened to white settlement on August 9, 1879 by an executive order of President Rutherford Hayes. Territorial governor William A. Howard appointed three county commissioners. They met, again established Brule City as the county seat, and issued two liquor licenses for $200 each.[34]

Charlie Collins returned from the Black Hills to promote his town. He set up a printing press on his claim and announced he would soon publish the *Brule City Times*. In typical Collin's fashion, he issued an advance prospectus proclaiming that he would print a million copies of the paper's first edition, which would have made it the largest paper in the United States.[35] The few copies of the first issue of the *Times* that were actually run described Brule City as having a boulevard two miles long and palatial steamboats that stopped every day. As a reward for his efforts, the county commissioners appointed Collins to be a judge in the 1879 election, one result of which was the retention of Brule City as the county seat.[36]

The rumor that Brule City would have a railroad seemed to be confirmed when F.W. Kimball, the Assistant Chief Engineer for the Chicago Milwaukee & St. Paul Railroad, arrived in town to assess the feasibility of running a railroad from Brule City to the Black Hills. Kimball departed for the reservation in August 1879 with a military escort of nine soldiers under the command of Lieutenant Armstrong and an interpreter, Alex Rencontre.

They traveled a good distance the first day and pushed on until dark before they made camp. Soon, a party of Indians, on their way back to the Standing Rock Reservation after attending a Sun Dance on the Rosebud Reservation, arrived and camped nearby. They warned Rencontre that some bad Indians had been at the Sun Dance, and that his party should be careful. Recalling that it had been only three years since the Sioux had wiped out Lt. Col. Custer and his entire 7th Cavalry, Kimball asked Lt. Armstrong whether he thought they were safe with only nine soldiers.

Armstrong admitted that he doubted it, but he was reluctant to send back for more troops because the request would cast aspersions on the post commander's judgment. Kimball announced he would personally ask the post commander for more troops and sent his interpreter on foot back to Fort Hall with the request. At dusk the following day, the interpreter returned with six additional soldiers. The reinforced party proceeded across the reservation without incident and in due time arrived in Rapid City. Still apprehensive about "bad" Indians, Kimball returned over the heavily traveled, and therefore safer, Fort Pierre-Deadwood Trail.[37]

Kimball reported to the Milwaukee Railroad officials that a railroad could be built up the White River valley and through the Badlands; but in his assessment, it was not suitable to bridge the Missouri River at Brule City. Therefore, Captain H.J. King was directed in the summer of 1880 to pilot his steamboat, the *Milwaukee*, past Brule City and proceed another 12 miles to the mouth of

American Creek. There, King unloaded the supplies to start the construction of a terminus of the coming railroad.[38]

F.W. Kimball arrived in Brule City that summer to survey the railroad's route across the Reservation and through the Badlands. To assuage his fear of "bad" Indians, Kimball had arranged for a large military escort; however, he arrived to find a telegram waiting for him from Carl Schurz, the Secretary of Interior. Schurz objected to any military units going onto the Reservation, and he demanded that Kimball use Indian police instead of U.S. Army soldiers. With reticence, Kimball went to the Lower Brule Agency to obtain Indian police. The agent told Kimball that to get any Indian police he must buy a steer and host a feast so the Indians would gather and King could explain the purpose of his trip onto the Reservation to them. This being done, the Indians agreed to provide ten Indian police with the stipulation that Kimball pay each man $1.50 a day (an exorbitant amount in 1881) and provide all rations.

The survey party had been on the Reservation only a few days when ten Indians arrived from the Rosebud Reservation saying that they had been instructed to serve as the survey party's escort. Kimball explained that he already had an escort of Indian police and did not need their services. The new arrivals refused to go back. Their orders, they claimed, came directly from their Agent, and they must follow them. Kimball acquiesced and hired the ten new Indians. This had hardly been done when another ten Indians arrived from Pine Ridge Reservation, bearing similar instructions from their Agent. Kimball had little option but to hire them also.

Kimball was now protected by 30 Indians, but he soon became concerned about his safety. A number of his "good" Indians, he learned, had taken part in the Custer Massacre. Around the evening campfire, several of them proudly announced that they had fired the shot that killed Custer.

Nonetheless, the survey party went on with its work under the watchful eye of 30 Indian police. In due time, the survey crew worked its way west to where the old Indian trail between Rosebud and Standing Rock reservations intersected the intended rail line (probably near the mouth of Black Pipe Creek). The survey crew arrived at this intersection just as the Sun Dance at Rosebud was concluding. Many Indians were passing down the trail on their way back to the Standing Rock Reservation. They informed Kimball's Indian policemen that Spotted Tail was angry with them for escorting the survey party onto the Sioux Reservation. With that information, the 30 Indian policemen who had been protecting the survey party now would not allow the survey to proceed with its work.

Kimball and a small escort of Indians left at once for Rosebud to get the matter resolved. After a journey of 50 miles, they arrived at the Agency about 9:00 p.m.; but they had to wait until the next day to see the Agent. The next morning, Kimball explained the situation to the Indian Agent, Wright. Kimball thought that Wright ran the Agency, and that he would immediately order Kimball's escorts to allow the survey to proceed. Instead, Agent Wright told Kimball that if Spotted Tail was against the survey, he [Kimball] might as well abandon the effort and go back east.

Kimball asked the Agent to go with him to see Spotted Tail, but Wright curtly refused. Exasperated, Kimball took the agent's interpreter and went to see Spotted Tail—the source of his problems.

All of the reason that Kimball could marshal had no affect on Spotted Tail. The Chief knew that President Garfield was up for re-election in the fall and there probably would be a new "Great Father" in Washington next year. Spotted Tail told Kimball that he'd go to Washington next summer to talk to the Great Father, and the survey could wait until then.[39]

Even with this setback, the town of Chamberlain quickly sprang up. If there was a town to promote or a cause to champion, Charley Collins was sure to get involved. Collins signed on with the Chicago Milwaukee & St. Paul Railroad and went to Ireland, his native country, to recruit settlers for the Chamberlain area.[40] The tracks reached Chamberlain that October. The *Rapid City Journal* reported:

> As a railroad terminus, Chamberlain is able to match Pierre stride for stride. The shooting begins shortly after dark and lasts until morning.[41]

As Chamberlain flourished, Brule City dwindled. Chamberlain replaced Brule City that November as the county seat. A year later, December 6, 1882, the Brule City post office closed – permanently.[42]

Chamberlain in 1881.
Photo courtesy of South Dakota State Historical Society.

Chamberlain was off to an auspicious beginning, but sustained growth depended on diverting at least some of the lucrative freighting business from Pierre, the terminus of the Chicago Northwestern Railroad. It proved difficult. Pierre was 60 miles closer to Deadwood. The Fort Pierre-Deadwood Trail was buttressed by six years of continuous use, and the railroad had arrived a full year earlier.

But the Fort Pierre-Deadwood Trail was not without its problems. The Northwestern Express, Stage & Transportation Company moved its entire operation down from Bismarck at considerable expense and invested heavily in building accommodations along the trail. Meanwhile, Fred Evans was in the Hills contracting with miners and merchants to deliver their freight at $2.00 per hundred weight. The Northwestern Transportation Company could not afford to haul freight for anything less than $2.50 per hundred weight. They were doomed unless Fred Evans' monopoly could be broken. Northwestern organized the small, independent operators into a union. The members agreed not to haul freight for less than $2.50 per hundred weight. When the next Evans' freight train rolled into Fort Pierre and parked beside 40 acres of freight waiting transportation to the Hills, no one would lift a finger to help them load. Empty wagons stood idle amid a sea of freight, but not for long. Evans hired Indians from the Reservation to load the freight, and he arranged for soldiers from Fort Sully to protect the Indian labors.[43] While Evans' freight train was loaded, someone (reportedly Noah Newbanks) slipped out to where Evans' oxen grazed and killed most of them.[44] Evans' men again proved resourceful. They unloaded the freight, sorted out the essentials, reloaded, and hitched the remaining oxen. The freight train did not go a mile before wheels rolled loose and axles smashed to the ground. Someone had removed the hub nuts.[45]

Freighting over the Fort Pierre-Deadwood trail suffered additional setbacks in 1881. A fire of unknown origin swept through Fort Pierre that January. It destroyed George Haines' store, Louis LaPlant's house, a drug store, a barber shop, and a saloon. But nature delivered an even more devastating blow on March 28th. An unusually large spring flood swept away tons of freight, smashed steamboats, drowned hundreds of oxen and mules, and floated much of Fort Pierre down the Missouri River. The Northwestern Transportation Company delivered the final blow that summer when they became a subsidiary of the Chicago Northwestern Railroad, which had a monopoly on all the freight brought into Pierre by rail.[46]

Downer T. Bramble, co-owner of the Merchants' Transportation & Freighting Company, immediately looked into the possibility of operating out of Chamberlain. He telegraphed the influential John Brennan of Rapid City on August 22nd:

Rapid City around 1883.
Photo courtesy of the South Dakota State Historical Society.

I want to look up a road to Chamberlain (from Rapid City) that has wood, water, and grass. I think we can go down Rapid Creek and find a crossing and then keep down White River to the Missouri. Want to operate if practical this fall and winter.[47]

Mayor Chauncey L. Wood of Rapid City convened with interested citizens the next morning to discuss the proposed Chamberlain Road, as the trail was being called. Henry Leedy, who was in attendance, informed the group that a few weeks earlier he crossed the Missouri River at the mouth of White River and came up White River fifty miles to the divide between White River and Bad River. He followed the divide for 30 miles to the Badlands, passed through them and came to the crossing on the Cheyenne River, and then on to Rapid City. The distance traveled, he informed the audience, was 219 miles. In other words, the proposed Chamberlain Road was imminently practical. It was moved and carried that a committee of three be appointed by Ed Loveland, the chairman, to meet with a party reported to have begun from Chamberlain and conduct them to Rapid City.

John Brennan proposed that a finance committee be selected to circulate a subscription paper among the business community to defray the explorers' expenses. The chairman appointed Brennan, Louis Vollin, and M. Wilsie to the finance committee. John Brennan was appointed to go to Deadwood to visit with D.T. Bramble about the matter.[48]

Americus Thompson, an old bachelor who lived 18 miles down on Rapid Creek, wrote to Brennan offering his services to guide the Rapid City party.[49] A

John Brennan.
Photo courtesy of Minnelusa Pioneer Museum.

better guide could not have been found. Americus Thompson spent much of his time hunting and traveling with the Indians. The Badlands were his backyard.

The party from Chamberlain never arrived and no action was immediately forthcoming from Rapid City. An exasperated H.L. Dickinson, agent for the Merchants Line, wrote to John Brennan, asking him to prod the people of Rapid City into assisting with the development of the Chamberlain Road. Dickinson especially wanted people to start putting up hay along the line. He assured them that they would find a good market for the hay because nearly all the freight would be handled over the Chamberlain Road.[50]

Bramble sent William Burns, a freighter, to Rapid City to organize a party to explore the trail. A subscription paper circulated through Rapid City's business community raised $153 to defray the expedition's expenses.[51] With Americus Thompson guiding, the party left Rapid City around the first week in September and arrived in Chamberlain on September 16th. Thompson gave the *Chamberlain Register* a detailed description of the proposed route, the water sources, and the needed improvements. He pronounced that the route was better for both summer and winter pasture than the Pierre Road, and that it was much better watered, wooded and sheltered. The *Register* assured everyone that the managers of the Milwaukee Railroad were doing their best to establish the trail, and that freight would probably be traveling over the Chamberlain Road by winter.[52]

Fred Evans was also interested in freighting over the proposed trail. He left Chamberlain on September 19th with Captain John Daugherty, David Spaulding, and Zack Sutley to examine the proposed Chamberlain Road. Evans found that the route had fewer hills than the Pierre Road, more wood and water, and it was only 40 miles longer. In Evans' opinion, the better route would more than compensate for the extra distance. He transferred his extensive freighting operation to Chamberlain.[53]

The Lakota still claimed the land between the Missouri River and the Black Hills, and no freight could roll over the trail until Spotted Tail gave his approval. The Chicago, Milwaukee & St. Paul Railroad was working on the problem. John Lawler, of the Milwaukee line, personally accompanied a delegation of six Indian Chiefs, headed by Spotted Tail (who insisted that "Chief Bushy Eyes" [Lawler] accompany them), to Washington. They rode east during the summer of 1881 in a private railroad car provided by the Milwaukee Railroad. The Indians were given a royal welcome at every stop. Every evening they were treated to a banquet. Nothing was too good for the Indians. Lawler even bought the Chiefs new suits. Spotted Tail looked distinguished in his black derby, swallow-tail suit coat, vest, cravat, cane, and leather shoes.[54]

After meeting the President and with all the fanfare that accompanied these trips east, Spotted Tail and other chiefs put their name to an agreement that allowed the Milwaukee Railroad a 200-foot-wide right-of-way across the reservation. On October 20, 1881 H. Price, the Commissioner of Indian Affairs, telegraphed the Indian Agent at Lower Brule that the Chicago, Milwaukee & St. Paul Railroad Company could be allowed to open a road at once across the Reservation. The agreement required the Milwaukee Railroad to pay the Lakota $22,000 for the right-of-way across the Reservation, and it gave them permission to locate a ferry landing on the west side of the river, opposite Chamberlain.[55]

The Milwaukee Railroad contracted with Fred Evans to improve the creek crossings, put up sufficient hay for the coming winter, and build six way-stations along the route, Evans put enough men on the job to have the Chamberlain Road ready within 30 days. He also exhorted the people of Rapid City to prepare the road from their town down Rapid Creek to the Cheyenne River, where his improvements would terminate at the west edge of the Reservation.[56]

Rapid City responded. John Hall secured pledges from the businessmen for $150 to bridge Rapid Creek in two places, the only improvements deemed necessary.[57]

Fred Evans.
Photo courtesy of the South Dakota State Historical Society.

Evans left Chamberlain in mid-November 1882 with Captain John Daugherty and William Wells to inspect the work on the Chamberlain Road. Three gangs of men were putting up hay and hauling it into the way-stations. Other men were working on the seven remaining small bridges. Evans was satisfied with the preparations and immediately started two bull trains operating over the route.[58] One of the first bull trains made the trip from Chamberlain to Rapid City in 18 days, three of which were spent in the Badlands with a broken axle.[59] The good time confirmed the practicality of freighting on the Chamberlain Road. Bramble and Miner, owners of the Merchants' Transportation & Freight Company, announced they would close their store in Pierre and open an even larger store that spring in Chamberlain.[60]

Fred Evans, Bramble & Miner and Daugherty & Company, the three principal handlers of Black Hills freight, were ready to operate out of Chamberlain by the spring of 1882. However, the spring thaw delayed the start of the freighting season. Chamberlain filled with freighters who had time on their hands. They passed the warm spring days playing baseball, and eventually challenged the local young men to a game. Wagers were made and the game started. The freighters ran up such a high score that by the fifth inning the local boys called it quits. The victors went to town to celebrate. Anti, a saloon keeper, threatened to kick the freighters out when they got too loud. They didn't leave. Instead, the freighters took possession of the saloon. At house expense, they treated everyone who came in the door. The freighters eventually tired of the game and moved on, in turn, to each of the five other saloons. In due time, they came to the end of street. From there, they had only one place to go – the *sporting house*. They made a wreck of it. They broke up the furniture, drove the ladies out, and would have destroyed the piano except Zack Sutley intervened. "Boys," he said, "we had better leave the piano alone. We don't want to do any serious harm." Finally, the freighters stumbled back to their camp to sleep it off. The next day Sutley, Clark, Quinn, and the two other wagon bosses went around to saloons to settle up the damages. The madam of the sporting house wanted $200. They gave her $50.[61]

The trail finally firmed up. Evans' bull train pulled out of Chamberlain with machinery for the Barstow Mining Company, 800 kegs of powder for a hard rock miner, and several hundred ton of coal for the Homestake Mine. From then on, bull trains were a common sight pulling the Seven Mile Hill west of Chamberlain and heading toward the Black Hills.

The permanence of the Chamberlain Road seemed further confirmed when word spread that R.H. Elmer, assistant postmaster general, was going to establish a mail route between Chamberlain and Rapid City, The proposed route, mail route #35,262, was to begin July 1, 1883. A notice was printed in the paper for bids. Interested parties were instructed to send a check for $4,000 and a bond for $20,000 with their proposal.[62] A mail route portended stage service.

Bull trains headed for the Black Hills.
Photo courtesy of the South Dakota State Historical Society.

Passengers would soon be able to leave Chamberlain at 7:00 a.m. on the stage, travel to the terminus of the narrow-gauge railroad at Stagebarn Canyon at the foot of the Black Hills, and be in Deadwood within 48 hours.[63]

John Lane, the depot agent for the Milwaukee Railroad, received an invoice in August for over 1,000 tons of freight for the Fred Evans Transportation Company. The shipment included 40 carloads of iron rails for the Black Hills & Fort Pierre Railroad.[64] It was the first shipment of the 125 tons of rails that the Fred Evans' freight trains carried over the Chamberlain Road to the Black Hills.[65]

The rails were laid from Deadwood to the mouth of Stagebarn Canyon, just ten miles north of Rapid City. Evans asked the people of Rapid City to raise $200 to build a first-class road from their city up to the terminus of the Black Hills & Fort Pierre Railroad. The money was quickly put up by backers who saw the narrow-gauge railroad as another sign that the lucrative freighting business would continue to roll over the Chamberlain Road and through their town.[66]

The optimism seemed justified. All of Fred Evans' freight now went over the Chamberlain Road. He also bought a building site in Chamberlain for a large roller mill and transferred Charley Davis, his right-hand man, to Chamberlain to oversee the project. Davis projected the mill would grind out 50,000 pounds of flour a year, which Evans had contracted to deliver to the Sioux agencies in 1883.[67]

Outwardly cantankerous Americus Thompson even did what he could to promote the Badlands freight trail, which ran right by his cabin. He nailed a note on his door:

> Old Thompson is away, and damn you if you must go in, don't leave the cabin any dirtier than you found it. If you need hay, don't scatter it all over the country on account of danger of fire.[68]

Hundreds of freight wagons rolled over the Chamberlain Road in 1882. The wagons seemed destined to cut a ribbon of ruts deep into the Badlands—ruts that would indelibly blaze a permanent testament to freighting barons. However, trouble was coming. One evening in the fall of 1882, an Evans' bull train pitched camp for the night along the Chamberlain Trail. As usual, the oxen were put out to graze. The next morning, the herder found ten dead oxen. Indians had killed them. A few weeks later a band of Brule braves rounded up 16 of Witcher's oxen and drove them off. In December, Brule warriors gathered up Evans' oxen and held them for ransom. The wagon master had to pay a dollar a head pasturage to get the stock back.[69]

The Right-Of-Way Agreement between the Lakota and the Milwaukee Railroad provided the freighters a 200-foot-wide strip across the reservation. The freighters considered the right-of-way to be the 200 feet they occupied at any particular moment. But Spotted Tail applied a more concrete and correct inter-

Steamboat landing at Fort Pierre.
Photo courtesy of the South Dakota State Historical Society.

pretation of the right-of-way. As a result, the most of the freighters abandoned the Chamberlain-Rapid City Trail.

Although Fred Evans considered the Chamberlain Road to be the best freight trail to the Hills, he too abandoned it. As soon as the ice went out on the Missouri in the spring of 1883, Evans began shipping his freight by steamboat from Chamberlain, up to Fort Pierre, and from there overland to the Hills. Four steamboats, the *Kelly*, the *Terry*, the *Behan* and the *Milwaukee* hauled his freight between the two ports.[70] All totaled, the steamboats carried 12 million pounds of freight from Chamberlain to Fort Pierre that season.[71]

Yet, the steamboats did not carry all of Evans' freight to Fort Pierre. He moved the heavier material from Chamberlain to Pierre by bull train. Eight hundred additional oxen were shipped in from Iowa for the purpose.[72] These extensive measures were only temporary. Evans engineered a way that winter to break the monopoly the Northwestern Transportation Company had on the railroad into Pierre. Evans had his freight transferred at Mitchell onto the newly constructed Jim Valley Railroad, which carried the merchandise to Wolsey and then over Chicago Northwestern tracks to Pierre.[73]

However, it was the Sioux City & Pacific Railroad that spelled the end of the Chamberlain Road. The railroad (later called the Fremont, Elkhorn & Missouri Valley Railroad) bridged the Missouri River at Sioux City in the summer of 1882 and quickly laid tracks west. Charles Van Wyck, U.S. Senator from Nebraska, perceiving an opportunity for his state, demanded that the postmaster general justify the proposed mail route from Chamberlain to Rapid City. The postmaster general meekly replied that the route was about 200 miles long and ran principally through Indian country where no whites, save those in government service, resided. The postmaster general also reported that the route had been considered only because the postmasters at Chamberlain and Rapid City had recommended it. Mail route #35,262 was canceled before it even started.[74]

The Sioux City & Pacific Railroad reached Valentine, Nebraska in the spring of 1883. The Niobrara Transportation Company hauled the railroad's freight from Valentine to the Hills. A mail route and daily stage soon followed. Each summer, the railroad laid tracks closer to its ultimate destination, the Black Hills. The first train ceremoniously puffed into Rapid City on July 5, 1886 [D].[75]

The Chamberlain Road thus died. Its passing went unnoticed. The trail's promoters had moved on. After doing his best to promote the Black Hills, Charley Collins returned to Sioux City. He was mugged one night and never fully recovered. He went to California, became involved briefly in real estate and died in 1893.[76] M.H. Day was in Rapid City by 1883, where his political career fizzled.[77] Fred Evans plunged his considerable fortune into building and promoting the resort town of Hot Springs, and lost.

Spring run offs and flash floods cut away at the wagon ruts that marked the Chamberlain Road. White River transported the grit and gumbo to the Missouri where, as if by a grand scheme, the debris was deposited at Brule City's doorstep. In the Badlands, most traces of the promoters' trail soon vanished.

Notes

[A] John Brennan was a reporter for the Sioux City *Weekly Times*. He is not the John Brennan associated with the founding and development of Rapid City.

[B] There is confusion as to whether the name is "Harnett" or "Hodnett." A.T. Andreas in *A Historical Atlas of Dakota* gave the name as "Harnett." Jane Conrad in her article, "Charlie Collins: The Sioux City promotion of the Black Hills," also gave the name as "Harnett." David Kemp, in his meticulously researched book, *The Irish Experience in Dakota Territory,* stated the name as "Hodnett. "John Pope Hodnett of Chicago was appointed," Kemp noted, "Assessor of Internal Revenue for the District of Dakota Territory in 1869." Annie Tallent, in *The Black Hills or Last Hunting Ground of the Dakotas,* wrote that John N. Hodnett worked with Charley Collins to found Brule City, and stated that Hodnett was the U.S. Assessor of Dakota Territory. Bingham and Peters give the name as "Harnett" in their article "A Short History of Brule County." A plausible explanation for this difference in spelling of the name is that in about 1870 the Hodnetts Americanized their name to Harnett.

[C] Several anecdotal incidents reveal the nature of Jim Somer's character. As a member of the 1861 Dakota Territory Legislature, Somers made but one speech to the august body. As he rose to speak, it was clear that both he and the arsenal he carried were loaded. Somers proclaimed that he was in favor of legislation legalizing the marriage of white men and Indian women, and vowed to blow out the brains of the lawmakers if they killed the bill.[78] Later, while on a drinking spree in Yankton, he rode his horse into a saloon and shot the sheriff. Somers was jailed, but escaped. No one went after him. To add to his considerable stature as a desperado, he, Jack Sully, and William "Billy" T. McKay hanged William Holbrough and Henry Hirl. They claimed to be vigilantes ridding the country of horse thieves. Others knew that Holbrough and Hirl were hanged because they kept the authorities in Yankton notified of the trio's movements, the trio being the real horse thieves.[79]

[D] The Independence Day celebration was held on the 5th because the 4th fell on a Sunday in 1886.

CHAPTER 4

In Quest Of Gold

"There's gold in the Badlands!" Tell that to a crusty old geologist and he'll call you loco. "Gold," the geologist will instruct, "forms when chemically suitable magma, as it cools, hovers between the critical temperatures of 400 and 120 degrees Celsius. Gold is found in Precambrian igneous rocks – granite. The Badlands is 600 feet of sediment laid down at the bottom of an ancient inland sea. It's dried mud. Only a romantic would search the Badlands for gold!"

South Dakota Badlands.
Photo courtesy of South Dakota State Historical Society.

Toussaint Langlois, a fur trapper for the American Fur Company, was the first person known to have prospected in the vicinity of the Badlands. He came into Fort Pierre in 1860 with a quill full of gold and told company officials that he found the small nuggets while searching for beaver. Company officials bluntly told Langlois that he was hired to obtain furs – not gold.

Langlois was standing in the south fork of the Cheyenne River at the time of his gold find. From the east, dry-wash creeks drained into the Cheyenne from the rugged Badlands. Cool, clear streams flowed in from the west. Langlois found the gold at the mouth of one such stream, Amphibious Creek (now called Lame Johnny Creek). He never thought for a minute that the gold had washed out of the Badlands. Instead, Langlois concluded the gold had been washed into the river by streams that rose in the Black Hills, 30 miles to the west.

By 1874, the year Lt. Colonel George Custer made a reconnaissance of the Black Hills, most people living on the edge of the Great Sioux Reservation knew about the gold in the Hills. Many would-be prospectors anxiously waited for Custer to confirm its existence. When he did, thousands of prospectors, merchants, freighters, derelicts, and prostitutes trespassed into the Hills to get gold from the streams or from those who panned it.[1]

The placer mining quickly played out. By 1883 most of the gold coming out of the Black Hills was extracted by hard-rock mining, which required expensive machinery and scores of organized laborers. The old-time prospectors became store keepers, ranchers, or freighters. A few chased rumors of gold to Alaska;[2] But apparently, some prospectors went to the Badlands to search for gold.

Leonel Jensen, a man whose veracity is beyond reproach, related a story that had been told to him about gold prospectors in the Badlands. The story was that a young cowpuncher working in 1888 for the Duhamel outfit north of the present-day town of Wall took advantage of a break in the fall roundup to ride into the Badlands. He rode about 16 miles and spent the day in the Sage Creek Basin. The weather had been rainy, and the sloughs and ponds were full of water. The ground was soft. After riding a distance into the Badlands, the cowboy dismounted. Picketing his horse, the cowboy walked about two miles and came upon some old sluice boxes, piles of rock, and other evidence that considerable digging had been done and considerable dirt had been washed. The cowboy wandered farther into rougher county. He came to a level table about an acre and half in size that was covered with tall grass. On top of the table, the cowboy found a five-foot-deep shaft. Dropping into the shaft, he found two tunnels, one of which had caved in.

The cowboy followed the open tunnel until he came to a room about 20 feet by 30 feet and 10 feet high. The place was dark. He found a piece of wood and made a torch. In the light, the cowboy discovered the room was furnished with crude, homemade furniture. In the center of the room was a large, roughly-hewn table. A kerosene lamp and some tin dishes sat on the table. Several chairs and a dresser completed the furnishings. Everything was covered with a half-inch of fine dust. The room appeared to have been abandoned several years before. The occupants had left without taking their personal belongings. Clothes hung on pegs driven into the dirt wall and tools stood in the corner ready for use. The evidence suggested that the prospectors had been discovered by Indians and killed. Rain was falling when the cowboy went outside. By the time the cowboy reached his horse, it was dark. He returned to the roundup camp in the dead of a starless, dark night.

After a week of inclement weather, the cowboy and several companions went back to the Badlands. They tried to relocate the cave, but heavy rains had washed away the landmarks. The numerous, small, grass-covered mesas all looked alike. They were not able to find the site. Later, the young cowboy spent several weeks combing the area, but he was never able to re-discover the cave or the gold diggings.[3]

The next person to look for gold in the Badlands was a prospector by the name of William W. Challis. He was living in Harney (now a Black Hills ghost town) when the Badlands were opened for white settlement. Challis, Bill Roy, and Ed Purcell probed the area in the spring of 1890 for ore deposits.[4] They found specimens of iron ore along White River and worked diligently at their mine throughout the summer, coming to town only for groceries and supplies. But their work came to an abrupt end on November 20, 1890 when U.S. Army troops moved onto the Rosebud Reservation and Pine Ridge Reservation in an effort to stop the Ghost Dancing that prophesied the death of all white men (see Chapter 5). Thousands of Lakota fled from the Agencies to the isolated corners of the reservation and commenced frenzied Ghost Dancing.[5] The unrest drove Challis and Bob Bennett out of the Badlands. Challis aptly summed up the sudden turn of events: "The Indians are scared and they're running, and the whites are scared and they're cunning."[6]

Challis returned to the Badlands the next summer, 1891. By July, he was one of a company of men developing an iron ore deposit along the White River.[7] The mining venture did not pan out. By fall, Challis was back in the Black Hills.[8]

A party from Pierre went into the Badlands to search for treasure in the fall of 1890. But they were not looking for gold or other valuable minerals. Thomas Phillips, Pete Lear, and Joe Wandall, well known old-timers in the Pierre area, came to the Badlands in September 1890 to procure fossils that Phillips sold to museums and collectors. While exploring along Sage Creek, Phillips thought he saw "color." Phillips, who had panned nuggets from Deadwood Gulch in 1876, was irresistibly drawn by the prospect of gold. He made a roughly improvised mining pan and washed some dirt. The trio returned to Pierre with startling news. There was gold in the Badlands![9]

Phillips had conducted a simple test while he panned along Sage Creek. He washed steadily for 20 minutes and saved all the gold panned from those washings. He showed the gold to Fred Huggins, a jeweler who managed the Gallett Jewelry Store in Pierre. Huggins determined that the gold was worth $1.40. Every miner knew that if $4.20 could be made in an hour with a gold pan, tenfold that amount could be made with a sluice box.

A sense of the prospectors' excitement is best conveyed by converting Phillips' findings into today's currency. Gold sold for $20 an ounce in 1890. Today (2008) it sells for roughly $900 an ounce. If Phillips had panned for an hour, he would have obtained about a fifth of an ounce of gold. At today's price, Phillips panned gold at a rate of $180 an hour.

Thomas Phillips Sr., Tom Phillips, Jr., George Ingram, Pete Lear, George Parody, Joe Wandall, and Fred Huggins, the requisite number for forming a mining company, soon left Pierre for the Badlands. They took a surveyor with them. After prospecting most of the Sage Creek Basin, they determined that the gold was in an area 30 miles long and of unknown width. Twenty-one claims of 18 acres each were staked out along the middle fork of Sage Creek (now called Johnson Creek). They also laid out a town on a beautiful sloping plateau in the center of the gold district. They called their envisioned town Logan.

Little more could be done that fall as it was too late in the year to find the water they needed for sluicing. Moreover, an Indian outbreak appeared imminent. The men prudently returned to Pierre. There, they filed papers to establish the Wandall Mining District. They built sluices that winter, anxiously waited for spring, and thought much about gold.

Word of the gold strike was picked up by the *Rapid City Journal* and the *Hot Springs Star* in the fall of 1890 and spread throughout the Black Hills.[10,11] However, interest in a rumored gold strike was overshadowed by the developing Indian unrest. No one in the Hills was going to risk his scalp wandering the Badlands in search of gold.

A.D. "Tony" Hengel ran a clothing store adjacent to Phillips' furniture store. He had bought a gold nugget from an Indian about five years previously and had stashed it in his safe. All of Phillips' talk about gold put a devilish idea in Hengel's head. Tony set a practical joke in operation one day in early March when Phillips made his daily sojourn into Hengel's store. Approaching Tom with a serious air, Tony handed him the nugget and said, "I found this the other day. Is it gold or just a piece of copper?" Phillips knew it was gold, but he wanted it tested. He convinced Hengel to let him run the nugget down the street to Fred Huggins for an assay.

Tony Hengel feigned surprise when Tom Phillips came back a half-hour later to announce that the nugget was gold, and Hengel suppressed a smile as Phillips gave him a pitch about forming a gold mining company and making a fortune. When Hengel agreed to Phillips' plan, Tom pressed Tony as to where he found the gold nugget. After extracting Phillips' promise to never tell another soul, Hengel told Phillips that he had found the nugget while grading one of his lots in town.

Phillips put his son, Thomas Phillips, Jr., in charge of the store for the rest of the day. He hitched up his delivery wagon and drove out to Hengel's lot, Sampling here and digging there, Phillips filled the delivery wagon with dirt and took it home. He spent most of the night washing through a wagon-load of dirt, a pan at a time. The next morning, exhausted from a lack of sleep and the work, Philips came to see Hengel. "I got only one or two nuggets about the size of a pin head from the entire wagon-load of dirt!" Phillips confided. Hengel burst out laughing. Putting a table of clothes between them, he confessed.[12]

While Phillips was in Pierre being victimized by his own greed, Joe Wandall and another member of the party were in the Badlands guarding the group's interests. When weather permitted, they prospected. Wandall found a rich bed on his claim. He returned to Pierre in late February for supplies. Before returning to the Badlands, Wandall confided to a friend that he could make a hundred dollars a day working his claim.

By mid-March, all of the members of the mining district were in the Badlands working their claims. Phillips struck a rich-paying ledge in one of the gullies leading into Sage Creek, from which he panned seven to eight dollars of gold a day. Knowing that they could find more gold with sluice boxes, Phillips and most of the mining company came into Pierre for lumber with which to build a bulkhead for a dam and sluice boxes and, not incidentally for a hot bath and good meal. While in Pierre, Phillips proudly and widely displayed the specimens of the gold dust that he had panned, claiming that he could pan $7 to $8 dollars a day. To add veracity to his claim, Phillips displayed a sample of his findings. Some of the particles were quite large and contained fifty cents to one dollar worth of gold. As soon as Phillips and Company purchased their lumber and stocked up with enough supplies to last the summer, they returned the Badland gold fields. Upon their return to the Badlands, the prospectors intended to build a dam 20 feet long and 30 feet high, and they counted on June rains to fill the dam. Through the bulkhead, the dam would provide water throughout the summer to run their sluices.[13]

Buck Williams also came into Pierre with Phillips. He was on hand when Phillips was displaying the results of his panning. Looking at Phillips' sampling, Williams told the onlookers, "If that is gold" (and it was) "I know where I can get a bushel of it." He then invited the several newspaper reporters into jewelry store where Fred Huggins was assaying the sample of gold that Buck had brought in from the Badlands. Higgins informed the reporters that Williams the bright particles in Williams' were a very fine article of gold. The jeweler was also analyzing a sample that George Parody had sent in with Williams. According to the Williams, Parody got that particular sample of gold from two scoops of earth washed in common bread ban. The jeweler confirmed that Parody's sample was also gold. According to Williams, Parody wanted the town folk to know that he'd soon come in from the Badlands with a $100 worth of gold dust. Buck Williams was so confident that there was gold in the Badlands that he offered to pay anybody's fare both ways if they didn't find paying quantities of gold.[14]

Having seen Badland gold with their own eyes, a number of Pierre residents, all of them respectable citizens and heretofore thought to be of sound mind, caught gold fever. George Ingram and several men left for the Badland gold fields on March 20, 1891. Ben Arnold, John Isele, Joseph Wandell, and Van Moore set out from Pierre for the gold fields on March 25, 1891. Arnold and party traveled through snow and wet gumbo for six days, arriving at Sage Creek on March 31st. However, the water from the melting snow was too high for them to do any prospecting. The Arnold party also attempted to build a dam. But everything was so wet that they were not able to get much dirt moved, and they abandoned the effort. So they prospected widely throughout the area. They were able to find gold, about 40 colors, on top of gravel knolls far out into the Badlands.

Then adversity struck. While Arnold's party was prospecting on April 10th, a fire started in their camp. Their tents, bedding, clothes, and food burned up, along with fifty dollars in paper currency belonging to Joseph Wandell. Some of Ingram's party saw the smoke and rushed to the scene, but exploding cartridges made them keep their distance, preventing them from putting the fire out or saving any of the supplies. In western spirit, George Ingram and members of his mining party came to the relief of Arnold and company, providing the hard-luck prospectors bedding, clothes, and shelter. The members of Tom Phillips, Pete Lears,' and George Parodys' mining company did likewise.

Ben Arnold and the members of his mining party immediately returned to Pierre to resupply. When he got to Pierre, Arnold was a sober but not a reluctant prospector. To encourage other would-be miners, Arnold reported to the editor of the *Pierre Daily Capital* that there is a good road to within fifteen miles of the gold fields:

> From Pierre to Sage Creek and the Sure Thing mines follow Bad River Valley as far as Napoleon Deschaneaux's (22 miles) and then on to Midland. Here you will find a general store (Charley Russell's) where anything needed can be bought at Pierre prices and also a post office. Distance from

Fort Pierre – 57 miles. The next day drive up the valley and you reach the forks of Bad River: distance 25 miles and 82 from Fort Pierre. Here, you leave Bad River and follow Cottonwood, a tributary for 25 miles. Where there is a haystack and dug out. Follow the trail to the head of Cottonwood. You strike the Fort Laramie and Fort Pierre wagon road, and then following this road 12 miles you arrive at Bull Creek. Here you cross the stream and about three miles further on the road forks, and taking the left fork for five miles you reach the north fork of Sage Creek – in the mining district. Total mileage – 129. You are never away from wood, water, or grass and can camp anywhere.

Any sane reader of the *Pierre Daily Capitol* would have been asking himself, "How likely is it that a miner would be announcing the road to the mother lode?" But Ben Arnold was not a man without a conscience. He went to went on to tell to report:

anyone who is doing well need not go there and think to pull up the grass and shake the gold out of the roots nor rake it off the top of the ground.. But there are eight men there at present. In my opinion, something rich will be struck before long. As for me, as soon as I can procure another outfit, I will return and hold what I have.[15]

Interest in the Badland gold fields was stirred in the Black Hills when Bradford Johnson came into Rapid City from his ranch, located opposite the mouth of Sage Creek. Bradford reported to the R*apid City Journal* that 14 men were busily panning gold along Sage Creek. They have been camped about 12 miles up Sage Creek for some time and they went to Link (the first name used for the little town of Creston – a town that once existed near the mouth of Rapid Creek) for their mail and provisions. Johnson stated that the men were making about two dollars a day while working under the adversity of bank-full flood waters in Sage Creek.[16]

Two weeks later, Johnson was in Rapid City to reiterate his favorable report about the gold fields along Sage Creek. He intended, he confided, to go there himself next week with an experienced miner.[17]

Word of the gold strike in the Badlands spread east. The *Sioux City Journal* informed its readers that gold in paying quantities had been discovered along Sage Creek in the Badlands. "Out of two pans of earth washed," the article related, "eighty cents in gold were taken."[18]

A party set out from Rapid City in mid-May to investigate the reputed gold finds in the Badlands. They returned with disappointing news. There was no evidence of extensive mining along Sage Creek. They had found only a dugout occupied by a lone prospector. The prospector affirmed that gold was in the Badlands, but it would take a quart cap full to weigh an ounce. The prospector related that the other miners had already left and he would be gone by the end of the week. "It may be set down as a fact," the *Journal* concluded, "that the Sage Creek mines are no good."[19] The *Pierre Daily Capital* concurred. "The gold hunters in the Badlands have forgotten what they went after and are now taking up homestead claims."[20]

However, the Badland gold would not be forgotten. Louie Blummer moved to the Badlands in 1909 with his mother and stepfather. The family homesteaded along Sage Creek. But Louie did not get along with his stepfather, so he went to live with Charley Wyant, a homesteader on the upper part of Sage Creek Basin whose son, Clive, was about Louie's age. Louie earned his keep at Wyant's by working. One task was to dig a well.

Louie had dug down 12 feet. The last two feet had been in wet sand. Clive was handing down flat stones so Louie, who was at the bottom of the hole, could build a curb, As Louie worked, water trickled in at his feet, and the sand walls slowly crumbled. While fitting a rock, Louie noticed a bright flash. He reached for it and picked up a bright, pea-sized rock. It looked like a gold nugget!

"Watch out! It's coming in!" Clive suddenly shouted. Louie scrambled to get out, as he did, he dropped the nugget The cave-in was minimal, and Louie was soon back down at the bottom of the hole. He tried to find the supposed gold nugget, but he could not.

That was the last time Louie thought about gold in the Badlands for the next 25 years. Then came the dirty thirties – drought and depression. There was no grass, no money, and no work. Louie had time on his hands. He got a gold pan and set out to search for Badland gold.

Forty years later, a few old-timers in the Badlands could recall that in the 1930s Louie Blummer had looked for gold along Sage Creek. Some swore he found it; other said he did not.

Louie graciously related the details of his search for Badland gold during an interview in 1973.[21] Louie said that as a kid he had discovered the remnants of prospecting years earlier on Johnson Creek – a crude rocker made out of a cottonwood log and signs of excavations. So 25 years later he went back to that area to search for gold. It was at the height of dirty thirties – a severe drought on the Great Plains. So, as Louie explained Sage Creek was bone dry. The nearest water hole was three miles away, and it was little more than a damp spot in the creek. But being determined to see if he could find gold, Louie dug down to just below the grass roots and shoveled the dirt into gunny sacks. He loaded the sacks on a pack horse and transported them the water hole. "Using a big, cast iron frying pan, I washed the dirt, looking for gold." Then Louie stopped talking and his mind seemed to get caught up in its own, long ago reverie. I could not take the suspense. "So," I blurted out, "did you find any gold?"

Louie's blue eyes twinkled. Then without another word, he went to a desk, opened a drawer, and carefully removed a small glass vial tightly capped with a cork. In the bottom was an inch of yellow flakes that glittered in the sunlight – Badlands gold!

CHAPTER 5

The Last Cowboy and Indian War

The once mighty Teton Sioux were struggling to survive by 1890. They retreated to the edge of the Badlands to engage in an emotionally charged spiritual quest for an answer to their plight. When 6,000 soldiers came to end that quest, thousands of Lakota gathered on Stronghold Table, a natural fortress in the Badlands. From there, young warriors proved themselves by making daring raids on cowboys who ranched on land taken from them. In turn, these frontiersmen went "Indian hunting;" and so it was that the last cowboy and Indian war was fought in the White River Badlands.

The Treaty of 1868 granted the Teton all the land from the Yellowstone River south to the North Platte River and from the Missouri River west to the Big Horn Mountains for, in the words of the treaty, "as long as the grass shall grow and the rivers shall flow." By 1890 the U.S. Government had taken nearly all of that land from the Indians through a series of cede-or-starve agreements and had confined the Sioux to five small reservations, located principally in western South Dakota. The last Agreement went into affect on February 10, 1890. It opened all of the land from the north bank of White River to the south bank of the Cheyenne River to white settlement – 11 million acres. The ink on the Agreement was barely dry when the Lakota were hit with a devastating drought, a reduction in their rations, a black leg epidemic that decimated their cattle herds, and outbreaks of measles, whooping cough, and influenza. Sick and malnourished, they died in record numbers. Records from the Pine Ridge Agency indicate that 45 Indians (approximately one person in every 100) died every month.[1]

In desperation, the Lakota leaders sent 11 emissaries to Pyramid Lake in Nevada in early November 1889. The emissaries and representatives from most other western tribes met with a Paiute medicine man named Wovoka. Wovoka supposedly had great powers and a message for the Indian people.[2]

The Teton representatives returned to the Pine Ridge Reservation in mid-March 1890, and thousands of Lakota gathered to learn about Wovoka's teachings. The emissaries showed the Lakota the prescribed designs and colors for special shirts, called *ghost shirts*, and taught them a new ceremony, the Ghost Dance. Ghost – shirted Indians, both men and women, danced continuously in a circle. They moved around the circle as the sun moves across the sky until they dropped from exhaustion and lapsed into a trance. Upon waking, a dancer often reported seeing and talking with relatives who had died.

According to the emissaries, Wovoka promised that if Indians faithfully performed the Ghost Dance, the Messiah would come. Because the whites had killed the Messiah the last time he came, this time he was coming to save the Indians, his chosen people. Whereas Wovoka's message putatively was one of peace, the emissaries, particularly Kicking Bear and Short Bull, turned it into something quite different. The ghost shirt took on the power of being impervious to the white man's bullets. By the fall of 1889, many Lakota believed the Messiah was coming in the spring, and that he would cause all white men and any Indians who did not practice the Ghost Dance to die.[3]

White settlers who lived adjacent to the reservations detected the unrest among the Indians. Early that fall, they learned early about the Ghost Dance and the Indians' belief that all whites would soon die. Joseph Gossage published this information about the Indian's activities in the *Rapid City Journal*.[4] The article elicited a wide array of emotions among the whites on the frontier. Recent settlers who had little experience with Indians were apprehensive, to say the least. Merchants fanned the settlers' anxiety in anticipation that the U.S. Government would send soldiers to hold the Indians in check, which would expand the merchants' market for their goods. Speculators promoted the perception of an Indian uprising in hopes it would result in a further reduction of the size of the Sioux reservations.[5]

Feeling this pressure, officials at the Department of Interior felt they had to show that they were in control of the reservations. In the fall of 1890 Robert Belt, Acting Commissioner of Indian Affairs, ordered the Indian agents on Sioux reservations to put a stop to the Ghost Dance ceremony. All tried. Their success was temporary, at best. Seasoned Indian agents like James McLaughlin at Standing Rock and Hugh Gallagher at Pine Ridge argued that increasing the rations and the coming winter would end the unrest.[6]

However, there was another factor stirring the Indian unrest. In 1889 South Dakota became a State, and the voters sent Richard Pettigrew to the U.S. Senate. Having campaigned on the slogan "Dakota for Dakotans," Senator Pettigrew set out to remove every Democrat and every non-South Dakotan in the state who held a federal job on any Indian reservation in the State. Pettigrew engineered the removal of competent Indian agents at five reservations in South Dakota and replaced them with local, Republican politicians. He then pillaged the reservations for jobs. Nearly every employee, from store clerks to teachers' assistants, was dismissed and replaced with a South Dakota Republican.[7] The ideological new comers knew nothing about Indians or the Lakota culture, and they could care less. They intended to "civilization" the Lakota and teach them how to work and live like white men. Worse, the new comers replaced seasoned Agency employees, many of whom had a Indian wife. They were sympathetic and understanding of the Lakota, and most were part of a tiospaye (extended family).

Daniel F. Royer was Pettigrew's most fateful appointment. Royer was born and raised in Pennsylvania. He came to the little town of Alpena in the 1880s, and quickly became active in politics, being elected to the Dakota Territory Legislature in 1887 and campaigning vigorously for Pettigrew's election in 1889. For his support, Pettigrew arranged for Royer to become the Indian Agent for the Pine Ridge Reservation. Royer assumed the job on October 9, 1890. By a combination of blatant graft and obvious timidity, Royer quickly lost control of the Oglalas.

Richard F. Pettigrew.
Photo courtesy of South Dakota Historical Society.

Following an incident at Pine Ridge on November 12th, Royer and his family fled to Rushville, Nebraska. There, he wired Washington. "We have no protection and are at the mercy of these dancers," he telegraphed. "It does not seem to me to be safe any longer without troops..."[8]

Army troops arrived at Pine Ridge and Rosebud in the early morning darkness of November 20th. Six thousand Indians camped at the two agencies hastily struck their tepees and fled into the Badlands. General Brooke, who was in command of the troops on the two reservations, sent couriers across the Reservations. All the Indians were to come into their Agency. Those who came in would be regarded as "friendly." By implication, the Indians who did not come to their Agency would be regarded as "hostile." The couriers also urged settlers living along the border of the two Reservations to abandon their places and seek the safety of settlement some distance for a reservation.

Brook's Camp on the Pine Ridge Reservation.
Photo courtesy of the Department of the Interior, Badlands National Park.

It was near midnight on November 24th when a courier rode reached the newly established ranch of Henry Smith and his brother Ben on the north bank of Whiter River, just across from the mouth of Bear-In-The-Lodge Creek.[9] It was not first word the ranchers had received of Indian unrest. The Smith brothers thanked the informant and went back to sleep. In the morning, Henry shouldered his axe and went into the wood to cut fence posts. Ben rode to Lodge, a general store, five miles down-river to learn the latest on the supposed Indian uprising. Ben came back with word that the situation was serious. Like many ranchers, the Smith brothers went to store, which was considered to be a better point of defense. All day, armed Brule Sioux continually passed along the south bank of White River. The settlers along that stretch of White River congregated at Lodge and spent two days strengthening their fortifications and posting 24-hour guards. But nothing happened, and in two days they went back their ranches and resumed their daily activities

William Challis lived six miles up river from Henry and Ben Smith. Challis, a bachelor and one-time gold prospector in the Black Hills, came to the

Soldiers and government officials at Pine Ridge, 1890.
Photo courtesy of South Dakota Historical Society.

Badlands in the early spring of 1890 to prospect for minerals. He found a deposit of iron ore that he thought could be mined; however, it was not a paying deposit of ore. Seeing the hundreds of cattle coming into the Badlands that summer, Challis realized that in the Badlands there was more money to be made from the grassroots up. He took squatter's rights on a place a mile up-river from Guy Trimble's place and spent the summer of 1890 cutting and stacking all of the hay he could. That fall, he sold the hay to Bud Holcomb, owner of the 6L.[10] When the Indian scare came, Challis was not willing to bet his life on a peaceful outcome. He went back to Black Hills. There, Joseph Gossage, the owner of the *Rapid City Journal*, asked Challis for his assessment of things on the northern border of the Indian Reservations. "The Indians are scared, and they're running" Challis reported, "and the whites are scared and they're cunning."[11]

Even though 3,000 Indians passed within miles of the settlers in the Badlands, and many of them were well-armed warriors, not a shot was fired at a white man and not so much a single calf was stolen. Whereas the Lakota could have easily killed every white man up and down White River, they didn't.

Nonetheless, the whites panicked. Nearly every town within a hundred miles of an Indian reservation formed a home guard and besieged their governors with requests for guns so they could protect themselves.[12]

These sudden developments placed the governor of South Dakota, Arthur Mellette, in a dilemma. He was reluctant to contribute to the settlers' hysteria by distributing guns. Yet, he was fearful of not arming the citizens if an Indian outbreak was imminent. He needed information.

Mellette sent a telegram to V.T. McGillycuddy, president of the Lakota Bank in Rapid City and a former Indian Agent at Pine Ridge, asking him to go to Pine Ridge and make an assessment of the situation.[13] A few days later, Mellette dispatched Scotty Philip and John Holland, west river ranchers, and an Indian named Crow Eagle to the Badlands to reconnoiter a large encampment of ghost dancers.

The three scouts departed Pierre on November 27th. They reached the mouth of Pass Creek, the site of the ghost dancers' encampment, on the morning of November 29th. What they saw stunned them. The large camp of nearly 3,000 Indians was abandoned. A trail, only hours old, indicated that the Indians had gone west, up the south side of White River. Just across the river lay the isolated homes of white settlers who had located on land recently taken from the Indians. Fearful the Sioux might be massacring whole families of new settlers, the scouts rode hard for Pierre. They reached the governor's house shortly after dusk and reported their findings.[14] Mellette immediately wired the information to General John R. Brooke at Pine Ridge. In response, Brooke ordered the cavalries at the Agency to be ready to move at a moment's notice. A rumor spread among the large contingent of reporters at the Agency that the long-awaited Indian war was about to commence.[15]

Short Bull, a Brule Sioux medicine man, led the 3,000 Brule Sioux at Pass Creek west to Wounded Knee Creek. At the same time, Chief Two Strike led 1,000 Oglalas down Wounded Knee Creek. To punish the Indians who had shown their submission by going into the Agency, Two Strike's band pillaged and plundered the abandoned placed they came across. Two Strike and Short Bull met at the mouth of Wounded Knee Creek. The formidable force headed for Stronghold Table.[16]

Stronghold Table, spanning a half-mile from north to south and running a little more than a mile from east to west, was a natural fortress. The only easy access to Stronghold Table was a narrow neck of land 30 feet wide leading to a much larger table, now called Cuny Table. The

Short Bull.
Photo courtesy of the South Dakota Historical Society.

Indians dug a trench in front of this access, making it possible for a handful of warriors armed with repeating Winchesters to defend access to Stronghold Table. At other points, Stronghold Table dropped 300 feet into the Devil's own labyrinth of Badlands canyons. The only means of ascending Stronghold Table was a narrow animal trail on the north face. A small boy with a handful of rocks could defend the position. The Indians were prepared to stay on Stronghold Table indefinitely. They had brought the agency's entire beef herd and many privately-owned cattle and horses. A good spring off the west face of Stronghold supplied plenty of water, and the numerous cedar groves on the sides of Stronghold supplied sufficient wood.

Governor Mellette decided that the situation now warranted arming the settlers. He sent over 400 guns and 20,000 rounds of ammunition on December 4th to small communities across South Dakota, the first of many such shipments.[17] On December 6th, he sent 100 guns, 5,000 rounds of ammunition and a telegram to Merritt H. Day, the former promoter of Brule City and now a Rapid City attorney. "You are hereby appointed my aide de camp to manage the Hills campaign," he informed Day.[18]

It was a curious appointment. M.H. Day hardly looked the part of an Indian fighter. He was short and misshapen. His huge belly protruded out mere inches below his shoulders and barely managed to tuck back in by the time it reached his short legs. His symmetry, not to mention balance, was achieved by an equally large posterior, so large it could be accommodated only by a saddle with 22" tree (a 14" tree fit the typical cowboy of the day). But M.H. Day and Governor Mellette were long-time friends, dating back to 1877 when Mellette was in charge of the land office in Springfield, Dakota Territory and Day was a young aspiring attorney. And how could Governor Mellette refuse to throw his old friend a political plum now? After all, Charley, Governor Mellette's son, had been a dinner guest at the Day home that summer.

M.H. Day and Charley L. Allen departed the next morning for the Cheyenne River with a wagon load of rifles and ammunition. There, Day found the ranchers anxious to join a militia authorized by the governor to fight Indians. Most of the ranchers had suffered losses at the hands of the hostiles. A small group of warriors from Little Wound's band had set up camp along Corral Draw. They crossed the Cheyenne River daily and ran off stock. They made off with most of the cattle on the Reed spread and stole many of Sam McCormack's cattle. A small party of Indians had attempted to take stock from H.M. Steele's ranch on Battle Creek, but a group of ranchers had run them off. Dan Phinney was hit particularly hard. He had moved his family into Hermosa for protection, and his abandoned ranch sat exposed on the flat south of Spring Creek. The Indians looted the ranch. They ran off the stock, and stole all the Phinney's blankets, much of their clothing, and their winter supply of food. The Indians demolished the furniture and took the saddles. However, what really made Dan Phinney furious was that an Indian took his top hat. Almost every day thereafter, one rancher or another ribbed Dan about having seen his top hat bobbing over the range.[19]

According to accounts of locals, the Indians destroyed what they could not use—a purely malicious act in the rancher's eyes. If stolen cattle were too far from Stronghold Table, the Indians shot them. They killed cows for their unborn calves, a delicacy to the Sioux, and shot unruly horses to recover a 75-cent lariat.[20] The ranchers were grateful that the State was finally going to help them.

M.H. Day distributed the governor's guns and cartridges widely. He left ten rifles at Box Elder, a little town 15 miles east of Rapid City. He passed out ten more rifles to the settlers at Creston, near the mouth of Rapid Creek, and he sent ten guns down-river to Link. Moving up-river, "Colonel" Day dispersed 20 guns to the ranchers along Spring Creek, five to the cowboys holed up at Reed's camp on the Cheyenne, and 15 to the people in the Centre precinct. By the time M.H. Day reached the ranchers on French Creek, those who were the closest to Stronghold Table, he had only ten rifles left. He placed those guns in the hands of ranchers who had fortified themselves at the Steward ranch on Harrison Flat by building a blockhouse.[21] They had found a straight cottonwood log, painted it black, and mounted it on two wheels so that from a distance it looked like a cannon.[22]

Merritt H. Day not only armed the cowboys, he organized them into the Dakota Militia. Ninety-six cowboys put their name to an "official" oath, but many others rode with the Dakota Militia.[23]

Day placed George Cosgrove in charge of 50 men stationed at the Frank Stanton ranch on Spring Creek. They were ordered to patrol from Rapid Creek south to Battle Creek. Gene Akin was placed in command of the 46 cowboys stationed at Joe McCloud's place on Battle Creek. They were instructed to patrol south from Battle Creek to Beaver Creek.[24] Day wrote the Governor of the preparations, telling him: "The men are good ones... if the Indians attack, God help them."[25] In response, the Governor sent out an additional 140 guns and 5,000 rounds of ammunition to such communities as Fort Pierre, Nolan, Hermosa, and Buffalo Gap.[26]

Day was soon back in Rapid City, where the *Rapid City Journal* applauded him for arming the ranchers along the Cheyenne River and organizing them so they could protect themselves and their property from marauding Indians. The resultant public support enabled Day and Frank Stanton to collect $184 from the business community with which to buy supplies for the Dakota Militia.[27]

An 80-car train carrying Colonel Eugene Carr's Sixth Cavalry arrived in Rapid City from Fort Wingate, New Mexico at midnight on December 8th.

Brig. General Thomas H. Ruger, commander of the Department of Platte, wired Colonel Carr that the Sixth's first duty was to "see that no parties of Sioux Indians... commit depredations or roam about the settlements along the Cheyenne River." Colonel Carr promptly dispatched Major David Perry and two troops to the mouth of Battle Creek and three troops under Major T.C. Tupper to the mouth of Box Elder Creek.[28]

With troops in place along the Cheyenne River, it could have been argued that there was no need for the Dakota Militia. Concerned at this prospect, Day wrote the Governor on December 11th to shore up his support. "As soon as the troops [the Sixth Cavalry] pass by," he informed Governor Mellette, "the Indians slip in behind them. The troubles will commence and we must rely upon ourselves for protection."[29] Day then left for the Cheyenne River to command the Dakota Militia and, in his mind, prevent the Sioux nation from overrunning the settlements along the edge of the Black Hills.

The first clash between the cowboys and the so-called "hostile" Indians occurred during Day's absence. Jack Daley and Nelse Torkelson had a ranch four miles above the mouth of French Creek. They were preparing breakfast on the morning of December 9th when a half-dozen armed Indians burst into the cabin. The Indians held the ranchers at gun point while they ransacked the place. They took $150 from Daley and almost everything of value, including the ranchers' hats, coats, and every horse on the place. Daley and Torkelson walked to the T.M. Warren ranch on Battle Creek.

The next morning, Joe McCloud rode with Daley and Torkelson back to their ranch. Indians had taken it over. Two Indians were in the corral working a herd of stolen horses. Smoke coming from the chimney indicated the Indians had a fire going in the cook stove, but the cowboys had no way of telling how many Indians were in the cabin. In time, one Indian came out. When the cowboys realized that only three Indians were holding the ranch, they rode down on the place, firing their guns and yelling as if they were leading a cavalry charge. The ruse worked. The three Indians jumped on their horses and fled across the Cheyenne River. Once safely across the river, the three Indians looked back at the ranch and realized they had been chased off by only three cowboys. The Indians reined up their horses and shot at the cowboys. The cowboys returned fire. No injuries were inflicted to either side, but that was due to distance and marksmanship—not intent. The war between the Sioux and the Dakota Militia had started.

The cowboys rode back to the Warren Ranch and boasted of their accomplishment. Gene Akin brought them up short by pointing out that the ranch was again abandoned and would soon fall back into Indian hands. He ordered Sam Bell, Gus Haaser, Ike Miller, Lew Peck, T.M. Warren, Alex Webb and Shorty West to ride back to the ranch and hold it.

The six cowboys arrived at the Daley-Torkelson ranch late that afternoon. They went into the cabin to cook some coffee. Just as the water came to a boil, they heard the hooves of galloping horses. The men rushed out the cabin door to get a fleeting glimpse of three Indians herding their horses across the river. They reluctantly walked back to the Warren ranch to confess that a few Indians had set them afoot.

Captain Akin decided to set a trap for the Indians. He, George Tarbox, Will Brisbin, Jim Ferguson, Charley Edgerton, Farley Sprague, Mac McGregor, and H.J. Sprague rode back to the Daley-Torkelson ranch later that night. They hid their horses in the barn and slipped into the cabin. They passed a cold night, because they did not want smoke from the chimney to reveal their presence.

Unaware of the planned ambush, George Cosgrove and five men patrolled up the river early the next morning. When they reached the Daley ranch, Cosgrove posted Neal Dennis on a high knoll to stand guard while everyone else went into the cabin to have lunch. They swung the door open on a cabin full of grinning cowboys, who kidded them about ruining their ambush. Joe McCloud, Jack Daley and Nelse Torkelson rode in at this time with lunch for the six men hidden in the cabin. Coffee, bacon, and biscuits were being served when Dennis rushed in to report that a bunch of horsemen were riding fast toward the ranch. Cosgrove grabbed his binoculars and announced the riders were 17 Indians. He ordered everyone to hide behind something and not to shoot until he hollered.

Pete Lemley hid behind a wood pile in front of the house. Charley Edgerton ran for a downed cottonwood tree about 200 feet north of the cabin. Riley Miller, a crack shot, found a good position, and Francis Rousch ducked behind the door frame and continued chewing on his biscuit.

The renegade Indians galloped to the entrance of the horse pasture. A brave reached down from his horse to slide back the poles. At that instant, the leader realized that they had ridden into an ambush. He raised his gun in the air and fired a warning shot. Charley Edgerton did not wait for Cosgrove to holler. He shot the Indian, who fell from his saddle and sprawled across the wooden gate poles. Two warriors instantly rode up, leaned down from their saddles, and picked up the dead man between them. A withering barrage of rifle fire came from the cabin and the Indians immediately retreated toward the river. Akin thought the men could get off some good shots, so he ordered everyone to rush to the corral. Joe McCloud reluctantly moved into the open. As he did, an Indian's bullet plowed a furrow down the middle of his head. A quarter of an inch lower and it would have killed him. That night McCloud made out his will.

The sound of rifle fire carried to the Z Bell ranch at the mouth of French Creek. A lot of men were there: Ed Lemmon, Bill Lindsey, and Warren Cole had just ridden in with extra horses; M.H. Day and Frank Stanton had just returned from Rapid City with a wagon load of supplies and rifles; and Captain Eugene Wells and a dozen cavalry soldiers had ridden down from Buffalo Gap that morning.

Captain Wells ordered everyone with a saddled horse to ride immediately for the Daley place. Lemmon, Lindsey, Cole, and four other cowboys were instantly in their saddles and out of the corral. Behind them, the excited cavalry horses snorted around the corral, uncatchable. Lemmon and the cowboys had covered a half-mile before the cavalry rode out of the corral at a trot! Sam Bell, who was riding with the soldiers, urged his horse into a gallop, but Captain Wells admonished Bell not to get too far ahead or the troopers might get lost.

The Indians had returned to the reservation by the time the rescue party arrived. Judging from the number of horses that crossed the river with empty saddles, the cowboys concluded that four Indians had been seriously wounded or killed. [30]

The next day M.H. Day decided to reconnoiter the Indians' position on Stronghold Table. He and a party of 18 men crossed the Cheyenne on Sunday morning, December 14th, and rode onto the Reservation. They climbed the northwest face of Plenty Star Table and advanced along the top to the southeast end. From this vantage they saw a great number of lodges on Stronghold Table. Looking through their field glasses, the cowboys saw Indian women butchering cattle and hanging the meat to dry, and the watched young braves training their stolen horses for war by shooting under their neck while galloping the horses around the perimeter of the camp.

Suddenly, the militia realized that they had been spotted by the Indians. Ed Lemmon believed that the steep, bare walls of Plenty Star Table gave the cowboys a strategic advantage, and he advised the group to stay put and see what the Indians were going to do. But there was no holding M.H. Day back. He ordered a hasty retreat.[31]

Some of Major Perry's soldiers were hauling hay from the Daley-Torkelson ranch to the Z Bell ranch when the Dakota Militia rode in from their reconnoiter of Stronghold Table on lathered horses. Bullets began kicking up dust under their hay wagons. The Indians who had chased the Militia off the Reservation were shooting at them from the bluffs across the river. The soldiers had orders not to fire on Indians who were on their own Reservation, so they merely took cover. The Dakota Militia was under no such constraint, and they returned a fusillade. The Indians eventually tired of the game and drifted back into the Badlands.[32] That night the Indians set fire to the grass east of the Cheyenne River. Some believed it was the Indians' signal for an imminent attack.[33]

Monday morning, December 15, 1890, was a day of bloodshed. The sun had not yet risen when a young Indian brave swung open the barn door on M.D. Cole's ranch on Spring Creek. The intruder struck a match. Cole, who lay hidden in the hay loft, pulled the trigger. His 10-gauge shotgun blasted the would-be horse thief into the barn yard.[34]

One hundred-fifty miles to the north, on the Grand River, 43 Indian police slipped into Sitting Bull's camp at sunrise. Lt. Bull Head and two sergeants entered Sitting Bull's cabin and informed the recalcitrant, old medicine man that he was under arrest. They were going to take him to Fort Yates. Sitting Bull agreed to go. The rest of the camp awoke. A crowd of Hunkpapas were waiting for Sitting Bull and his captors when they emerged from the cabin. A few bystanders chided the Indian police for doing the white man's work. Some taunted Sitting Bull for meekly accepting his arrest. Sitting Bull called for his rescue. Two Indian policemen were shot. Lt. Bull Head, on being fatally wounded, whirled and fired his pistol into Sitting Bull's chest. At the same instant Red Tomahawk shot Sitting Bull in the back of the head. Gunfire erupted from all quarters. The aftermath found seven of Sitting Bull's people and five Indian police dead. The rest of Sitting Bull's band, about 330 men, women, and children, fled south toward the Cheyenne River.

Later that morning, Second Lt. Joseph C. Bryon of the Eight Cavalry led a detachment of a dozen Cheyenne Indian scouts and three local cowboys, who went along as guides, across the Cheyenne River and onto the Pine Ridge Reservation. Bryon wanted to determine if a cannon could be brought within range of Stronghold Table. The party rode to the west end of Cuny Table and found it could be easily ascended by a team of horses pulling a light cannon. They then turned west and began a circuitous route back to camp. Traversing along the edge of Squaw Humper Table, Bryon's patrol saw a small party of Indians between them and the Cheyenne River. Lt. Bryon intentionally cut the Indians off and killed them. As the action was a direct violation of orders, mention of this incident was suppressed until years later.[35]

Most whites on the frontier were pleased with the events of December 15th. When word reached Rapid City that M.D. Cole had killed an Indian attempting to steal his horses, the *Rapid City Journal* proudly announced, "The ball which made him a good Indian struck him in the left temple."[36] The *Battle River Pilot* lauded Cole for "letting the settlers know what a good Indian looks like."[37]

The frontier also welcomed Sitting Bull's death, S.G. Dewell, editor of the *Pierre Weekly Free Press*, wrote:

> The decisive action will go far toward putting a stop to the rebellious actions of certain Indians. Sitting Bull has been a disturbing element ever since the memorable Custer campaign of 1876 and should have been hung fourteen years ago.[38]

General Nelson Miles, the overall commander of the campaign, announced: "The killing of Sitting Bull will have a rather disheartening influence over the Indians... and will be favorable to an amicable settlement of the present trouble."[39]

The Dakota Militia, possibly inspired by the slain Indian in Cole's corral, planned a daring escapade. They rose before sunup on December 16th and rode out from Frank Stanton's place on Spring Creek toward the reservation. Their destination was a place where Big Corral Draw narrows into a canyon with steep Badlands walls on either side. Here, George Cosgrove, Roy Coates, Joe Erdman, Frank Lockhart, Charley Allen, Bill Lindsey, Riley Miller, John Hart, and a dozen other cowboys turned up a steep, cedar-covered ravine. Near the top, an animal trail wound its way over 20 yards of bare Badlands. The men tied their horses out of sight at the base of the trail. If necessary, the trail would be their escape route. The cowboys then hid among the big rocks and cedars.

Pete Lemley, Frank Hart, Paul McClelland, and Francis Rousch continued up Big Corral Draw to a broad Badlands basin to where the hostiles grazed a big herd of horses. The four men slowly worked their way into the herd and remained undetected until they stampeded the horses toward the river. Almost immediately, Indians were in hot pursuit.

The four young cowboys hazed the herd toward Big Corral Draw where the other cowboys waited. After the cowboys and the horses passed, those waiting in ambush opened fire on the pursuing Indians.[40]

Those involved in the ambush knew the Indians would seek revenge. The first confrontation occurred about noon. A patrol led by M.H. Day spotted a party of Indians trying to slip up Spring Creek. With Day in command, caution prevailed. The patrol fired at the Indians from a distance and without affect.[41] A few hours later, government supply train moving hay to Colonel Carr's camp at the mouth of Rapid Creek was ambushed on Spring Creek. No soldiers were hit in the first volley, but the Indians pinned the men behind the protection of their wagons. The Indians dispersed quickly when 100 troopers led by Major Tupper arrived.[42]

The cowboys who had staged the ambush realized that the greatest danger of attack would come at Dan Phinney's place, where the Indians' horses had been brought. By nightfall, 14 Dakota Militia men had gathered there. Joe Erdman stood first watch.

About 10:00 p.m. an Indian sneaked to the corral where the horses were being held. He smeared a corral post with grease and lit it. Erdman ran to the well, drew a pail of water and doused the burning post, but the fire did not go out. Erdman got on his hands and knees to smear the post with mud. While he was attempting to put out the fire, an Indian rode out of the darkness right up on him. Erdman saw the horses' feet and looked up just as the Indian fired at the back of his head. The bullet plowed a furrow across the front of Erdman's chest. Riley Miller fired the next shot. The Indian slumped in his saddle, and his horse turned and disappeared into the darkness. The Indians then attacked in force. They fired the grass around the buildings and pinned down the cowboys with heavy gun fire.[43] The cowboys were in serious trouble.

Luckily for them, the sound of rifle fire carried to the Cole ranch. Coles' 18-year-old daughter, Maggie, volunteered to ride the two miles to Col. Carr's camp on Rapid Creek while her father remained at the ranch to defend his family and property. Colonel Carr immediately dispatched Major Tupper with 100 cavalrymen. The Indians, who had just mounted a second attack, withdrew when the troopers arrived.[44]

Events were happening more quickly than word-of-mouth communication could carry news up and down the Cheyenne River. Unaware of the ambush in Big Corral Draw and the Indians' night attack on the Phinney ranch, Gene Akin's men planned a daring escapade for the next day.

The Indians always waited until mid-day before they left their sanctuary on the Reservation to cross the Cheyenne and raid the ranches. Through observation, the men of the Dakota Militia discovered that when the Indians crossed the river, they left a signaler behind. The signaler used powerful binoculars to scan the countryside, and then he bounced the rays of the afternoon sun off a mirror to signal his comrades if a patrol came along.

Farley Sprague decided to use the same tactic to foil the Indians. He sneaked onto the Reservation the next morning, December 17th, Farley picketed his horse in a depression and hid amongst some cedar trees. About noon, he spotted three warriors making their way toward the river. He signaled Gene Akin and his men that he had spotted some Indians. The Militia men circled south around the Indians and joined Sprague.[45]

At this same time, Pete Lemley and Frank Hart were on the Reservation looking for a steer to butcher. The two cowboys were herding a suitable animal back to Phinney's when they headed down the draw below where the three Indians that Farley had spotted sat planning their raid. As Lemley and Hart passed below the Indians, they unleashed a barrage of rifle fire at the two cowboys. "Get a rope on this damn steer," Lemley hollered at Hart, "and let's get out of here!"

Hart scoffed at him. "Ah, they can't hit us, Pete. Hell, they're way up in dem cedars," Frank replied as bullets ricocheted under them.[46]

Akin's men were surprised to hear gunshots coming from the suspected location of the three Indians. Akin advised that they hold their position until the reason for the gun fire could be determined. But Joe McCloud thought otherwise. "Those shots mean but one thing," McCloud said as he spurred his horse toward the gun fire. "It means some cowboys are in trouble!"

The three Indians were unleashing such a fusillade at Lemley and Hart that they did not hear Akin and his men ride up behind them. After a brief skirmish, the Militia men killed the three Indians.

At this same time, V.T. McGillycuddy, John Brennan, and Will McFarland were at Cole's ranch investigating the death of the Indian killed there three days earlier. John Farnham and his Indian wife went with them. They found the young Indian warrior still laying in the corral wearing his ghost shirt. Cole had taken his scalp. Mrs. Farnham recognized the dead Indian. His name was Istok-ta (Dead Arm). He was a nephew of Kicking Bear and, Mrs. Farnham announced, her cousin. He was only 19-years-old. Brennan later reported to the *Rapid City Journal* that "Dead Arm had died of exposure-exposure to buck shot."[47]

The next day, V.T. McGillycuddy, John Brennan, and Will McFarland set out from Carr's camp on a peace mission to Stronghold Table. Americus Thompson guided them. The party approached within three miles of Stronghold Table, and they were close enough to make out about 100 tepees at the base of the table. Suddenly, an uncomfortably close human voice said, "Hau! Putin Cigala," ("Hello, Little Beard," which was the Indians' name for McGillycuddy, their former Agent). Following the sound, the men saw a solitary old Indian sitting motionless not 25 yards away. The man, an old friend of McGillycuddy's, told them the Indians would continue fighting unless the soldiers were taken away, and the little band of whites (the Dakota Militia) were in a dangerous position and should get out of there. He said the hostiles knew Sitting Bull had been killed and their hearts were bad. He also said that the warriors on Stronghold Table vowed to kill the next white man who came to them talking about peace. On the old Indian's advice, McGillycuddy and his party turned back. As if to underscore the old Indian's admonition, an Indian scouting party fired on McGillycuddy's party as they retreated from the Reservation.[48]

The weather turned unseasonably warm the following week. On December 21st, General Brooke took advantage of the temperate weather to send a peace delegation of about 130 Indians with three wagon loads of rations to Stronghold Table.[49] General Miles notified M.H. Day on December 22nd of the peace initiative and requested that he not cross the Cheyenne River until receiving further instructions.[50] Knowing that Day was not under his command and might disregard the order, Miles asked Governor Mellette to bring Lt. Col. Day into line. Accordingly, Mellette telegraphed Day on December 22nd to "strictly prohibit your men from going on the Reservation. You will understand the necessity of this order and it must be strictly enforced."[51]

The peace delegation returned from Stronghold Table several days later, accompanied by a fair number of hostiles. Only about 250 Indians remained on

Stronghold Table and even those ardent ghost dancers seemed on the verge of coming in.[52]

That left only one large band of ghost dancers—the Minneconjou people in Big Foot's village just below the forks of the Cheyenne River. Even there, events seemed to be moving toward a peaceful conclusion. On the morning of December 15th, Big Foot sent word to Lt. Col Edwin V. Sumner, who was camped near the forks of the Cheyenne, that he was taking his people to Fort Bennett for their annual annuities.

The band broke camp on December 17th and started down-river toward Fort Bennett. They camped that evening along the Cheyenne River. An elderly Indian came in a few hours later with word that three companies of soldiers had crossed the Missouri River and had started up the Cheyenne toward them. The next morning, two Hunkpapa men, one with a bullet in his leg, stumbled into Big Foot's camp. The Hunkpapa men informed Big Foot that Indian police, backed by Army soldiers, had killed Sitting Bull. Big Foot and his headmen decided to return to their village until the Army's intentions became known.

As Big Foot's party passed through Touch-The-Cloud's deserted village on the morning of December 21st, they met Lt. Col. Sumner and a large detachment of the 8th Cavalry. Sumner, who was searching for Big Foot because he had orders to arrest him and bring him into Fort Meade, informed Big Foot that he would escort him back to Camp Cheyenne, the soldiers' encampment. However, as the caravan neared Big Foot's village young warriors rushed to the head of the column and charged past the soldiers. Big Foot's people broke rank and each family scattered to their log cabin. Sumner was faced with two unpleasant choices. He could rout the Minneconjou from their cabins, which might result in dead Indians and dead soldiers, or he could acquiesce. After Big Foot promised to come into Camp Cheyenne in the morning. Sumner left the Indians and continued to Camp Cheyenne.[53]

The next morning, December 23rd, Big Foot did not come in. Instead, the band hastily loaded their belongings and headed south. By 7:00 p.m. Sumner realized that Big Foot had struck out for the Pine Ridge Reservation. He instructed Jack Hinkley, a local cowboy, to inform Colonel Carr of the development and to advise Carr that if he [Carr] set out immediately, he could probably intercept Big Foot.

Hinkley reached Carr's camp at 10:00 the next morning. Carr's troopers struck out within a half-hour for the Badlands, guided by two local men, Americus Thompson and Jack Reed. The patrol rode 18 miles east into the Badlands and struck the old Fort Laramie-Fort Pierre Trail, the only known trail within 40 miles on which wagons could be taken over the Badlands wall. Expecting to meet Big Foot's band at any time, Carr followed the Fort Laramie-Fort Pierre Trail as far as Sage Creek. There was no sign of Big Foot and it was dusk. Carr stationed some troops to cover the main trail and positioned others to watch a branch in the trail that led to Sage Creek Pass. The ill-prepared troops pitched camp and spent a miserably cold Christmas Eve night.[54]

Big Foot, possibly anticipating Carr's actions, led his people straight south. Traveling much faster than the Army thought possible, Big Foot's band struck the Badlands wall about mid-afternoon on December 24th. Several hundred feet below them and nearly straight down lay the floor of the Badlands. They had come directly to a little-known spot where a saddle horse could precariously wind down a narrow spine of Badlands to the floor below. The Minneconjou lowered their wagons one at a time down the wall on ropes, and then urged their horses and cattle down the path. They crossed White River about dusk and camped for the night on the northern edge of the Pine Ridge Reservation. Knowing the troops were close, they did not build fires.[55]

Gus Craven, a local rancher working as a scout, rode under the light of a full moon into Colonel Carr's camp on Sage Creek about midnight. Carr immediately sent him through Sage Creek Pass with instructions to locate Major Adams, commander of A Company, and tell him to scout up-river for Big Foot. (Big Foot was then less than ten miles down-stream from Adams' camp.)

Americus Thompson, the old man who had piloted Colonel Carr, wandered the Badlands alone that Christmas Eve night. The Indians were his friends. Thompson knew that Carr would soon figure out that Big Foot had not taken the Fort Laramie-Fort Pierre Trail, and he would ask Thompson where Big Foot might be. It was a question Americus Thompson probably did not want to answer, so he deserted.[56]

Big Foot's band broke camp Christmas morning and headed southwest, toward Medicine Root Creek. Reaching Medicine Root Creek, the Indians were hidden by the surrounding Badlands, and they camped for several days. Runners were to sent Stronghold Table. The runners came back with word that the Indians on Stronghold Table were planning to come in on December 29th. They wanted Big Foot to meet them just south of the Pine Ridge Agency so they could go into the Agency together.

At this same time – December 27th – Lt. Edward Casey and his Cheyenne Indian scouts were huddled around a campfire along the Cheyenne River.[57] Suddenly, horsemen approached. The soldiers reached for their rifles, but just as quickly they put their weapons down. It was Second Lt. Joseph Byron and a detachment of Cheyenne Indian scouts. They were returning from a reconnoiter of the large encampment of hostile Indians on top of Stronghold Table, a natural fortress deep in the recesses of the rugged Badlands. The patrol had exciting news. The several thousand hostile Indians on Stronghold Table struck their tepees that afternoon as if they were preparing to leave. It was surmised that they intended to go into the Pine Ridge Agency and put themselves in the custody of Brigadier General John Brooke, commander of the Eighth and Ninth Cavalry as well as the Second Regiment and the Eighth Regiment of Infantry – all bivouacked at the Agency since November 20, 1890.[58]

Lt. Byron's news suggested that, if handled properly, the Sioux Indian Uprising could be drawn to an end with no more bloodshed. Lt. Casey immediately put a courier on a fast horse and sent him down the Cheyenne River to Colonel Offley's camp of Seventeenth Infantry, bivouacked a few miles up from the mouth of Battle Creek.[59] From there, a rider carried the auspicious information into the little railroad town of Hermosa and telegraphed it to Major General Nelson A. Miles, who was coordinating the massive effort to squash the Sioux uprising from his suite of rooms in the Harney Hotel in Rapid City.[60]

Late that night a courier rode into Lt. Casey's bivouac with urgent instructions. Lt. Casey was to set out at first light for Stronghold Table. If the hostiles had departed Stronghold Table, Casey and his Cheyenne scouts were to follow them at a prudent distance. But under no circumstances were Casey and his Cheyenne Scouts to initiate any hostile actions against the retreating Indians.[61]

The sun was barely awake when Lieutenant Casey led his Cheyenne scouts five miles down the Cheyenne River. A mile above the mouth of Battle Creek, a half dozen cowboys, members of the Dakota Militia, waited for Lt. Casey and his Cheyenne scouts. The cowboys hoped they could retrieve some of the stolen livestock. Lt. Casey probably welcomed the cowboys' accompaniment because they knew the Badlands like the back of their hands.

The cowboys guided Lt. Casey's detachment to the northwest corner of Stronghold Table. There, a narrow path wound its way to the top. The passage was steep and ice covered, making the trail up so precarious that it could have been defended by a few Indian boys with a handful of rocks. But no one was there to offer resistance. The detachment dismounted and led their reluctant horses up the treacherous path.

On top, the cowboys did not find any of their cattle or horses contentedly grazing. Instead, they were found hundreds of carcasses. "It looks like a slaughter house," one of the cowboys commented, "for which we provided the cattle."[62]

The patrol then crossed the narrow neck of land that connected Stronghold Table to the big table immediately to the south – now called Cuny Table. The Cheyenne scouts set fire to the tall, winter-dried grass that grew on top of the Table, sending smoke high into the air. Lt. Casey hoped that retreating hostiles would see the smoke and realize that the forage for their horses was burned up, which would encourage them to keep going and relinquish any thoughts of coming back to Stronghold Table.[63]

This being done, the detachment rode south across Cuny Table at a rapid trot. From the rim of the mesa, they could see clear to White River, eighteen miles away. But they did not have to look that far to find the enemy. Just below them a cloud of tan-colored dust caught their eye. It was the hostiles. They were heading toward the Agency.

Dropping off the edge of Cuny Table, Lt. Casey's patrol fell in behind the hostiles and followed them at a prudent distance. When the hostiles crossed the ford on White River, which was four miles above the mouth of White Clay Creek, Lt. Casey's detachment stopped on the west bank of the river. They were soon joined by Captain Almond Wells and the two companies of Troop A of the 8th Cavalry. If the hardened Cheyenne scouts thought that the cavalry soldiers looked soft and unfit for hard riding, they weren't wrong. Troop A had passed the last seven months encamped on the Oelrichs fairgrounds, drinking in the town's saloon, dancing with the local girls, and playing baseball.[64]

Meanwhile, Chief Big Foot's band broke camp on December 28th and headed for the Pine Ridge Agency. In route, he was intercepted by Major Samuel M. Whitside. Whitside escorted Big Foot's band to Wounded Knee Creek, where they camped for the night under guard of the 7th Cavalry. The next morning, December 29th, the Army attempted to disarm Big Foot's band. A scuffle broke out over some hidden guns. A shot was accidentally fired. Pandemonium erupted. Troopers on the hill to the west rained a withering barrage of rifle fire and Hotchkiss cannon shells on Big Foot's encampment. When it was over, Big Foot and most of his band lay dead in the snow.[65]

Wounded Knee Battlefield, December 30, 1890.
Photo courtesy of South Dakota State Historical Society.

78   *Philip S. Hall*

The booming of the Hotchkiss cannons reverberated across the frozen prairie. The Indians who had occupied Stronghold Table but were on their way into the agency, heard the sounds of battle. A small group of young warriors rode to Wounded Knee to engage the soldiers, while the rest of the hostiles, joined by most Indians at the Agency, fled down White Clay Creek. However, Captain Wells and a detachment of the 8th Cavalry had moved in behind the Indians as they deserted Stronghold Table on the morning of December 28th and had followed them as far as White River. There, at the only decent ford on White River, Wells positioned his troops to prevent the Sioux from returning to Stronghold Table.[66]

The hostiles, who again numbered nearly 3,000, moved half-way down White Clay Creek and went into camp. They commenced frenzied ghost dancing. Daily, young warriors rode out to attack supply trains and engage the soldiers in running battles. But the Indians were greatly outnumbered. They no longer had a limitless supply of beef or the protection of the Badlands. The Army tightened the net around the hostiles a little each day. The Indians had few options. In parade style, they came into the Agency on January 15, 1891, and Kicking Bear ceremoniously laid his rifle at General Miles' feet. The Ghost Dance uprising was over.[67]

**Indian Chiefs and U.S. Officials of Pine Ridge, January 16, 1891.
Indians left to right: Two Strike, Crow Dog, Short Bull, High Hawk,
Two Lance, Kicking Bear, Good Voice, Thunder Hawk, Rocky Bear,
Young Man Afraid of His Horses, and American Horse.
U.S. Officials left to right: W.F. Cody, Major J.M. Burk,
J.C. Craiger, U. McDonald, and J.G. Worthy.**
Photo courtesy of South Dakota State Historical Society.

CHAPTER 6

The First Family of the Badlands

The Badlands were uninhabited at the beginning of 1880. But destiny was at work drawing a poor Norwegian family across an ocean and over half a continent to this barren, inhospitable land. The Badlands would eventually come to represent the fulfillment of their American dream. They would build log homes from its cottonwoods, bury their kin in its gumbo, and bring forth children along its river bank. The family would become the cornerstone of white civilization in the Badlands. They could rightfully be called the first family of the Badlands.

The Ludvig (Nels) and Margaret Johnson family, taken in
Chamberlain, South Dakota, about 1888.
Front row: Mary (Oliver) Johnson, Ludvig, Margaret, and Louis A. Johnson.
Back row: Lena, George, Emma Wells, and Christina Jacobs.
Photo courtesy of Mary Peterson.

When the Civil War concluded in 1865, America set out to bind her wounds by directing attention and capital toward the development of the West. A transcontinental railroad was built; millions of acres of land were opened for homesteading. People from the depression-ridden East, the war-torn South and Europe came west by the hundreds of thousands. Over 100,000 people came from Scandinavian countries alone. Among them was a poverty-stricken family from Eidsvold, Norway.

Ludvig and Margarita Rustaad and their seven children boarded the *Atlanta*, a sailing ship anchored in Oslo's harbor, and departed for America on May 17, 1867.[1] The sailors manning the *Atlanta* could not remember the immigrants' foreign-sounding Norwegian names. So they called half of the several hundred immigrants by the name of *Olson*, and the other half *Johnson*. When Ludvig and Margarita Rustaad landed in Quebec City, Canada, they were Nels and Margaret Johnson. They had but $15.00 between them.

The family traveled by way of Lake Ontario, the Welland Canal and Lake Erie to Milwaukee, Wisconsin. There, Margaret's aunt and uncle, the Larsons, had jobs for them on their three farms. Louis, the couple's eighth and last child, was born on the Larson farm in 1868. The Johnsons were not paid wages. Instead, they were provided with food and shelter while they worked off the price of their passage from Norway. When this was accomplished in 1872, the family moved to Menominee, Wisconsin where jobs were plentiful. Nels worked as a carpenter; George, their son, worked in a brick yard; Mary, who was only 13 years old, did baby-sitting. Although everyone worked, they did not have enough money to rent a home of their own. They lived with neighbors.

Nels obtained his citizenship in 1874 and took out a 160-acre homestead that was heavily timbered and had to be cleared before crops could be planted. The Johnsons sold syrup from their maple trees and saw logs to tide them through until they had a crop to sell. Nels felled the trees and a lumber company sent several teams of oxen to skid them to a steam-powered saw mill. One of the bull whackers was a young man named Oliver Johnson. Like Nels and Margaret, he was of Norwegian stock and Lutheran religion. Oliver took a fancy to Mary Johnson, and the couple married in 1879.

Unbeknown to Mary, her new husband was a born wanderer. Oliver would, over the next 36 years, strike out for the Montana gold fields, live near the banks of the Missouri River, haul freight to the Black Hills, homestead in the Badlands, own a general store in Nebraska, ride a mule deep into Mexico looking for a home, temporarily settle on disputed Indian Territory in Oklahoma, and farm on the shores of Horse Shoe Lake in northern Alberta, Canada. Where he moved, Mary followed, usually just one step behind.

82   *Philip S. Hall*

Oliver's penchant for rambling first surfaced in the spring of 1882. Holiver Johnson, his father, returned that year from the gold camps of Montana after a 25-year absence. When Holiver found he was no longer welcome at his wife's home, he suggested to his sons, Jenner and Oliver, that they accompany him to Montana. Oliver did not seem concerned that he had a wife and a one-year-old daughter, Mina.

The trio set off across the grass-covered, trackless prairies of northern Dakota Territory toward Montana. The temperature dipped so low one summer night that the picket ropes froze. The cold was too much for Oliver. He bid his father and brother goodbye and turned south.

Oliver Johnson arrived in Chamberlain, Dakota Territory in the early fall of 1882, The frontier town was the terminus of the Chicago Milwaukee & St. Paul Railroad. Soldiers from Fort Hale came into the town's six saloons to blow off steam. Drovers left town with herds of cattle bound for the lush grass in the Black Hills. Steamboats, plying freight and passengers up and down the Missouri, tied up at Chamberlain's dock. Railroaders brought in supplies and merchandise. Freighters hauled goods and materials to gold camps in the Black Hills. The booming town was even vying for a college.

Oliver filed on a homestead eight miles east of Chamberlain, near Pukwana. He built a small, sod shack and then returned to Wisconsin for his wife and Mina. A new daughter, Helen Elizabeth, had been born in his absence. Oliver told such glowing stories of Dakota Territory that Mary's entire family, with the exception of her two older sisters Martha and Anna, moved to Chamberlain. Nels found work as a carpenter. The twins, Lena and Christina, worked as waitresses in a hotel restaurant. Emma Johnson was soon being courted by a handsome widower, William "Wallace"

Oliver and Mary Johnson, taken in 1890 at Rapid City.
Photo courtesy of Mary Peterson.

Wells; and they were married in 1883. He was 37 and already had three young children from a previous marriage. She was 19.

Oliver and Mary tried farming. Oliver attempted to hand-dig a well, but got only a dry hole in the ground. Their crops failed. Three more children, Arnold, Emma, and Elizabeth, were born. The homestead was not able to produce enough to provide for seven people. Oliver needed a way to earn money.

Johnson received a break of sorts when the big operators abandoned the freight trail from Chamberlain to the Black Hills in the spring of 1883 because of problems with the Indians.[2] The Chicago Milwaukee & St. Paul Railroad still brought in freight slated for the Black Hills, and soon John Hart, a small independent freighter who was still operating over the Chamberlain Road, had more freight than he could carry. In the fall of 1883, Wallace Wells made a business proposal to his new brother-in-law, Oliver. Wells said he would supply the wagons and oxen if Oliver would ramrod the teams to and from the Hills.[3] As part of the deal, it was proposed that George and Louis Johnson move into one of the six, abandoned way-stations along the trail. They looked after foot-sore oxen, put up hay for the winter, and provided the freighters shelter during bad weather.

George and Louis Johnson were placed in the way-station that was half way between Chamberlain and Rapid City. The way-station was in the middle of the Badlands. It was a harsh land. The temperature rose to 115 degrees during the summer and dipped to 30 degrees below in the winter. Rattlesnakes were plentiful. Drinkable water was not. Yet, the young Norwegian immigrants loved the Badlands because it offered them a chance to be something more than penniless foreigners.

George and Louis remained at their way-station in the Badlands until the

Wallace Wells and Emma Johnson Wells, taken at Fort Thompson, November 12, 1884.
Photo courtesy of Mary Peterson.

Fremont Elkhorn & Missouri Valley Railroad reached Rapid City in the summer of 1886. The days of hauling supplies to the Hills with oxen were then over. The brothers returned to Chamberlain where they built a peddler's wagon and went about town selling wares and homegrown vegetables.

For a few years the Badlands reverted to an isolated, uninhabited land. Then in 1889, the Crook Commission convinced the Lakota to cede eleven million acres of the Great Sioux Reservation. The ceded land, which included the portion of the Badlands north of White River, was opened to homesteading on February 10, 1890, but word that the President signed the Agreement did not reach South Dakota for two days. At the firing of a gun, 5,000 would-be homesteaders gathered in Chamberlain rushed across the frozen Missouri River to stake a claim on 160 acres. At Pierre, a like number did the same.[4]

The Oliver Johnson family and the Johnson brothers, George and Louis, were among the first to settle on the newly ceded land. The Johnson brothers returned to the way-station they had previously occupied. Oliver, Mary, and their five children built a log cabin a half-mile up-river. Charley Gallagher was already living in the area. In 1889, he squatted on a piece of land four miles up-river from the way-station. Guy Trimble came to the Badlands in 1890 and lived with Charley Gallagher that winter while he built his own place. John Black and his two adult sons, Phil and Barney, settled on a place another mile and a half up-river; and Henry Hurley and his son Charley settled three and a half more miles up-river.[5]

The settlers' first year in the Badlands was adventuresome. Frank Lynn killed a grizzly bear that fall just down-river from Johnsons' way-station.[6] But the excitement of killing a grizzly paled in comparison to the shock the settlers received the day before Christmas. Major Emil Adams and two troops of 6th Cavalry rode in from the east on December 24th with disconcerting news. Adams informed the settlers that nearly the entire Lakota nation had risen up against the whites. Many of the hostiles had gathered on Stronghold Table to Ghost Dance. Adams also related that

Guy Trimble about 1890.
Photo courtesy of Hallie (Trimble) Young.

Guy Trimble ranch in approximately 1894.
Photo courtesy of South Dakota State Historical Society.

Sitting Bull had planned to join the hostiles on Stronghold, but was killed resisting arrest. More to the point, Major Adams told the settlers that Big Foot's band on the Cheyenne River had eluded the U.S. Army troops. Adams believed that Big Foot's band was now on the warpath and headed for Stronghold Table. He thought that the hostile Indians were probably heading the settlers' way.[7]

The men hastily constructed a fortification on top of a butte five miles northeast of the way-station and laid in ammunition, drinking water, food, blankets, and other provisions. That evening, Christmas Eve, the settlers climbed the precarious path to the top of the butte and prepared for the worst.

The night grew bitter cold. Early in the morning, just before daybreak, they heard what sounded like cannon fire. They surmised that Major Adams' patrol had located Big Foot and a fierce battle was underway. They listened and peered into the pre-dawn darkness looking for hostile Indians.

The sun finally rose, but the temperature continued to plunge. The booming still reverberated down the river. The settlers realized that the booming was not the sound of cannons. It was the river ice contracting. The cold settlers disregarded their fear of Indians and went back to the comfort of their cabins.

Big Foot's band had camped just five miles west of the way-station. The Indians rose Christmas morning and headed southwest. Four days later, December 29, 1890, soldiers of the 7th Cavalry killed most of the men, women, and children in Big Foot's band. Within a month, all the ghost dancers surrendered.[8]

That spring, settlers along White River again turned their thoughts to civilizing the Badlands. Mail service was one their first concerns. Edward Asay

Jr.'s trading post, across from the mouth of Bear-In-The-Lodge Creek, was designated a post office on December 8, 1890; but it was not on a government mail route.[9] Mail destined for the settlers in the Badlands reached them only intermittently through a series of convenient arrangements among the settlers. Specifically, it is surmised that Ed Asay received the goods for his trading post on White River from his father's (James Asay) general store in Pine Ridge, and that mail destined for settlers along White River was brought down from Pine Ridge with the supplies. The arrangement was good for business. Everyone who stopped at the trading post for mail was a potential customer.

Phil Black, an early settler in the Badlands, took a job in 1891 as a bronc buster for Missouri John Massengale.[10] In those days, a bronc was a four-year-old gelding who had been running wild on the range. He was caught, put in a small round corral, saddled, and cheeked while a rider climbed aboard. After a few trips around the corral, the bronc rider yelled, "Open the gate!" The trick was to tire the horse as quickly as possible. As the saying went, a horse with a wet blanket was a poor bucker and quick learner. It is likely that Phil Black tired each bronc by riding the horse from Massengale's place the 22 miles up-river to his father's place, which was five miles upriver from where the Johnsons settled. It is likely that Black delivered the mail that came into Lodge addressed to settlers who lived farther upriver. Delivering mail gave Phil Black, a bachelor, an excuse to stop at a settler's place about meal time. Hence, the mail that came to this cluster of settlers settled within five miles of George and Louis Johnson's former waystation was addressed "c/o Black"; and for a time, Black was an unofficial but workable U.S. Postal Service designation

On behalf of his constituents in the Badlands, Congressman John R. Gamble urged the Post Office Department to establish a mail route along White River.[11] The Post Office Department responded by advertising in July 1891 for bids on a contract to carry mail between Chamberlain and Rapid City. The successful contractor would carry mail three times a week from Chamberlain to Earling, Presho, Moore, Westover, Stearns, Whitfield, Lodge, Black (meaning Oliver Johnson's Store), Casey, Creston, Farmington, and Rapid City.[12] The government also established post offices at these locations. Christian Hellikson was named as the postmaster at Presho, Joseph Moore at Moore, E.C. Kelly at Westover, David S. Johnson at Stearns, Robert Whitfield at Whitfield, Ed Asay at Lodge, Mary Johnson at Black and John Roth at Casey. Mail service began September 1, 1891.[13]

A small town soon built up around the Black post office. Oliver and Mary operated a general store and the post office out of two connected log cabins. Oliver was so often away from home that it was convenient to make George and Louis partners in the store. Remembering the tornadoes in Wisconsin, the Johnsons built six dugouts along the banks of the adjacent creek. The dugouts were cool in the summer and warm in the winter; and they were used for storing fruit from their orchard, vegetables from their garden, and blocks of ice taken each winter from the river. Two mail carriers, one from Creston and the other from Westover, exchanged parcels and letters in Interior and used one dugout as place to rest.[14]

The twins, Lena and Christina, (who were elective mutes all of their lives but communicated almost telepathically with each other) came out from Chamberlain in the fall of 1890 to keep house for their brothers. Their parents, Nels and Margaret, followed in the summer of 1891. Oliver's mother, Randine, came to the Badlands from her home in Capron, Illinois in 1892. She was old and frail, and she died in 1894. Randine Johnson was buried on a buffalo grass-covered prominence a mile northwest of Black. Most people in attendance knew that they eventually would be buried there, so a fence was built to delineate the graveyard from the surrounding prairie.

The town of Black slowly grew. Mary gave birth to the couple's fifth child, Ruth, in 1892. Emma and John, twins, were born in 1894. A stone mason, who had just been released from prison for selling whiskey to Indians, and his wife located in a dugout on the east edge of town, across the creek. Jimmy Six moved to the town around 1894 and started a saloon. Johnny Valentine operated a blacksmith shop. Frank Turner arrived in 1895, and he started a butcher shop. His wife, Bertha, came to the Oliver Johnson home during the winter months to teach school.[15]

Interior about 1890.
Photo courtesy of The Department of Interior, Badlands National Park.

Black soon had a population of 20, and it was a trade center for several hundred square miles. Indians from Wanblee and Potato Creek, small villages 20 miles south of the White River, came to Black to shop. The Johnsons suspended a cable above the river. A eight foot by three foot box was attached to the cable by two pulleys, one at the front of the box and the other at the back. The arrangement made for a suspended ferry over the river. A megaphone hung from a cottonwood tree on the south bank. Anyone wanting to cross the river in the suspended ferry yelled into the megaphone until someone in town heard them and brought the cart across the river.[16]

Each year, the spring roundup was wrapped up by July 3rd so the cowboys could gather at Black for a big Fourth of July picnic. Any gathering of cowboys with a remuda of maverick horses inevitably led to challenges and bets about someone's ability to ride a particularly mean-spirited horse. Every picnic eventually evolved into a rodeo.

All this activity made for good business. The Johnsons eventually had four, four-horse teams going to Gordon, Nebraska for merchandise for their store. One outfit or another was always on the trail. The wagons came back to Black full, but they went to Gordon empty.

About this time, 1894, a banker in Colorado called in a bad debt and ended up with only the collateral – 3,000 sheep. The banker convinced Oliver Johnson to sign the note and take the sheep. Oliver Johnson knew nothing about sheep, but they came with a herder, Martin Johnson (not related). Sheep fit Oliver's needs. He could collect wool and haul it to Gordon in the otherwise

Hauling wool to Gordon, Nebraska.
Photo courtesy of A.E. "Doll" Johnson.

empty wagons. But sheep brought problems. The cattlemen along White River hated sheep, and they disliked any sheepman who grazed on their land. Oliver Johnson was forced to graze his sheep north of Cedar Pass, in the Bad River watershed. To give his sheep operation the force of law, Oliver Johnson filed on a quarter of land near Big Buffalo Creek. His sheep herd soon expanded to 4,000 head, and they ranged along Bad River from present-day Midland to the Cheyenne River. Oliver was good at delegating work, and he often had his young children, Mina, Helen, and Arnold tend a band of sheep. Each camped alone far from home with only a horse, tent, and dog.[17]

The post office at Lodge was discontinued on July 20, 1893.[18] The next year, 1894, Phil Black stopped breaking horses for Missouri John Massengale and went to work for the 3S outfit, located ten miles up-river from Johnson's post office.[19] Phil Black no longer regularly rode by the town of Black and the adjacent cluster of settlers. Soon, Mary Johnson received a letter from Washington asking her to change the name of her post office. The Johnsons searched for a suitable new name. Most of the letters arriving at Black were for Oglala Indians and came from the Department of Interior. George Johnson thought the name described their isolated setting deep in the recesses of the Badlands. He concluded that the post office should become known as Interior.[20]

Oliver Johnson was ready to move on by 1897. He and his family re-located in Gordon, where he bought a general store.[21] By then, Interior was well

Mike Miller (L) and Herman Jacobs (R) herding Oliver Johnson's sheep.
Photo courtesy of the Department of Interior, Badlands National Park.

established. It had a general store, a blacksmith shop, a butcher shop, a saloon, a school, and a graveyard. The town started by poverty-stricken Norwegian immigrants had become the cornerstone of civilization in the Badlands.

CHAPTER 7

Missouri John Massengale and the 15 Ranch

Legend has it that a cowboy was ready with his fists, fast with his gun, and deadly with his aim. He could ride anything that could be saddled and rope any critter his horse could outrun. The cowboy earned his living punching cattle from one horizon to beyond the other as he lived with an uneasy peace with the Indians. Well, if those are the qualities of a cowboy, then Missouri John Massengale and men who rode with him were the fabric for legends.

John Massengale

John Massengale came to the White River Badlands via a long road. That road began in Nashville, Tennessee, where he was born on December 10, 1840 to John and Celia Massengale. Shortly thereafter, the family moved to Kentucky. Life for the Massengale family was tough, allowing young John Jr. to attend school only two months of his life. Despite a reservoir of intelligence, he remained illiterate all of his life.

When John was only nine-years-old, tragedy struck. His father and his only sibling, an older brother, were killed by a bolt of lightening. His mother later remarried, but Jesse Brewster, the step-father, did not accept young John. At twenty years of age, John Massengale left Kentucky and found his way to Macon, Missouri. There, he was taken in and raised as a son by Jefferson Morrow, a friend of John Massengale Sr. when both of them lived in Kentucky.

Abraham Lincoln took the office of President of the United States on March 4, 1861. Thirty-nine days later the Confederate Army attacked Fort Sumner and the Civil War began. Missouri was a border state. Some residents were passionately abolitionists. Others were staunchly loyal to the Confederacy. But there was little doubt about the allegiance of the residents of Macon, Missouri. Union General Henry Halleck, head of the Department of the Missouri, regarded Macon to be a hotbed of southern sympathizers. As the owner of 12 slaves, Jefferson Morrow was among those gave their loyalty to the Confederacy.[1]

Kansas was on Missouri's western border and just across the Missouri River; it was brought into the Union in 1861 as a free state. That set the stage for bitter acrimony between the anti-slave residents of Kansas and the pro-slave citizens of Missouri. When the Civil War broke out, homegrown militia groups, known as Jayhawkers, formed to defend Kansas from Confederate loyalists living in Missouri; but they also made raids into Missouri. A particular notorious Jayhawker act was a raid on the town of Oscelola, Missouri in 1861. In that raid, the Jayhawkers executed nine Oscelola men and presumed Confederate sympathizers after a farcical trail. The town of Oscelola was then pillaged, looted, and burned to the ground. The Jayhawkers carried off a tremendous load of plunder.

For their part, the Southern sympathizers in Missouri gave their allegiance and support, be it often covert, to the Missouri Partisan Rangers. The Partisan Rangers were led by William Quantrill. Beyond Missouri's borders, the Partisan Rangers were better known as Quantrill's Guerillas. Some ruthless men rode with Quantrill's Guerillas: Jesse James, Frank James, Cole Younger, and Bloody Bill Anderson. The Union Army and most people in Kansas considered William Quantrill and his men to be nothing more than outlaws, and they came to regard Quantrill as the bloodiest man in the annals of American history. Because

Quantrill's guerilla raiders depended on the support of the local citizens, Union General Thomas Ewing ordered the arrest of anyone giving aid and comfort to Quantrill's raiders. Ewing confined those arrested, all of them women and children, in a make-shift prison in Kansas City, Missouri. Five captive women and a sixteen-year-old girl died when the dilapidated building collapsed. Many southern loyalists believed that the foundation of the make-shift prison housing the women had been deliberately weakened.

Still furious about the Oscelola raid and now the deaths of six women, William Quantrill plotted revenge. He decided to make a raid on Lawrence, Kansas, the center of the Jayhawkers. Many incensed Missouri farmers' joined Quantrill, swelling his official force of 250 to 450. As enrolled members of the Partisan Rangers, Benjamin Morrow and George Morrow, Jefferson Morrow's nephews, almost certainly participated in the Lawrence Raid of August 21, 1863. Subsequent events and associations suggest that John Massengale also accompanied the Raiders to Lawrence. The raid quickly got out of Quantrill's control. There was much looting, cold-blooded murder, and mayhem. Over 150 citizens of Lawrence were killed. Many who rode with Quantrill to Lawrence were sickened by the slaughter.

Shortly after the raid, Judge Jefferson Morrow was arrested by the local militia on the suspicion of being a Quantrill supporter, and he was imprisoned.[2] Hearing rumor of his pending arrest, Jefferson Morrow advised John Massengale to leave Missouri as quickly as possible.

The spring of 1864 found Massengale and a small group of young Missouri men on their way to the newly discovered gold fields of Idaho Territory [A]. As Massengale later put it, "I went West before anyone could catch me and nail my hide to a barn door."[3] Massengale's party followed the newly laid out Bozeman Trail. Starting in northwest corner of Nebraska, the Bozeman Trail followed the North Platte River through central Wyoming, along the eastern edge of the Big Horn Mountains and across the Powder River Basin into Montana Territory. While the Bozeman Trail was shortest most convenient route to the new gold fields, it went through the heart of Indian Country, evoking the wrath of the Lakota, the Cheyenne, and the Arapaho. Traveling by ox team, it took Massengale and his party four months and sixteen days to reach the newly found gold fields; and they almost didn't make it. On one occasion they were surrounded by Indians, who attacked them without let up for two days and two nights.

Massengale spent three years searching for gold in the vicinity of Virginia City and Bannock. He found some, but not enough to offset the sky-high prices: $150 for a barrel of flour. So in 1867, Massengale returned to Macon, Missouri. There, he engaged in farming with Jefferson Morrow for several years. During this time, the country's first transcontinental railroad was being built. Upon the completion of the railroad in 1869, the federal government awarded the Union

Pacific every odd-numbered section of land bordering ten miles on each side of the railroad. Seeking to make money from their extensive land holdings, the Union Pacific joined with investors from Missouri to get into the cattle business. In 1869, John Massengale went to Wyoming to take charge of the Union Pacific's livestock interests, a position he held for the next four years.[4]

The Union Pacific branded its cattle UP, which when scorched on a calf, looked like a beer mug. Hence, the headquarters for the Union Pacific Railroad livestock interests became known as the Beer Mug Ranch. The ranch headquarters was located in the foothills of the Seminole Mountains at the confluence of Difficulty Creek and the Medicine Bow River. The cattle's principal range was the Shirley Basin and the southeast slope of the Shirley Mountains. In those early days, no attention was paid to whether the cattle were running on UP land or on government land. It was all considered to be open range.

The Beer Mug Ranch got its supplies in Carbon. Founded in 1868, Carbon was a railroad town. The town was built for one reason and one reason only – coal. There was a seam of exposed coal in the hills above Carbon. The steam-powered locomotives that pulled the Union Pacific train east and west needed coal. Using horizontal drifts, seven mines were sunk into the side of the hill above Carbon. Some of the miners came from Lancashire, England, and they were called Lankies. Other coal miners were from Finland, and they were called Finns. The miners and their families dug caves into the sides of a nearby ravine, covered the fronts with boards or earth, and called it home. The demand of coal spurred the growth of Carbon. The town soon boasted a state bank and a weekly newspaper, and the population grew to 3,000.[5]

In 1873, Massengale stepped down as the manager for the Union Pacific Railroad's cattle operation, and he went into the cattle business with James Ross, the owner of a profitable saloon in Carbon, a prominent businessman, and in 1877 a member of the Wyoming Legislature.[6] They called their headquarters the 15 Ranch and branded their livestock 15. But Massengale so often left the ranch in charge of his capable foreman, "Dude" Rounds, that in 1878 he found it convenient to buy a 16 foot by 24 foot long house in Carbon complete with a corral & stable and three milk pails from J.G. Yost. The price for the package was $650. In 1882, the Union Pacific Railroad decided to get out the cattle business. Records suggest that Massengale and Ross added to their holdings by buying the Beer Mug Ranch. That year, Massengale and Ross also bought a large herd of cattle from Carl Vagner, a prominent Carbon business man. However, the 15 Ranch was known more as a horse ranch than a cattle ranch, running 1,000 head of horses in Shirley Basin.[7]

For nearly 20 years, Massengale and Ross prospered in Wyoming. They made good money running both horses and cattle on the open range. In addition, they lent money to neighboring ranchers at a fair rate of interest, which brought them even more money.[8] The saloon that they now jointly owned in Carbon provided Massengale and Ross a good cash flow.

A Soft Heart

John Massengale had an uncommon empathy for people, especially those who were having a hard time of it or whose life might be in peril. The story of a train trip back to Missouri makes the point.[9]

Late in the winter of 1888, Missouri John, as he came to be called, decided to make a trip back to Macon City, Missouri to visit his adoptive family, the Morrows. Boarding the train in Carbon, he struck out for Missouri. The train was not yet out of Nebraska when a furious blizzard brought it to an abrupt stop. After being stuck fast on tracks for a week, the train finally limped into Hastings, Nebraska. There, a woman boarded the train. She was wearing a thin dress, and she didn't have a coat. The woman was shivering badly and turning blue. "Madam," Missouri John said to her, "You're chilled. Take my coat until you get warmed up a little." The woman objected, but Missouri John insisted. It wasn't long before Missouri John started to shiver, and he shivered all the way to St. Joe, Kansas. There, the woman returned the coat as she got off the train.

Massengale intended to stay in Macon City for two months, but he was there only three weeks when a telegram arrived for him. James Ross, his partner, had been shot and was seriously wounded. Massengale took the next train back to Carbon.

When Massengale boarded the train, he saw an old woman sitting alone in a seat. In the seat behind her sat a weasel-eyed man who appeared to be her husband. The woman looked pathetically sad. Missouri John took the seat in front of the woman, which faced her, and they struck up a conversation. Grateful for a listening ear, the woman told Missouri John her story. Ever since she was old enough to remember, her life had been tough. But now, it was even worse. She was at the lowest possible ebb. After her first husband died, she remarried. Her second husband, the man sitting behind her, had spent all of her money and was too lazy to earn any of his own. For some time, they had been living on what money her children could send them. Now, she and her second husband were going to live with another one of her children. "I wish I could die," the woman said, her eyes welling with tears, "rather than take my new husband onto my children."

"Don't ever wish to die, Madam. Never even think about dying," John replied. "I've never seen the other place, but I think we should stay here as long as we can." With that, John got up and returned to his seat, but not before slipping the woman a sizeable amount of money.

When Missouri John's feet hit the ground at Carbon, his first steps were toward the hotel where his partner, James Ross, lay recovering from his bullet wound. "Well, ol' partner," Missouri John said when he saw Ross, "it looks like the old man is after both of us. Last fall I got cut in the belly when that colt we were castrating kicked and drove the cutting knife I was holding into my belly. It took all Doc Ricketts could do to keep me from being planted. And now you've let somebody shoot you. How did it happen?"

"I was in Mandy Petersen's saloon," Ross replied. "A young fellow was showing off, trying to prove how good he was with a gun. He was shooting out the open window of the saloon at something in the street. I was sitting right behind him – a stupid place to be. As the young fellow threw his six-gun back, his finger touched the trigger. The barrel was pointed right at me. Jumping up, I yelled, 'My God, man! You've shot me.' The young man looked around. Seeing the blood on my shirt, he fainted."

Deputy Sheriff Fisher immediately arrested the young man and threw him in jail on the charge of attempted murder. However, Ross refused to press charges. "He's learned his lesson, Sheriff. Maybe he'll make a good cowhand now that he's over playing the part of a bad man."

Leaving Wyoming

In the spring of 1889, a guest in the hotel in Carbon knocked over the kerosene lamp in his room. The fire quickly engulfed the wood structure, and the constant wind that blew through Carbon spread the fire from one wood building to the next. Having no city water with which to fight fire, men dynamited several buildings in attempt to control the inferno. It did no good. When the fire finally burned itself out, most of the town's business district lay in ashes, including Massengale and Ross' saloon.[10]

To add to those woes, there were the sheepmen. They began moving into Carbon County as early as 1880, and every year thereafter they increased in number. The cattlemen made a final struggle for supremacy by posting signs on the open range that no sheep were permitted. But it didn't work. The sheepmen were as entitled to the open range as anyone else. By 1890 sheepmen had a firm foothold in Carbon County;[11] and Massengale couldn't stand them.

Hearing that eleven million acres of the Sioux Reservation in southwestern part of the new State of South Dakota had been opened to white occupation, Massengale decided to investigate. He sent Dude Rounds, James Ross, and George Porch to take a look at the White River Badlands. Traveling by horseback, the trio crossed into South Dakota on December 29, 1890 – the very day of the Wounded Knee Massacre. They camped that night with the troops on a hill overlooking the dead bodies of Big Foot's band. The next morning, the three well-armed men continued across the Pine Ridge Reservation and into the Badlands.[12]

Liking what they saw, the trio scoured the Badlands for the ideal location for a ranch. They selected a place along White River that was sheltered on the north by a high table and on the south by timber. A creek came in from the northwest. It was one of the few places where White River ran over a gravel bottom and could be safely forded. The men hastily built a log cabin and log corral. Leaving James Ross to hold claim to the new ranch site, Rounds and Porch returned to Wyoming to tell Massengale the Badlands was a cattlemen's paradise.

Massengale made a big roundup in the late spring of 1891 that took nearly two months to complete. When the roundup was over, Massengale sold 3,000 head of cattle to cull the herd back to two-year-old heifers and young steers. He left for the White River Badlands in early July with the 2,000 head of cattle and 500 horses. "I leave Wyoming with only one regret," Massengale told Dude Rounds as he left Wyoming. "I regret that I never got to kill one of damn smelly sheepherders."[13]

Massengale left Dude Rounds in Wyoming to wrap up his business interests and look after the remaining horses, and he set out for the White River Badlands. On the trip, George Porch served as Massengale's right-hand man. Frank Robinson came on the cattle drive with understanding that he could bring a dozen of his horses. A man known only as Ladigo was hired to look after the cattle. Johnny Livingston, who was but eighteen years old, and Bob Ellis were hired to assist Ladigo.

Striking out to the northeast, they herded the livestock east-northeast through the Laramie Mountains. Hitting the headwaters of the Laramie River, they followed it to the site of old Fort Laramie. Here, they struck the old Cheyenne-Deadwood Trail, which they followed to near the headwaters of Hat Creek. Veering east, they passed into the northwest corner of Nebraska and passed near the little town Whitney. As they camped for night on the banks of White River, a severe hailstorm passed overhead, missing them by mere feet. At the Nebraska-South Dakota border, they left White River, taking an easier route that went through the heart of the Pine Ridge Indian Reservation. After being on the trail for 40 days and 40 nights, they arrived at the new location for the 15 Ranch on August 26, 1891. When winter came on, Missouri John left for Macon, Missouri and James Ross went to visit his relatives in Philadelphia. They left Ladigo, Porch, Robinson, and Livingston to look after the livestock.

Wintering in the White River Badlands in 1891 wasn't easy. "Durin' da nights," Porch related, "we listened to the howlin' of the coyotes and the roarin' o' the gray wolves, known they was makin' havoc amongst the cattle. Often I'd git up and git on my horse, an' ride out and sit until I could locate one by its howl. Then I'd ride over that way and shoot two or three times just to scare 'em into runnin' and maybe keep 'em quiet till daylight. Come daylight, it was pretty discouraging to ride out a few miles and come on a good, two-year-old steer pulled down by a pack of wolves and almost ate up, and go another mile or so and find another, and then another." For a single man who just lost the love of his life, the Badlands was also lonely. There weren't ten white people living within 15 miles up and down White River, and not an unmarried woman within 50. The closest settlement worthy of being called a town was more than a hundred miles away. There were only a few Indian trails and virtually no roads. On the plus side, the winter of 1891–1892 was open, allowing the livestock to graze contentedly on the protein-rich buffalo grass that carpets much of the Badlands.[14]

Back in Wyoming, Dude Rounds was busy. He found a buyer for the Beer Mug Ranch – a man by the name of Pompell, a pioneer sheepman in that part of Wyoming. As soon as the ranch was sold, Rounds then hired John Burke and a man by the name of Amoss to help him move the 15 horses from Wyoming to the White River Badlands.[15] It was tough trip. There was a heavy snow on April Fools Day. The sun completely disappeared for day after day, and it snowed almost constantly. After Rounds and his crew arrived at the new 15 Ranch in the Badlands, they didn't see the sun for a month and half. On the fifteenth of May, Dude Rounds stuck his head into the bunkhouse door. "Come outside quick,

The 15 Ranch in 1894. Dude Rounds is to the left and George Porch is the right.
Photo courtesy of the South Dakota State Historical Society.

boys!" Dude exclaimed, "I want to show you something." When everyone had gathered outside, Dude pointed up at the sun. "What's that?" He asked.[16]

A Grizzly Bear

In the summer of 1893, Missouri John and George Porch were riding on the Fifteen Table about opposite of Long Creek. Suddenly, Missouri John pulled up on his horse. "What's that lone horse doing over there?" He asked, pointing across the river.[17]

"That ain't no horse, John. It's a bear!"

"Too big for bear," John said, laughing. "There ain't no bear around here that big, especially at that distance."

Porch pulled out a pair of field glasses. Clear as day, he saw it was a bear. It was nosing along digging up roots. "See if yuh can make out the brand on that horse," George said, handing the field glasses to Missouri John.

"My God, Porch! That's the biggest grizzly bear I ever saw." The bear stayed in sight for quite a while, but they didn't try to get any closer to him as they were carrying only pistols.

The bear was next seen on the Gannon Ranch. The Gannon boys were building a shed. Cowie Gannon and Clare Denton went after some cedar poles. In their search for good poles, Gannon and Denton came across bear tracks – big ones. They immediately returned to the ranch for the Winchester rifle and reinforcements. Four men went back to the bear's trail, and they followed it on foot for two miles. The tracks got fresher. Finally, the tracks headed up into thicket of cedar trees. "Boys, we'll get him pretty soon. These tracks have just been laid down, Henry Gannon exclaimed." At that instant, the grizzly bear burst out of the cedar thicket and bounded past them. Then the bear stopped, turned, and faced them. The four men ran.

Denton was in rear, but he didn't have a gun. The bear bounced on him. Seeing the bear attack, Cowie yelled for help. Turning, Henry Gannon saw the fix that Denton was in. He fired three bullets. Every one of went into the bear's massive head. As the bear reared up, Henry put another bullet into the bear's body, and that bullet hit the bear just right. The bear fell dead, but right across Denton. The three of them managed to pry up the bear and pull Denton out from under the grizzly. Denton was bleeding profusely. One of the bear's swipes had taken most of the skin off Denton's ribs and broke some to them. Another swipe had tore off Denton's knee cap. However, Denton was Badlands tough. Without any professional medical attention, he pulled through.

The Horse Race

True to his Tennessee origins, Missouri John loved a fast horse. In 1893, he had bought a blooded and fleet-footed horse from a man named Blossendaller from Beulah, Wyoming. The horse, Sorrel Tom, was incredible fast in a half-mile. In his time, Sorrel Tom showed his heels to many so-called fast horses in western South Dakota and eastern Wyoming and Montana. Missouri John raced Sorrel Tom in the summer of 1895 against a horse named Two Bits, owned George LaPlant and Ed Jones. The race took place on flat bottom of Bad River five miles east of Midland.

On the day set for the horse race, a lot of ranchers were there to watch the race. George Porch, Tom Jones, Harry Hopkins, Kruse Madsen, Bradshaw, and Pearsall were among the several hundred spectators. Each owner bet $500 on their respective horse. In addition, there was lot of money bet on the side by the on lookers. Kruse Madsen bet every cent he with him on Massengale's horse, Sorrel Tom; he even got LaPlant to wager money against Madsen's six-shooter.[18]

It was a good race, but Sorrel Tom once again proved he was the fastest horse west of the Missouri River. LaPlant and Jones immediately challenged Missouri John and his horse to a rematch. The race was scheduled to be held in Fort Pierre. Missouri John hired Rome Glover, who weighed less than 110 pounds, to train Sorrel Tom and climb aboard as the jockey on the day of the race [B]. In its August 20th edition in 1895, the *Pierre Daily Capitol* noted that great enthusiasm was building in over the prospect of a horse race between Massengale and Ross' horse and LaPlant's horse. Elaborate preparations were made for the grudge match. A subscription paper circulated amongst the businessmen in Fort Pierre and Pierre secured $200 to prepare the kite-shaped race track four miles north of Fort Pierre.[19] Initially, the owners each deposited $500 with the Stock Grower's Bank in Pierre; but as the race grew near, Massengale and LaPlant increased their wager to $2,000. Their agreement called for the Stock Grower's Bank to pay out the money to winner upon the presentation of results bearing the signatures of all three judges. George Porch was one of the judges. A reporter for *Pierre Daily Capitol* speculated that with the side bets included, more than 10,000 dollars and a good amount of livestock was going to change hands at the end of the race. The race was held on September 17, 1895. More than 1,000 people turned out for the event, making it the largest gathering that the area had ever seen. So many people went to watch the horse race that the editor of the *Pierre Daily Capitol* pronounced Pierre to be depopulated.[20]

When the horses came out on the race track, George Porch noticed that Sorrel Tom's reins were tied together and closer up one side than the other.[21] Despite that handicap, at the sound of the starting gun Sorrel Tom shot out to a two hundred yard lead and held it for a long time. Then as the race neared the finish, his head commenced to come up and up and he ran to the side with his mouth open. Sorrel Tom lost ground, and Two Bits finished 30 yards in the lead. In George Porch's eyes, "It was the plainest piece of crooked ridin' I ever seed, an' the rottenest. It didn't take no two eyes to see that race was a sell out, and some that watched it said it was the rottenest they ever saw. And I wisht that Missouri John an' James Ross had stayed more sober so da could have seen it as it was."

Following the race, George Porch refused to sign the decision that allowed the Stock Grower's Bank to release the money to LaPlant and Jones. Nonetheless, Missouri John and James Ross agreed to pay LaPlant and Jones. Everyone went into Jim Hall's saloon in Fort Pierre, where Missouri John, James Ross, and the rest of the Fifteen cowboys started drinking again.

After a time, Rome Glover came into the saloon. "Porch," he said, "I want to see yuh outside." George followed Glover out the backdoor. Glover said, "I hear yuh told Massengale that I pulled his horse."

"I ain't told Missouri John or anyone else what I think about the race," Porch replied, and he turned to go back inside. Glover followed Porch back inside. As they passed a table where a card game was going on, Glover said, "I can find a man that can lick yuh so damn quick yuh won't know it till it's over." Porch saw the outline of a gun inside the jockey's shirt, and that only made him more angry. Stepping right up beside Glover, Porch said, "You're a damned son of a bitch. Yuh pulled that horse. I know yuh pulled that horse, and you know yuh pulled that horse!"

Glover quickly jumped back as he pulled out his gun. Porch wasn't more than five feet away, and running wouldn't have done any good. So he jumped for Glover and struck. Glover caught George's blow on the arm, and he tried to hit Porch on the head with the barrel of his gun. But every time Glover lifted his arm, George hit him. Porch hit Glover one more time, catching him good on the chin. Glover went down. Porch reached for the gun; but Lou Bennett, who was a Marshall, put a big hand on Glover's arm and squeezed down hard. Glover let the gun fall to the floor.

Glover started to get up, and Porch grabbed him by the overalls; but two men grabbed George from behind and pulled him over backwards. But while Porch was being pulled over backwards, he hung on to Glover's pants. When the two men hit the floor, George hit Glover again, knocking him unconscious.

Badlands Justice

In those early days, the only official law in the Badlands came out of Pierre, 130 miles to the northeast. Lawmen were seldom seen in the Badlands. As one cowboy put it, "The men with badges did not poke around too much just to see if they could find trouble." When the law was not around to deal with a problem, the cowboys in the Badlands often carried out their version of justice. The fate of Bill Newsome was a case in point.

Bill Newsome was a Texan who came to Dakota Territory in the 1880s. He probably arrived with an unsavory past, for his real name was Chatman.[22] Newsome worked in the fall of 1891 and the spring of 1892 for Scotty Philip, who was then located on Bad River at the mouth of Grindstone Creek. Newsome, like many other cowboys, started to run a few cattle of his own. However, he did not always have the proper papers for his stock.

As a cattle rustler, Newsome was smart. He never stole from the big ranchers, men who had the determination and the means to deal with cattle thieves. Instead, Newsome stole from small operators – young men just getting started in the cattle business who didn't have friends in high places; and once wiped out, usually pulled up stakes and went back to where they came from. Accordingly, Newsome made a midnight appropriation of 31 head of cattle that belonged to a young, would-be cowboy homesteading on Deep Creek. So it was that young Bruce Siberts woke one morning to find his cattle gone. With tears in his eyes and a colt pistol in his belt, Siberts trailed after his cattle. Being inexperienced, Siberts rode his horse hard – too hard, and his horse gave out. Despondent, Siberts led his tired horse home.[23]

Siberts learned through the grapevine in Fort Pierre that his cattle had been run into Scotty Philip's corrals on Grindstone Creek. There, his **A** brand had been converted to a ⇔ brand; and Sibert's stolen cattle had then been trailed into the Badlands. Siberts vowed he'd hunt down the cattle thief; but Siberts' neighbors advised him not to go into the Badlands in search of his cattle. His well-meaning neighbors told Sibert that some of the meanest men on the range work for an outfit along White River called the 15 Ranch. But Siberts would not be dissuaded. He rigged up a bedroll and cook outfit, and headed out. At Scotty Philip's corrals, Siberts picked up cattle tracks leading south and he followed them to Cedar Pass. There, he lost the trail. Siberts descended Cedar Pass onto the floor of the Badlands. He searched the ravines and canyons for a week, but found nothing. His cattle, he concluded, were gone. With thoughts of quitting and going back to Iowa reverberating through his brain, he slowly and dejectedly rode back to his homestead on Deep Creek.

However, Siberts did not abandon his homestead. Instead, he and a partner by the name of Fleming went back to the Badlands a few weeks later. Siberts had given up all hopes of finding his cattle, but thought he could replace them with sticks (unbranded cattle) and maverick horses that roamed the Badlands. The two, noticeably well-armed men stayed one night at the Midland Hotel, which was just down Bad River from Scotty Philip's ranch. The rumor went out far and wide that Siberts and Fleming had come to get the man who had stolen Siberts' cattle. Newsome laid low.

Siberts returned to the Badlands in the winter of 1893. He set up camp in the same place he and Fleming had camped the previous winter. The next morning, he set out to catch wild horses. He succeeded only in playing out his own horse, and he returned to camp empty-handed and tired. The next morning, he found that his horse had been stolen. The tracks in the snow indicated that a lone thief cut the picket rope and led the horse off.

Siberts started afoot on the thief's trail. By noon, the freshness of the tracks told Siberts that he was getting closer. Suddenly, the thief's trail circled back. Siberts realized his mistake. He ran as hard as he could for his camp. Arriving after dark, Siberts found his bedding, his grub, and his saddle had been burned. He had been left to freeze.

Fortuitously, Siberts had stored some food and a blanket in a small, nearby cave. He ate the food, wrapped himself in the blanket, and snuggled into the small cave. The morning sun found him alive, but his feet were badly frostbitten. He moved his camp to a big wash out, where he was able to get below the frost line. Siberts shot a rabbit for food, built a fire to cook it, and warmed his feet.

The next morning, Siberts headed for home. Siberts had not gone a hundred yards when he spotted a rider, and he hid. The rider passed within 100 feet, but he did not see Siberts. The man rode on for a short distance, dismounted, and tied his horse to a tree. He drew his Winchester from its scabbard and started slowly down the trail toward Siberts' first camp. When the man had gone about a quarter of a mile, Siberts ran for the man's horse. He jumped into the saddle and kicked the horse into a dead run. Siberts concluded that the thief would expect him to head north, toward his place on Deep Creek. So he headed south. Two days later he came to the little town of Merriman, Nebraska.

At Merriman, Siberts bought a ticket on the east-bound Fremont, Elkhorn & Missouri Valley Railroad. Eventually, he got back to Pierre. In Pierre, Siberts ran across a broke, young cowboy who was homesick for Arkansas. Siberts bought the man's horse, saddle, bedroll, and Colt six-shooter with a flashy ivory handle for $100. Then he stopped at Fletcher's Drug Store for salve for his sore feet. Several loafers were in the Drug Store. One of them asked Siberts where he was headed.

"I'm on my way to the Badlands to look for stolen cattle," he replied, sliding his coat aside to give them a glimpse of his fancy pistol. The words were no more out of his mouth than Siberts realized that one of the loafers was the man who had burned his camp and whose horse he had stolen. Both men were nervous. Each expected the other to go for his gun. Siberts kept up his bluff.

While never taking his eyes off Newsome, Siberts swaggered out the door. He lost no time getting out of Pierre. Newsome did the same.

Bill Newsome should have thanked his luck stars for getting out of Pierre alive. But he didn't. The episode only emboldened him. A short time later, Newsome went from being a little thief to being a big one.[24] He stole two carloads of cattle from Patterson's place on Bad River. Newsome altered Patterson's brand and then trailed the cattle to Pierre. There, Newsome put the cattle in the hands of a banker in Pierre by the name of Hayes. Hayes shipped the cattle to a commission firm in Kansas City. Kansas City was a long way to ship cattle, but it was necessary because the brand inspector at the Sioux City Stockyards and even the brand inspector at the Omaha Stockyards would recognize that the brand these cattle were wearing was Patterson's altered brand. However, the cattle were sold in Kansas City without question, and a draft for the selling price went back to the Pierre bank.

When Patterson discovered that his cattle had been stolen, he immediately suspected Newsome. Patterson's suspicion and Newsome's well-known reputation were all it took to get Newsome arrested. The alleged cattle thief was put in the Hughes County jail in Pierre to await trial. However, Newsome did not sit for long in jail. The banker, Hayes, posted Newsome's bail. More than one person saw what was about to unfold. Newsome would jump his bond. Sure, the banker would have to forfeit the bail. But the bail was small in comparison to the amount of money garnered by two carloads of cattle. Newsome would be loose and darn hard to find in the lawless, West River Country. Sure enough, that is exactly what happened.

So some Badland ranchers decided to take the law into their own hands. One night a pounding at George Porch's door woke him from a deep sleep. "Whose thar?" He called out. Without answering, an Indian opened the door. "From Whipple" the Indian said, handing Porch a letter.

"George," the letter read, "go down to Whitfield's and get his team and buggy, and have them here by two o'clock tonight – for sure!" That was all that the note said. But it was enough. If Jack Whipple wanted a team and buggy at two in the morning, Porch would get them there, and then he'd find out why.

Porch quickly put on his pants and pulled on his boots. In the dead of night, he struck for Whitfield's place, where he got a team and buggy. At ten minutes to two in the morning, Porch knocked on Jack and Sally Whipple's door. "I knowed I could count on you, George," Whipple said, inviting George into the log house. Bill Newsome was there. His feet were sticking out of the rag shoes he had on, and it looked like he had run the gauntlet. Kruse Madsen was also there. All three of them – Porch, Whipple, and Madsen – had lost some cattle to Newsome, and they were anxious to have him out of the country. Kruse gave Newsome $20, Porch gave him $20, and Jack Whipple drove Newsome to

Cody, Nebraska. At Cody, Whipple stayed with Newsome until the east-bound train arrived. He put Newsome on it, but not before giving the cattle thief some good advice. "Newsome, I'd advise you never to show your face in these parts again," Whipple said, "cuz if you do, the next time things will be settled more permanently."

Selling Out

Missouri John lived the good life at his ranch on the north bank of White River. There was a bunk house for the hired men. He and James Ross had the comforts of an adjacent log house, and they even had a full-time housekeeper and cook, Mrs. Patterson. She was a widow with a young daughter. Missouri John developed a romantic relationship with a good-looking widow woman in Rapid City, Mrs. Risor. And John found many reasons to make business trips to Rapid City. When he couldn't get away, Mrs. Risor frequently made the two-day, horse & buggy trip to spend time with John on the 15 Ranch. To cap things off, Missouri John kept an ample supply of good Kentucky whiskey in the cellar.[25]

But even these amenities could not put off old man time. By 1896, Missouri John and James Ross decided they were getting too old for rigors of ranching on the open range. Massengale was ready to return to Macon, Missouri, and James Ross wanted to live out his last days in Philadelphia. Besides, they had made their fortune. They decided to sell out.

The 15 Ranch organized a big horse roundup that summer involving nearly every cowboy within 20 miles. The horses were scattered in small herds along White River from Pass Creek to Interior. Most of the horses were across the river, on the Reservation, in an area that had come to be known as Wild Horse Basin. Dude Rounds divided the cowboys into teams. The plan called for the teams to spread themselves out along the south Badland wall and send every loose horse across the White River at a gallop. The feat was accomplished by the end of the first day. The second day, the men strung themselves along the north side of White River. Starting across from the mouth of Pass Creek, the cowboys worked their way up the river valley, driving every horse north up against the Badland Wall and then herding them west toward Chamberlain Pass. Three-and-a-half miles northwest of Chamberlain Pass, one of the few penetrable spots in the north Badland Wall, Massengale had a big corral on Little Buffalo Creek capable of holding several thousand horses.[26] By late afternoon, the cowboys had pushed 2,000 horses through Chamberlain Pass and had them headed into the corral on Little Buffalo Creek. Everything was going according to plan. But just as the horses reached the gate into the natural corral, something spooked them. They stampeded. The horses scattered in every direction. The roundup was never restaged.

Missouri John sold the 15 Ranch that fall with 5,000 head of cattle and 200 horses to Corb Morse. Corb Morse paid Massengale and Ross $55,000 in cash and gave them a note for another $20,000.[27] Massengale went to his long-time foreman, Dude Rounds. Handing his checkbook to Rounds, Missouri John said, "Dude, write yourself a check for any ranch you want and sign my name to it."[28]

Missouri John asked George Porch to drive him to Cody so that Massengale could catch the train to Missouri.[29] Porch felt honored to do so. The first night, Porch and Massengale got as far as Pass Creek. They stayed that night at Ed Amiotte's ranch. The next day, they came upon a herd of 900 horses that Corb Morse was having trailed to Cody, Nebraska for a big horse sale. Of course, every horse in the bunch had formerly belonged to Massengale and Ross. Corb Morse's foreman, I.J.M. Brown and few of the cowboys had gone ahead to Cody to make arrangements for 900 horses coming into town. Porch guessed that Brown and the cowboys would then get drunk. Hans Thode and few cowboys had been left on the range to look after the herd of horses. When Porch and Massengale came along, Thode asked them to stay the night. Initially, Massengale declined the offer. He and Porch had not put in a full day, and Missouri John wanted to keep going so they could reach Cody before night fall. But Porch prevailed on Massengale to stay. "John," he said, "You're leaving the range fer good. This will be the last time yuh'll have a chance to be with a bunch of cowboys looking after a huge herd of horses that just a few days ago was yours." They stayed. That evening, Thode said to Porch, "Let's go out and watch the horses. They will stampede at the least little thing; and when the boys get back from Cody tonight, there's no telling what will happen."

About midnight, the boys came back from Cody. They were drunker than skunks and just barely able to stay in the saddle. The commotion they made riled the horses. Thode rode around the horses, whistling to keep their attention. The horses milled around uneasy, but they did not bolt. All of the drunks from Cody went to bed – all except for one, Harry West. West insisted on going out to help hold the horses. But Porch gently pinned him to his bed and wouldn't let him up. All at once, West sneezed. Nine hundred horses broke like a cannon had been fired. In the dark, the horses ran into Cody Lake, which was shallow. The stampeding herd plunged across the lake; but several horses in the lead fell, and they were tramped to death by the ones following them. Once across the shallow lake, the horses lit out at dead run for their home range back in Wild Horse Basin.

Hans Thode plunged his horse into Cody Lake amidst the stampeding herd. He gained the far bank right with the lead horses, and turned them. Porch jumped on his horse and rode out to help. But the horses ran right into a bunch of saddle horses, and the saddle horses went right along with the stampede.

Some of the saddle horses had bells on. The clanging bells urged the stampeding horses to run faster and to keep running. When Porch got back to camp, Harry West, who had started it all with one sneeze was passed out, dead drunk. I.M. Brown was sleeping like a log. Porch shook him. When Brown raised his heavy eyelids enough to see, Porch said, "I.M., do yuh know your horses is gone?" Without answering, Brown rolled over and went back to sleep.

Hans Thode managed to bring back one bunch of mares that night, but that was all that were ever gathered. The large herd of 15 Ranch horses went back on their home range. For years, they ran more or less wild in the area of the Badlands aptly named Wild Horse Basin.

The Men Who Rode with Missouri John

Many of the men who came to the White River Badlands with Missouri John stayed. Together, they laid down a legacy of skill, toughness, and daring that made the 15 Ranch legendary in the Badlands.

Dude Rounds was born in Clarinda, Iowa in 1862.[30] His parents either thought their new son was special or they wanted to toughen him up for the life that lay ahead of him, because his given name was Julius Caesar Rounds. When Mrs. Rounds sent her red-headed, freckle-faced, blue-eyed boy to his first day of school dressed in a white suit, the older boys tauntingly called him Dude. The appellation sounded much better to the young boy than his given name. So Julius Caesar called himself Dude for the rest of this long life.

Getting Ready to Ride: 15 Ranch.
Photo courtesy of the South Dakota State Historical Society.

When Dude was 15-years-old, he was big for age. Knowing that there was a bigger world out there, he set out to see it. Dude walked five miles to the nearest railroad station and used his hard-earned money to buy a one-way ticket to Omaha, Nebraska. There, Dude worked for the railroad for a short time. His work ethic did not go unnoticed. One day a stranger asked the young boy to help him drive a herd of cattle to Wyoming. The man was John Massengale. Dude Rounds quickly became Massengale's foreman and his business assistant. It is told that Massengale had money in three banks, but he always had to ask Dude how much money he had and where it was located. It is also told that Dude wrote and signed every check that Missouri John issued.[31]

Even though Dude Rounds rubbed shoulders everyday with men who spent their lives on the range, he was known far and wide for his uncanny knack for

Julius C. (Dude) Rounds and an unknown 15 Ranch hand, taken in Rawlins, Wyoming in 1885.

working with cattle. George Carlbom summed it up best during an interview in 1974: "When I was but a kid," Carlbom related, "I got to ride the Badlands one day with Dude Rounds gathering cattle. I learned more about cattle in that one day of riding with Dude Rounds than I've learned since in a life time of ranching."[32]

Dude also had a way with men. By the age of 19, he was the wagon boss of the spring roundup on the Laramie Plains and carried a Deputy U.S. Marshall badge to back up his unchallenged authority over the reps from 50 ranches. After a roundup it was the custom for the cowboys to ride into town and get wildly drunk. But not Dude Rounds. While the other cowboys were throwing down shots of whiskey as if it was water, Dude Rounds took a table at the back of the saloon and drank Sarsaparilla or, if it was available, lemonade.[33]

Dude Rounds was adept at gauging the credulity of strangers. With a straight face and total plausibility, he could tell the biggest of fibs; and he loved to pull practical jokes. A cattle drive to Chamberlain is a case in point. After delivering the cattle to Chamberlain, the 15 hands went to celebrate at the best restaurant in Chamberlain. At Massengale's expense, they were ready to eat the biggest steak the house had to offer.

George decided it would be fun to play a practical joke on the waitress. "Let's fake that I'm deaf and dumb," he told the others. Dude assured everyone

Pontoon bridge crossing the Missouri River going west at Chamberlain (1901).
Photo courtesy of the South Dakota State Historical Society.

that it would not be too hard to pretend that Porch was deaf and dumb, and recommended that they play along with the idea. When the waitress asked the 15 hands what they would like to eat, Dude answered for everyone, "Let's start with a big bowl of soup." Everyone joked good-naturedly with the waitress. Well, everyone joked with the waitress except George Porch. He sat stone silent. When the waitress asked what they'd like next, Dude again ordered for everyone. "We'll have a salad of your freshest lettuce smothered by your juiciest red tomatoes," he said. Then he added, "Well, all of us will except this fellow here," he said pointing to George. "Bring him another bowl of soup." The waitress later came back to get their orders for the main course. "Bring us the biggest steaks you have!" Rounds requested. "Well, we will all have a steak except this fellow here," he said, again pointing to Porch. "Give him another bowl of soup." George had had enough. "No ya don't, by God," he roared, "I want a steak just like everybody else."

Ernest W. (Hans) Thode was born in Itachoe, Germany in 1868.[34] He and his brother, Emil, came to America with their parents in 1870. The family settled first in Omaha, Nebraska and later moved to Carbon County, Wyoming. In 1893, Missouri John Massengale hired Hans and his brother Emil to help him trail a herd of cattle from Carbon to the White River Badlands. In 1896, Hans made a trip back to Carbon to marry his girlfriend, Frances Stephenson. The couple settled along the White River south of the present-day town of Stamford. In time, they raised twelve children.

Hans was first and foremost a bronc rider – indisputably the best bronc rider in the Badlands. He may have been one of the best riders to ever straddle a four-legged thunderbolt. During the end of a long career on the range, Jay Seath wrote that he had seen 400 to 500 top bronc riders in his time. But five of them, he related, were in a class by themselves.[35] One of those was Hans Thode. Seath told about one of the best rides he ever saw. It was in 1900. Seath rode with Hans Thode to cut a —X horse out of Thode's horse herd. It was a long ride, and they didn't reach the horse herd until mid-day. Among Thode's herd was a big, six-year-old, blue roan horse. The blue roan had not been handled since he had been caught, branded, and castrated four years earlier. Hans said, "Jay, my horse is tired. I'm going to catch that blue roan. When the horse chokes down, you hold his head down."

Hans caught the horse with his first throw. Seath held the horse's head while Hans tied three of its feet together and put a saddle and bridle on him. Thode straddled the horse, untied the three feet, and told Seath to turn the horse loose. All around were Badland washes ten to fifteen feet across and 50 feet deep. "Ya ain't gonna ride him here, are ya?" Seath asked. "I don't see no plank floor to ride him on Jay," replied Hans.

Gray wolf in the Badlands in 1917.
Photo courtesy of the South Dakota State Historical Society.

Hans rode him out. "He was," Seath related, "the whole wild west show, and I was the only audience."

Charley Thompson was not a 15 Ranch man, but he often helped them on roundups. Moreover, because of his close friendship with George Porch, the 15 men knew they could count on Charley Thompson. He was a good ally. Thompson stood six feet four inches and weighed 230 pounds, and he did not like outsiders moving onto his range.

Thompson was born in Illinois in 1857 and came with his parents to the Nebraska frontier in 1872. He joined his first cattle drive from Texas at the age of 16. In 1884 his second trail drive brought him to the Pine Ridge Reservation. About this time, Charley married Ida Lotzenheizer from Pierce, Nebraska. According to family history, Charley was at the Pine Ridge Agency when Chief Big Foot surrendered to Major Whitside on December 28, 1890. Like many then at the Agency, Charley Thompson rode out to Wounded Knee Creek early on the morning of December 29, 1890, expecting to see the orderly disarmament of the Big Foot's band and to watch them being escorted in the Pine Ridge Agency. Instead, Thompson witnessed the Wounded Knee Massacre.

As soon as the newly ceded reservation was opened to white settlement, Charley located at the forks of Bad River, where the present-day town of Philip now sits. The couple's first child was born there in 1894 – John "Lloyd" Thompson. The Thompsons moved in 1896 to a place 12 miles north of Cedar Pass, just below the forks of White Water Creek and Big Buffalo Creek.

In 1892, the newly formed Stock Grower's Association assessed themselves ten cents a head for wolf control. The money was used to pay a $10 bounty for adult wolves and $5 for pups. Charley Thompson became a "wolfer," meaning he hunted wolves for a living. When winter came, Charley packed a camp wagon with 100 No. 4 Newhouse traps and enough food to last several months. Taking 15 wolf hounds, he would be gone for several months at a time covering western South Dakota and parts of Montana and Wyoming.

Once, Thompson saw a female wolf and her pups sunning themselves by their den just west of Cedar Pass. He shot the wolf, but the pups scurried into the den. Thompson threw his jacket over the hole and rode home to get his eleven-year-old son, Lloyd. Together, they went back to the den.

"Tuffy," as Charley called his son, "thar's six wolf pups down that hole. Ya shinny on down and pull 'em out so I can kill 'em."

Lloyd made six trips into the den and came out each time with a pup. On his final trip into the den, Lloyd came nose-to-nose with an adult, male wolf. The wolf snarled and bared his fangs, but it didn't attack, Lloyd backed out of the hole as fast as his limbs would carry him. Not even the assurance of his father's six-shooter could get him to go back in the den.

Not to be beaten, Charley Thompson squeezed his big body into the den, laid his pistol up against the wolf's ear and pulled the trigger. "Thar ya go, Tuffy. Now get in thar and put this rope around a foot so's I can pull 'em out."[36]

Some regarded Charley Thompson as the strongest man on the range, but there are those who argue that that distinction belongs to W.F. Bartlett. However, there was no question as to who was the best shot. It was Charley Thompson. He could outshoot anyone of them, and he could do it with either a rifle or pistol. He carried a 44-40 pistol around his waist and a 44-40 rifle in his scabbard, making the ammunition interchangeable. Western movies depict gunslingers who simultaneously draw and fire two pistols. It makes for a good Western. However, few gunmen were capable of that. But Charley Thompson was one who could. More than one cowboy marveled as Charley threw out a tin can. Before the can hit ground, Charley could draw both pistols and roll the can across the prairie, hitting it first with a shot from the pistol in his left and then with a shot from the pistol in his right hand. My grandfather, Joe Hall, told of riding along the headwaters of the South Fork Bad River with Charley Thompson in search of some cattle that were missing after a heavy rainstorm. Suddenly, they jumped two wolves. Pulling his rife from its scabbard, Charley kicked his horse into a dead run. While the horse jumped small washes and struggled to keep his feet from going out from under him on the rain-slick hard hardpan, Charley rose in the saddle and shot one wolf on the dead run. Turning to his left, Charley saw that the other wolf was a hundred yards away and running full tilt into the mouth of dry wash. Thompson quickly fired. The wolf dropped dead in its tracks. "By then," Joe Hall said, "I had my rifle out of its scabbard."[37]

Stories are still told along Bad River about the duel between Charley Thompson and a sharpshooter from the Remington Firearms Company. The Remington Company sent their marksman out across the country to promote Remington guns by putting on demonstrations of unbelievable marksmanship. In 1899, the renowned sharpshooter arrived in Pierre with amidst much fanfare. Word went out that the sharpshooter would put on public display of marksmanship in Fort Pierre such as had never been seen in that part of the country or, for that matter, any other place. Simply put, he was the best marksman in the world. Charley Thompson decided to attend the public exhibition. To draw a crowd, the Remington Firearms Company offered a thousand dollars to anyone who could outshoot their marksman. Of course, every area of the country had their exceptional marksman, and the Remington Firearms man was never without a challenger, and he never lost.

The targets were arranged and the rules for the contest were set. One man would shoot a hole through the bulls-eye, The other man then had to shoot his bullet thru the same hole. This being done, the targets were moved farther away, and then farther away, and then even farther away until someone missed. It was a close match; and just as advertised, the Remington marksman was good. But when the match was over, the famous Remington marksman took the first train leaving town and Charley Thompson went home with a thousand dollars.

When Charley was not trapping wolves, he and Ida were quite the socialites. Charley played the fiddle and Ida accompanied him on the piano. Their musical

Charley Thompson around 1894.
Photo courtesy of Lloyd Thompson.

talents made them a popular couple. Cowboys stopped at Thompson's place whenever there was a dance, helped load the piano into a wagon, and escorted the band across the prairie to the dance. The dances lasted until dawn.[38]

George Porch was regarded as the toughest man on the range.[39] Fear was not a word in his limited vocabulary. If he felt pain, no one ever heard him mention it. George's love of bear hunting often interfered with his work. Massengale more than once cursed George for his devil-may-care bear hunting. When a bear had been spotted Massengale would futilely yell after Porch, "Porch, I'm not paying you to hunt bear. If you get hurt, I'll never come get your damn hide. You can rot there for all I care."[40] By then, George was out of ear-shot.

One of the stories that George told and retold in his later years was about roping a bear. According to Porch, the 15 outfit had just set up in the Badlands in the spring of 1891 and had put their cattle out on the range when a bear was spotted along the north bank of White River. While Porch's horse snorted and crow hopped, George set the air singing with his lariat. He roped the bear. With 300 pounds of black fury on the end of his rope, he hollered for the others to help. The bear was soon stretched taut between three horses. George hastily built a fire and heated a branding iron. The bear was caught on Ganow's range, whose brand was ICU. So George scorched ICU2 into the bear's hide, and then he let the bruin go. As an old man, George loved to entertain people, especially young children, with tales of his exploits as a cowboy. So it might be that this story about roping a bear and branding it, is just that – a story. But if the story isn't true, it ought to be.

Epilog

Shortly after moving back to Missouri, John Massengale settled in the town of Bevier, just a few miles west of Macon. There, he enjoyed a dignified, genial lifestyle as the owner of 800 acres of top-quality farm land and one of the principal stockholders in the State Exchange Bank of Macon. James Ross died on December 2, 1899 in Philadelphia, Pennsylvania at the age of 61. At the time of his death, the Ross-Massengale partnership was still in tact. After the death of Mr. James Ross, Massengale carefully computed the assets of the firm, which were as follows:[41]

Cash on hand in the First National Bank of Macon, Missouri.	$ 3,810.00
Certificate of Deposit #20866 with the First National Bank of Rapid City, South Dakota	$ 20,010.00

Certificate of Deposit #588 with the Pennington
County Bank of Rapid City, South Dakota .... $ 10,180.00

Certificate of Deposit #11486 with the Pennington
County Bank of Rapid City, South Dakota .... $ 2,774.75

Certificate of Deposit #1728 with the Bank of
Chamberlain, South Dakota, dated March 29,
1900 due on demand... $ 4,085.76

Certificate of Deposit #1748 with Stock Growers Bank
of Fort Pierre, South Dakota dated March 29, 1900,
due March 31, 1901 with
Interest at 10% per annum .... $ 4,000.00

Certificate of Deposit # 1768 with the Stock Growers
Bank of Fort Pierre, South Dakota dated March 31,
1900 and due on demand .... $ 794.71

Draft #19818 with the Bank of Iowa and Dakota in
Chamberlain, South Dakota .... $ 80.00

Note on Johnson Bros. and George L. Johnson *(from
Interior, South Dakota)* December 22, 1898, due one
year after date, bearing interest of 10% per annum .... $ 1,000.00
Interest now due on same .... $ 129.85

Note on J. Frank Miller *(from Macon, Missouri)* dated
on January 24, 1899 due one year after date, bearing
interest at 8% per annum .... $ 125.00
Interest now due on same .... $ 2.10

Note on Wilbert Gorum with William Hickox as
security dated July 1, 1899 due one year after date,
bearing interest at 10% per annum .... $ 600.00
Interest now due on same .... $ 43.00

Note on C.P. Riger with William Hickox *(from Stearns,
South Dakota)* as security dated June 27, 1899, due two
years after date, bearing interest at 8% per annum .... $ 1,800.00
Interest now due on same .... $ 106.00

Note on Wm. Trister *(from Macon, Missouri)* dated
September 29, 1899, due one year after date, bearing
interest at 7% per annum .... $ 400.00
Interest now due on same .... $ 14.66

Note on Johnson Morrow *(from Macon, Missouri)* dated
August 14, 1899, due one day (error) after date, bearing
interest at 7% per annum .... $ 1,878.45
Interest now due on same .... $ 46.96

Note on J.P. Mason *(from Macon, Missouri)* dated
September 4, 1899, due day (error) after date, bearing
interest at 7% per annum .... $ 880.00
Interest now due on same .... $ 12.65

Note on Lenard Phipps *(from Macon, Missouri)* dated
October 6, 1899, due one year after date, bearing
interest at 7% per annum .... $ 112.50
Interest now due on same .... $ 3.95

Note on Hicks, Yuts and Company, G.W. Hicks, John M.
Lenden, and T.S. Lenden *(from Macon, Missouri)* dated
October 25, 1899, due one year after date, bearing
interest at 8% per annum .... $ 500.00
Interest now due on same .... $ 9.35

Note on Thelma Richards *(from Bozeman, Montana)*
dated January 4, 1900, due on or before three years
after date, bearing interest at 7% per annum .... $ 500.00
Interest now due on same .... $ 9.35

Note on Chas Pilsher dated October 1, 1899, due eight
months after date, bearing interest at 7% per annum ...... $ 1,200.00
Interest now due on same .... $ 44.10

Note on J.F. Lear *(from Macon, Missouri)* dated
January 1, 1900, due on or before December 1, 1900,
bearing interest at 8% per annum .... $ 60.00
Interest now due on same .... $ .00

Note on Annie Morrow *(from Macon, Missouri)* date
August 8, 1895, due one day (error) after date, bearing
interest at 8% per annum, payable to Wm. Trister and
by him endorsed in blank .... $ 300.00
Interest now due on same .... $ 15.65

Note on J.S. Mayfield and C.N. Mayfield, dated
February 8, 1900, due twelve months after date, bearing
interest at 8% per annum .... $ 100.00
Interest now due on same .... $ 1.00

Note on William Hickox *(from Interior, South Dakota)*
dated October 30, 1895, due twelve months after date,
bearing interest at 10% per annum, which is now due
and unpaid .... $ 1,117.80

Note on William Hickox dated October 17, 1896, due
one year after date, bearing interest at 10% per annum,
which is due and unpaid .... $ 318.00
Interest now due on same .... $ 47.05

Note on William Hickox dated June 23, 1897, due five
months after date, bearing interest at 10% per annum .... $ 100.00
Interest now due on same .... $ 28.00

Note on Corbin Morse *(from Rapid City, South Dakota)*
date July 20, 1896, due two years after date, bearing
interest at 7% per annum, which is due and unpaid .... $ 20,804.75
Interest now due on same .... $ 729.00

Note on James Ellefson *(from Rapid City, South Dakota)*
dated October 10, 1899, due one year after date, bearing
interest at 10% per annum .... $ 300.00
Interest now due on same .... $ 15.00

Note on W. Swigert and Mrs. Swigert *(from Gordon, Nebraska)* dated August 1, 1898, due one year after
date, bearing interest at 10% per annum .... $ 300.00
Interest now due on same .... $ 19.35

Note on Ed Peterson *(from Rapid City, South Dakota)* dated July 1, 1899, due one year after date, bearing interest at 10% per annum......$ 35.00
Interest now due on same......$ 8.35

Note on Oliver H. Johnson *(from Interior, South Dakota)* date October 27, 1897, due one year after date, bearing interest at 10% per annum, which is now due and unpaid......$ 3,781.40

Note on Oliver H. Johnson date November 17, 1897, due one year after date, bearing interest at 10% per annum, which is now due and unpaid......$ 948.30

Note on Johnson Bros. by George L. Johnson dated October 27, 1897, bearing interest at 10% per annum, which is now due and unpaid......$ 1,141.80

Note on Johnson Bros. by George L. Johnson dated October 27, 1897, bearing interest at 10% per annum, which is now due and unpaid......$ 1,735.70

Note on George Porch *(from Interior, South Dakota)* dated September 2, 1897, due one year after date, bearing interest at 10% per annum, which is due and unpaid......$ 943.20

Note on George Porch *(from Interior, South Dakota)* dated September 2, 1898, due one year after date, bearing interest at 10% per annum, which is due and unpaid......$ 348.15

Note on W.H. Ochsner *(from Chamberlain, South Dakota)* dated September 5, 1899, due one year after date, bearing interest at 10% per annum......$ 6,800.00
Interest now due on same......$ 383.10

Note on William H. Place *(from Chamberlain, South Dakota)* dated October 20, 1896, due one year after date, bearing interest at 10% per annum, which is due and unpaid......$ 6,888.35

Note on Elsie Place *(wife of Wm. Place)* dated
November 17, 1897, due one year after date, bearing
interest at 10%, which is due and unpaid....................$ 2,338.29

Note on Elsie Place dated April 27, 1898, due seven
months after date, bearing interest at 10% per annum,
which is due and unpaid ....$ 299.10

Note on Albert Dalloff *(from Hultman, South Dakota)*
dated October 7, 1897 with H.P. Smith as security, due
one year after date, bearing interest at 10% per annum,
which is due and unpaid ....$ 157.60

Note on P.B. McCarthy and C.J. Hergan *(from Rapid City,
South Dakota)* dated June 28, 1899, due sixty days after
date, bearing interest at 10% per annum, which is due
and unpaid..$ 129.40

Note on R.C. Blassingame *(from Fort Pierre, South Dakota)*
dated May 9, 1896, due November 1, 1896, bearing
interest at 10% per annum, which is due and unpaid......$ 1,471.00

Note on R.P. Whitfield *(from Stearns, South Dakota)*
dated January 27, 1897, due eight months after date,
bearing interest at 10% per annum, which is due
and unpaid..$ 264.00

GRAND TOTAL ....$ 106,172.48

Massengale sent a check for the executor of James Ross' estate for $53,086.24, which in 1900 was a lot of money. As per James Ross' written instructions in his will, the account provided by Massengale was accepted without question.

In October 1904, John Massengale married a woman whose first name was, according to census records, Parrell. However, other spellings of her name are variously Parrelee and Paralee. At the time of the marriage, John Massengale was 61 years old and Parrell was 42 years old. The census of 1910 lists three children in the Massengale household: Mary Row, age twelve; Charley Reed, age eight: and William Reynolds, age two. Family records note that the couple a son. One wonders whether Parrell was a widow who had a son from a previous marriage. A picture of Parrell and a young boy shows a striking resemblance between the two. On the back of the picture, the picture says, "Paralee and the son they adopted."[42]

John Massengale died on December 19, 1910 in Macon, Missouri. George Porch and Dude Rounds caught the train in Kadoka and went to Missouri to attend his funeral.[43] In his will, John Massengale left one half of estate to his wife, and the other half divided equally between three half-sisters. But there is more to the story. John Massengale was not childless. When he moved to Missouri in 1861, Massengale allegedly left a woman pregnant in Kentucky. A son was born to this woman, and he was named John Slagle. In time and probably around 1906, John Slagle went to Missouri and sought out John Massengale. It was agreed that if John Slagle lived on and worked an acreage for a certain number of years, John Massengale would sign the land over to him. This verbal agreement was in effect at the time of John Massengale's death. Finding that he was not mentioned in Massengale's will, John Slagle sued for title to the land and won.[44]

Notes

[A] In 1861, the area of Virginia City (Montana) was part of Idaho Territory. It was not until 1864 that then surveyor mistook the ridgeline of the Bitterroot Mountains for the Continental Divide and included the area east of the Bitterroot Mountains in Montana Territory, thus moving Virginia City from Idaho to Montana. During the 1860s, Idaho Territory and the newly found gold fields around Virginia City became a destination for a good many Southern Democrats who fought for the Confederacy during the Civil War.

[B] An account of the horse race between Sorrel Tom and LaPlant's horse is given in the book *Western Dakota Horse Stories* and also in Bret Hall's book, *Roundup Years: Old Muddy to the Black Hills*. In both accounts, Rome Glover was LaPlant's jockey. However, in his autobiography, George Porch related that Rome Glover was Massengale's jockey. Since Porch was an eye witness to the horse race and later got into a life-threatening fight with Glover, Porch's account is taken to be the correct version.

CHAPTER 8

George Porch: A Badlands Character

Some people claim that a certain kind of character is attracted to a particular type of land. But others believe that it is the land that selectively puts its brand on the people, accepting a few while sending others packing. As for the Badlands, the truth is right in the middle. When the White River Badlands was opened for white settlement in 1890, its isolation and desolation attracted very few people, but they all had one thing in common. They wanted elbow room, and they did not want anyone living amongst them who represented law, conformity, or the shackles of civilization. But the Badlands did not abide all who came. She accepted on the tough, sending the weak and faint hearted packing.

George Porch.

The Badlands had more than its share of characters. There was Charley Thompson, all six foot four inches and 230 pounds of him. Frank Hart was another colorful Badland character. He was as comfortable on the back of bucking bronc as most people are in a rocking chair. Speaking of characters, one cannot overlook Bud Dalrymple, the wolfer who lived in a dug out over on Spring Creek and had gray wolf called Bruno. There other characters – many of them. But one of the Badland characters was in a class by himself.

George Porch was born Tarkio City, Iowa in 1862 to dirt-poor parents struggling to eke out a living on a 160-acre homestead. Money was scarce in the Porch family. So by the age of six, George was doing any little job that would earn him a penny or two. Often, he walked into nearby Clarinda to see of a town merchant might pay him a little something to run an errand or do a small chore. While in Clarinda, George often hung out with a tall lanky, red-headed boy named Julius Rounds. The town boys often picked on George because he was always barefoot, the family being too poor to afford shoes. But when Julius and George stood shoulder to shoulder against the town kids, they were a formidable duo. Their friendship continued for the next eight years. But when Julius was fifteen, he stuck out for Omaha, Nebraska. While the boys had no way of knowing it at the time, fate was determined to bind them together for the rest of their lives

At the age of seven, George trapped gophers to garner the county-paid bounty of ten cents apiece, and young Porch fancied that he was on his way to getting rich. That fall, George worked side by side with his dad sawing fire wood to sell by the cord. George's maternal uncle, Zack Montgomery, lived just down the road on a fairly large farm. Uncle Zack often needed to employ a hired man. But Montgomery was a hard worker, and he expected his hired man to work as hard as he did. Most hired men couldn't, and the others wouldn't. So Zack Montgomery was often in need of help. Seeing that his nephew was a hard worker, Zack hired George that spring to help him plow. Montgomery put eleven-year-old George behind a single-row plow pulled by a team of horses. Three years later, Montgomery got a contract to build grade for the Burlington Railroad line from Claremont, Iowa to St. Joe Missouri. He took George with him, putting him behind a Fresno Scraper pulled by a team of green-broke mules. While George did not know it at the time, Uncle Zack was getting him tough enough to survive in the White River Badlands.

In 1876 the Porch family moved to a farm near Gaynor City, Missouri, just south of the Iowa-Missouri line. There, George went to school for the first time. He attended the Elm Tree County School. The school had a bully – Rufe Cook. Rufe was three years older than George and thirty five pounds heavier. From day one, Rufe harassed George. For a while, George took it. But the harassing only got worse. So George decided that the next time Rufe bullied him, he would fight back. George did not have to wait long. When George stood up to Rufe, the bully scratched a circle in the dirt and stepped inside of it. George stepped into it, too. "You're in my ring," Rufe called out, and he swung at George. George blocked the blow with his left arm, and he threw a hard right that hit the Rufe right between the eyes. Rufe swung again. Again, George blocked the blow and landed another punch. Before the teacher came out and put a stop to it, George knocked Rufe down several times and bloodied his face. Both boys were suspended from school for a while. At the end of his suspension time, George went back to school and finished his one and only year of school. Rufe never did show his face back at the Elm Tree Country School.

When George was eighteen, he and two brothers, Billy and Lew McCall, set out for Kansas to find work. In Kansas, the McCalls went to work for their uncle. George cut broom corn for neighboring farmer. When fall came, the trio set out for home. They were cooking their supper one evening when three men drove up in a buggy. The men asked a lot of questions, mostly about where the three boys hailed from and where they were going. While one of the strangers did the talking, the other two looked over their horses. When they left, George said, "Unless I miss my guess, they'll be back tonight to steal our horses."

The McCalls had an old shot gun, and George had a Hopkins & Allen 38 revolver. George gave his pistol to Billy and took his shotgun. They hid themselves and waited. Just before midnight they heard a buggy and a horse coming back. The buggy stopped almost beside them. Someone softly called out, "Hello, boys." They didn't answer, but cocked their guns. The buggy went on, but not before one man got out. Crawling along the ground, George followed the would-be horse thief as he slipped quietly toward where the horses were picketed. Seeing something move in dark, one horse snorted and pulled loose. Billy ran to catch the horse. The stranger walked over to Billy and said, "What are you doing up at this time of night?"

"Watchin' again horse thieves," Billy replied, waving his pistol.

"Good idea! Got yourself a gun there, I see."

"Sure do."

"Let me see it." Billy handed his pistol to the man. The man examined it. Seeing that the pistol was loaded, he pointed it at Billy. But before the horse thief could say a word, George stepped out of the darkness and leveled his shotgun at the stranger's back.

"Drop the gun, Mister." The man held the pistol. "I said drop the gun!" The man dropped it. The man lamely explained why he was out so late at night, saying he was on his way to Frankfort. "Well," George replied, "Yuh better lope right along cuz if ya show up back hereabouts, you'll get a hole bored right through yuh."

The Love of His Life

In the summer of 1884, George put up a hundred acres of timothy grass and clover for a farmer, Tim Clark. The farmer had a daughter, Carrie. In George's eyes, "Carrie Clark was da prettiest girl in da whole county."

At the end of the summer, Tim's oldest son, Henry, came home from Wyoming in order to marry Melissa Owen, the daughter of a nearby farmer. The wedding put ideas in George's head. "So fur as I was concerned, George later confessed, "Carrie was the only woman in the world. But I held back from askin' her ta marry me fur the reason that I hadn't much money, and Carrie had eight hundred dollars o' her own and a good education so's she could teach music an' make more money. I couldn't see myself askin' her ta marry me till I had at least as much as she did."

After the wedding ceremony, Henry and his new wife departed for Wyoming. Before leaving, the young couple convinced Henry's sister, Carrie, to go with them to Wyoming. George drove the three of them to the train. At the train station, George pulled Henry aside. "If ya run any kind of work I could do," George quietly told Henry, "I wisht yuh'd let me know."

Two weeks later, George got a letter from Henry. "I've found a job for you George if can come right away." George borrowed two hundred dollars from Horace Jones and boarded the Union Pacific train the next day. His destination was Carbon, Wyoming. As the train rolled across the Nebraska prairie, George formulated his plan. Right away, he'd start saving as much money as possible. The first two hundred dollars would go to paying back Horace Jones. After that, he would save most everything he earned. When he had eight hundred, he'd ask Carrie to marry him.

Early the next morning, George reported to Jim Fisher, his new employer. Fisher owned the livery stable and the only hotel in town. He was a big man, weighing 220 pounds without an ounce of fat. Fisher acquainted George with his several jobs. One job was do the stable work. Another of George's jobs was to deliver water to the cave-like homes of the miners. When the water arrived on the Union Pacific Water Car, George pumped the water in 50 gallon barrels and then hauled the barrels, three to a load, around to the houses in town and the miners and their families living in cave-like homes up the ravine. At each house, George dipped the water into the house's private barrel. It was impossible to do the job without getting sopping wet. To make matters worse, winter was approaching. It was only a few weeks and the thermometer dipped below freezing, and it kept falling. Between pumping the water into 50 gallon barrels, hauling it, and dipping it into smaller barrels, George was so wet that by the end of his rounds he had to thaw his coat off of him. His pay was thirty-five dollars a month and board and room.

When George got his first paycheck, he did not put aside one cent toward his going-to-get-married fund. Instead, he sent a money order for thirty dollars home to his mother and kept back five to live on. Porch did this with every check he got from Jim Fisher. "I wasn't too keen 'bout the job, but I needed the money and I felt I ought ta help my folks back in Missouri." Money wasn't the only thing standing between George and Carrie. "I was so busy that I ner got time to keep in touch with Carrie, an' she was teachin' down by Cheyenne."

Fisher had a third job for George. Two days a week Porch carried the mail by horseback up to Leo, a post office, general store, and saloon all rolled into one at the foothills of the Shirley Mountains. Leo was thirty-five miles away, and it took a day to get there and a day to get back. As the winter came on, the trips to Leo became increasingly arduous. One trip to Leo was particularly hard. The snow lay heavy on ground. As Porch's horse climbed higher and higher, the bottom dropped out of the thermometer. George was nearly frozen to death, and he was still seventeen miles from Leo. A half mile ahead was a ranch. Hunkering down in the saddle, George headed for the ranch. Just as Porch got off his horse, a fellow ran out of the ranch house for fire wood. As the man gathered up an armful of wood, he spotted Porch. "Come on in stranger and get warm," he said, running for the warmth of the house. When the cowboy opened the door, his mouth dropped to the floor. "George," the cowboy yelled like he had seen a ghost. It was Porch's boyhood friend, Dude Rounds. Dude ushered George to a chair near the stove, sat him down, and yanked off his boots. "My God, George," Dude exclaimed, looking at Porch's bare feet, "What do you mean going without socks in this weather? You're in Wyoming, man!"

"Is thar any partickler reason fer puttin' on style in Wyomin,' Dude?"

Dude was the foreman for John Massengale's 15 Ranch, and it was arranged so that if no one from the 15 Ranch came into Carbon for mail, George would deliver the mail on his way to Leo. One such mail delivery to the 15 Ranch the following spring changed the course of George's life. As Porch rode into the ranch, he saw a huge roundup unfolding before his eyes. "Dar was cattle all over the lan'scape. A couple of cowboys was holdin' a big herd of cattle, but dar was more cattle pourin' in from every direction. Horses were runnin' and bucking ever' whar you looked. In the mittle of it all, dey was ropin' and an' brandin' calves. The whole thing knocked my eyes out and sucked my breath away. The smell o' the cookin' was mixed wit' the smell o' burnin' calf hide an' hair. The cook was dishin' out grub to the furst bunch o' riders. One of 'em yells ta me, 'Hi Mail Carrier, get off that horse and grab a plate and pour yourself some coffee. Here, everyone eats.'"

A cowboy sailed a plate toward George. George caught the plate and got in line. Just has the cook was about to put food on George's plate, a big fellow standing right behind George called out, "Why is this damn mail carrier eating?" When George looked over his shoulder, the big man pushed up close to his face and stuck his whiskers against George's nose. "Who hired you into this outfit?" He snarled.

"I was asked to eat," George replied. "In fact, I was ordered to eat, and bein' hungry, I obeyed doz orders."

"This is a cow roundup," the big man replied. "It ain't no mail carrier's picnic!" And he stuck a fist against George's nose and ground it around. George backed out line, but the big man kept following him, grinning and keeping his fist right against George' nose. Porch flung his plate back into the box. "Keep your feed!" George said. "An' keep your fist outta my face. There's your pack of mail of over thar, and it's the last mail of yours that I'll fetch up here!"

George went for his horse, but the man followed him. "Porch, come and eat. I was just having a little fun with you. You know me, Porch. I'm John Massengale. We're both from Missouri, and I want you to stay and eat," the big man said with tears in his eyes.

George went back and ate. No one seemed surprised at what had just taken place. Besides that, the food was good. Seeing a roundup and feeling its energy hooked George. Then and there, Porch knew that he wanted to become a cowboy.

In the spring of 1886, George made a short visit back to Missouri to visit his parents and siblings. While George was in Missouri, Stephen Gay, the foreman for the Long Nine Ranch, trailed in a bunch of Texas longhorns and put them on the range beside the North Platte. Gay offered George a job as a cowboy. "I don't know a thin' 'bout ridin' horses nor a thing 'bout handling stock on the range cuz I has been prutty much a farmer all o' my life," Porch confessed to Gay.

"But you're a hard worker, and so you're hired."

Deputized

While Porch was working on the Long Nine for Stephen Gay, John Massengale made verbal agreement with Joe Lee and his sons to build him a log house in Carbon. The Lees were to get the logs in the mountains and Missouri John was to furnish the teams to haul the logs into Carbon. It was agreed that the cost of the house would be 403 dollars.

The Lees built the house, and it was satisfactory in every way. But when it came time to close the deal, Joe Lee wanted 603 dollars for the house. Missouri

John won't pay it. So the Joe Lee moved into the house, defying anyone to stop him. To George's surprise, Missouri John didn't force the issue.

Several months later, George went to Lee's place to purchase a tanned, buckskin hide. At the time, George was wearing a fancy six gun. While Porch and Lee talked, the old man kept looking at George's pistol. Finally, Lee said, "I'm expecting most any time fer someone to come out from Carbon and try to arrest me. But that can't be done by no man." George didn't say anything, but old man Lee continued. "Maybe they'll press you inta service. If you come fur me, Porch, I'll have that gun your wearin.'"

"Mr. Lee, I don't want anythin' to do with the business between you and the law. But if I'm pressed inta service by the law, I'll be here with this gun. If you get it, you'll earn it."

Suddenly, Joe Lee's son, Hank, grabbed George by the back of his shirt collar and tried to pull George to the floor. But he only succeeded ripping George's shirt down the shoulder. George grabbed Hank by the throat, flung him into wood box, and proceeded to choke Hank nearly to death. "Boys, boys, stop!" old man Lee called out. "What's da use of fighin'?" George jerked Hank up out of the wood box, shook him like a pup, and flung him backwards.

"Let's settle for the tanned hide," Porch said to old man Lee.

Several weeks later word reached Carbon that the Lees were coming to town to get supplies and to see whether anyone was going to try to arrest them. Missouri John pounced. He got the judge to issue a subpoena for George, requiring him to testify that John Massengale entered into a verbal contract that called for Joe Lee to build the log house for 403 dollars. To make sure that the subpoena got delivered, Massengale arranged for Dude Rounds to ride up the Long Nine Ranch and personally deliver it to Porch. As Rounds put the subpoena into Porch's hands, he made it clear that George was supposed to immediately come to town. When George arrived in Carbon, Deputy Sheriff James Finch was waiting for him. Finch deputized Porch and handed him a warrant to arrest the Lees when they got to town. "If you can't bring them in alive, their bodies will due," the deputy sheriff said.

"I don't pertickler like the job," George replied. "But if I'm paid fer doin' it, I'll do it."

George was standing on the corner when the Joe Lee and two sons rode into town. Porch waved to them. The old man pulled up his horse. Waving his Winchester over his head, Joe Lee said, "If anybody tries to arrest me, there'll be blood flowing in the streets."

George thought he could have got everyone of them right there, figuring that Hank Lee was only one he'd have to kill as the others wouldn't have found their guns before the job was done. But not wanting to kill anyone, George let them pass.

The Lees went into Mandy Peterson's saloon. In time, George went in too and bought a round of drinks for everyone in the saloon. After getting tanked up, the Lees went over to their new log house in Carbon (the one they had built for Missouri John) and went to bed. In the morning, a blizzard had set in. Even the miners couldn't get out their jobs. By noon, Mandy Peterson's saloon was packed. Men were there not so much to drink as to keep warm from the big, coalstove that heated the place.

George saw that situation as a good opportunity to arrest Joe Lee without any bloodshed. He told Jim Finch, the deputy sheriff, about his plan to get the drop on the Lees in the crowded saloon. "Ya just be close by to take 'em off my hands when I get 'em," Porch told the deputy sheriff.

George went into the saloon and shuffled amongst the miners crowded close the stove. All the time, George edged toward Hank Lee, who was packed in among the crowd and couldn't move very fast. Looking out the window, George saw Jim Finch's hat pass by. Finch was heading toward the saloon door. Slipping out his pistol, George stuck the 38 into Hank's ribs. "Put up yer hand's, ever' damn one of ya," he said to the Lees. Everyone in the saloon froze. Finch came in and relieved the Lees of their guns.

The Lees were put in jail in Rawlins until their trial. However, they never went to trial. Instead, Massengale paid Joe Lee $403, and Lee signed over the house. Missouri John dropped the charges.

The Winter of 1886–1887

In the fall of 1886, the snow came early and it came often. Winter set in hard across the Northern Great Plains. The mercury slid to the bottom of the thermometer, and it stayed there. The wind blew hard out of the northwest, almost endlessly and relentlessly shifting the drifting snow across the prairie. When spring was supposed to come in 1887, it didn't. All across Wyoming Territory, Montana Territory, the Dakota Territory, and the prairie provinces of Canada, hundreds of thousand of cattle perished. Most of the dead cattle belonged to English aristocrats and other titled foreign investors who thought that raising cattle on the Northern Plains was a sure way to add to their wealth. But the winter of 1886–1887 taught them that it took more than capital to gamble successfully in the cattle business with Mother Nature. When spring finally came in 1887, most of absentee rancher owners sold their few remaining cattle and withdrew from the West. The owners of the Long Nine were among them. After the roundup, George Porch was out of a job.

Like many unemployed cowboys, George rode the grub line during the winter of 1887–1888, going from ranch to ranch. The drifters stayed in the ranch's bunk house, ate a few meals, did any odd job that needed doing, then rode to the next place. When spring came, there weren't wasn't much demand for cowboys.

Late one Saturday night in the spring of 1888, Porch sat In James Ross' saloon, drowning his sorrows in whiskey. Seeing no other way to survive, George dejectedly decided that come Monday he would take a job in one of Carbon's seven coal mines. As George poured himself another shot of whiskey, he saw John Massengale come into the saloon. Spotting Porch, Massengale immediately came up to Porch's table, pulled out a chair, and sat down. "George," Missouri John said, getting right to the point, "Henry Clark told me that come Monday you're going to work in the coal mines."

"I has got be doin' somethin,'" George sighed, "and there's nothin' else to do."

"Porch, don't you do it. You're too good a man to go into the mines and get all crippled up. I'm going to Missouri pretty soon. You come along, Porch. You can stay here at the hotel until I'm ready and . . ." At this point, George started to protest, but Massengale held up his palm, informing George to hush. "I'll take care of your bill at the hotel until I'm ready to go. We can go down together. You visit your folks, and I'll go on to Macon. About the first week in April, we can meet somewhere and come back together."

"But maybe I won't be able to get on at the mine when we get back. With all the big ranchers sellin' out, thar might not be any ranch work, and men will be standin' in line to work in the mines."

"The hell with the mines" Massengale exploded, "I was figuring on hiring you on at the Fifteen!"

Dealing with a Bad Character

In the spring of 1888, Massengale and Ross held a big roundup on the Beer Mug Ranch. Additional riders were hired. One of them was Clabe Young. Young came to Wyoming Territory from Texas. He arrived with reputation of being a bad man who knew how to use a gun. It was widely rumored that when in Texas, Clabe Young had killed a man.

By asking the various ranch hands, Clabe Young learned that George Porch was the toughest man on the 15 Ranch, and that he was also a pretty good shot with both a rifle and a pistol. That was probably why Clabe Young sought out George and boastfully told Porch that he could out shoot him. Not one to back away from anything or anyone, George said he would take that challenge at a dollar a shot. A target was set up. Each man shot fourteen rounds. George beat Young every round. That evening in the bunk house, Clabe told some of the boys that someday Porch would go riding out in the prairie, and he wouldn't come back. The cowhands told Missouri John about Young's threat. Missouri John worried about it, and passed the information on to Porch. "I wish you wouldn't go anywhere with Clabe Young," Massengale told Porch. "I'm scared he'll leave you out on the prairie if he gets a chance."

The next morning, Clabe Young said he didn't have a horse that was up to a day of hard riding. Pointing out Porch's horse, Blue Jay, Clabe asked George if he could use the horse. Porch allowed it. However, noting the double rigging on Young's saddle, Porch added, "I has allus ride him wit' a single rig. If he was double girted, he might not like it."

Swinging his saddle on the big blue roan, Young replied, "If he pitches with me, Porch, I'll kill ya." Young's tone suggested that he meant what he said.

Clabe Young rode with George that day. They soon came across four wild horses, including a big stallion. Young and Porch set in after the wild horses. In chasing the horses, they became separated. At the end of the day, Young returned to the 15 Ranch. Porch was still out on the prairie and night was approaching. Massengale was worried. He wondered whether Clabe Young had shot George. However, long after sunset Porch came in, driving the big, six-year-old stallion into the 15 corrals.

The next day, Clabe Young again told George that he wanted to ride with him. When George said that he could, the ranch hands looked at Porch like he was loco. Porch and Young rode along that morning right beside each other for quite a spell, neither saying a word. Young pulled out a bottle of whiskey and took a long drink. He put the bottle back without offering George a drink. Again, they rode in silence. As they rode, Young gradually edged his horse closer and closer to Porch until Young was crowding him. Again, Young got out his bottle. While Young took a sig from his bottle, George discreetly pulled back the hammer on his pistol. As Young put his bottle away, his hand came up over his hip and Young suddenly pulled his gun. "Porch," he said, "I'm gona kill. . ." But Young stopped right there. George's gun was right under Young's arm.

"Clabe, if yuh ever make to pull a gun on me agin, I'll drill yuh."

"Oh Porch, ya know that I wouldn't shoot yuh for the world," Young said, shaking like an aspen leaf in the fall wind. Again, Young reached into saddle bag for the bottle of whiskey, and he drank from the bottle until he was wobbling in the saddle. George veered his horse off to the right and kicked him into a lope.

By sunset, all of the riders had returned to the ranch except Clabe Young and George Porch. Every man wondered what had happened to them. For hours, Missouri John walked around the outside of the house, taking his hat off, putting it on, looking at the prairie, and fighting back tears. George was the first to come back. He was driving three wild horses. Upon seeing George, Missouri John walked over to the corral and swung the gate open. As George got close, he saw tears Missouri John's eyes. "Glad to see you, Porch. How did you get back?"

"Clabe couldn't git his gun up quick enough and I just happened to have mine ready," Porch replied. Missouri John thought that George had killed Clabe Young, but while he was searching for a way to ask that question, Young rode into sight. "I'd appreciate it if no one made mention of this," George said to Massengale and men standing by the corral.

A few days later the roundup was over, and Missouri John terminated Clabe Young's employment.

The End of an Illusion

When Missouri John decided to relocate in the White River Badlands, Porch was running 15 wild horses with the 15 horse herd. Massengale told Porch that if George helped the 15 Ranch move to the Badlands, Porch could throw his horses in with the 15 Ranch stock. As arrangements were being made that spring to move to the Badlands, a heavy snow arrived. A few days later, it got warm enough to melt the top of the snow, which then froze that night, covering the heavy snow with a thick coat of ice. Several weeks later, word came that George's horses were snowed in up in the mountains and they had been without grass for two weeks. Their ribs were showing.

The fifteen horses represented all of George's wealth. So the next morning he struck out for the snowbound horses. The deep, ice-covered snow made it tough going. It was late in afternoon before Porch a broke a trail to his horses and started driving them home. It was 40 miles to the 15 Ranch. The horses were so starved down that they would die if pushed hard. George urged them gently and slowly through the deep snow. He was only half way down the mountain when it got dark. There was no moon. The wind came up strong, whipping up a blizzard. To get out of the wind, George herded the horses into a deep canyon. It was a mistake. The snow in the bottom of the canyon came up the horses' belly, and there was no broken trail. Fortunately, George was riding a particularly tough horse aptly named Headlight. Headlight broke the trail, and the other horses followed. It was now pitch black. Wind-driven snow swirled through the night air, completely obscuring George's vision. Nonetheless, Headlight plowed on for hour after hour. All of a sudden, the horse stopped dead in its tracks. George got off. Putting out a hand to feel his way, George touched a gate post. Immediately, Porch knew where the horse had taken him. The gate led into a corral and then to an old barn. George put the horses into the dilapidated barn and felt his way to the log cabin. Finding the door to the cabin, George went in, taking Headlight with him. Feeling around in the dark, Porch found a cedar log that someone had dragged into the cabin. A hatchet was buried into the log.

George cut a few slivers from the log. He put the shavings into the fireplace and lit them. The heat felt good, and it gave off enough light for George to see a hay-filled tick. He cut the tick open and fed the hay to Headlight. Feeling warmer, George rolled up in his saddle blanket and went to sleep.

When morning came, George poked his head out the door. The sky was clear. A bright sun glittered off the pure-white snow. George's horses were standing in the barn, but their heads stuck out through the roof poles. Sixteen-feet-high Quaking Aspen grew beside the barn, but only the tips of trees stuck out of the snow. Porch gathered up his horses and struck out for the 15 Ranch. Luckily, the frozen crust on the snow was so hard that the horses were able walk over the top of it all the way to the 15 Ranch.

"As I come inta sight o' the 15 Ranch House, I seen someone walkin' back and forth between the house an' the yard gate. It was Missouri John. Taking off his hat to shade his eyes from the bright sun, Massengale saw that it was Porch, and he heaved a sigh of relief. 'Porch,' he whimpered as George rode up, "I thought I'd never see you again." Later, the boys told George that Missouri John walked the floor most of the night, saying over and over that he'd never again see Porch alive.

The cook gave Porch a big meal to break his long fast. Afterward, George got a bucket of water and took a sponge bath. Then he flung himself across his bed and fell into a deep sleep.

The next morning, Porch rode into Carbon to get the ranch mail. It was mid-afternoon when George topped the hill that led down to Carbon. As Porch approached the post office, the jingle of sleigh bells, a most unusual thing in Carbon, fell on George's ear. Looking up, he saw a perfectly matched team of bays with bells that kept time to horses' hoof beats as they pulled a swan-body cutter. As it flashed by, a red mitten waved and a woman's voice rang out, "Hi, George!" It was a voice that George had not forgotten, nor would he ever forget. A half strangled cry rattled out of Porch's throat. "Carrie," he called out. If she heard him, the cutter never stopped. Carrie Clark, the love of his life, rode off with a potato farmer from Torrington.

Sipping on a glass of whiskey at the saloon, George convinced himself that Carrie had come to Carbon to see her brother, and that coming to town with the potato farmer from Torrington was simply convenient. Two days later, George had another chance meeting with Carrie. Carrie told George that she was going to marry the man from Torrington. "I'd like your blessing, George."

"Carrie," George managed to say after a long pause, "God knows that your happiness is the greatest wish in my heart." But when George related this fifty years later, sobs shook his granite frame. "Oh," he whimpered trying to hold tears, "if I'd only said, 'Haven't I a chance, Carrie?'"

More Guts than Brains

When the snow finally melted in the spring of 1892, George set out for Rapid City to see if he could find a banker who would lend him money with which to buy cattle. Missouri John told Porch to go to Belson's place on the east bank of the Cheyenne River and to ask Belson the best place to cross the river. When Porch got to the Cheyenne River, he found it bank full, making the river two hundred yards wide. Belson advised Porch to go back home and come back in a week or two. George won't do it. Relenting in the face of Porch's determination, Belson said, "See that little rise on the far bank. It slopes out into river, and it's pretty firm. It would probably give good footing for your horse if you can hit it."

George could not swim a lick. Nonetheless, he jumped his horse off the bank and plunged into the raging river. Immediately, he and his horse went under. But the horse came up swimming. George hung onto the horse and got towed across the river. However, the current was stronger than George had anticipated, and the rushing water swept him and the horse past the intended landing point. About ninety feet from the west bank, the horse got his feet into quicksand. The strong current instantly rolled the horse over on his side, forcing George to let go of his grip on the saddle. The current swept him away, and George was certain he was going to drown. But his feet hit the bottom. Standing up, George found that he was in chin-deep water. Tying his thirty-foot lariat to the horse's hackamore, George floundered to the end of rope. Still, the water was chest deep. Tugging on the lariat, Porch helped the horse advance toward the shore. As the horse moved closer, George used the slack to walk toward the shore. Eventually, George reached solid ground. Still, it took another half hour to get the horse out of the river. The horse was played out, and George was chilled to the bone. Leading the horse, George walked to Bill Charles's place on Spring Creek, where he stayed the night.

Becoming a Cattleman

George Porch realized that the untamed and basically uninhabited land in the Badlands offered a rare opportunity to became a cattleman. So in 1892 Porch set out to find a place of his own. While George was looking for a place, he stayed with Robert Whitfield. Whitfield had been the former Boss Farmer for the Pass Creek district, but due to Pettigrew's insistence on employing only South Dakota Republicans, Whitfield lost his job in 1890. In 1891, Whitfield relocated on the north bank of White River at the mouth At the time, a young man by the name of Bill Hickox was working for Whitfield [A].

To pay for his keep and also for the pasturage of the 16 horses he brought with him, Porch helped cut hay that summer for Whitfield. Hickox assisted him.

They cut the hay on the large flat to the southwest of Whitfield's, hauled it down a steep hill, and unloaded the hay next to the corral. A team of stout draft horses was hitched to the hay wagon by a set of tugs. There was no britching on the harness, so the horses could not hold back the load when they went down the steep cut into Whitfield's corral. To make matters worse, there was steep cut bank on the south side of the hill.

When they came to the hill, Hickox always jumped off the hay wagon and walked down the hill. "Porch," he said, "I wouldn't ride to the bottom of hill with you at reins of a wagon load of hay for a million dollars." One time Hickox and Porch got more hay down the two of them could handle. So Whitfield hired Richard Lip, an Indian who lived not far away, to help. When Hickox slipped off the wagon at the brow of the steep hill, Lip gave him a confused look as if to wonder why a tired man would walk when he could ride. But Lip didn't ask Hickox why he decided to walk down the hay corral, and Hickox didn't warn Richard Lip that his life was in immediate peril. When Porch and Lip got to bottom of the hill, so much blood had drained from the Indian's face that he could have passed for a white man.

Bill Hickox regularly talked in his sleep, and he could carry on quite a conversation with himself. One night Hickox had a nightmare about Porch driving that team down the steep hill. All at once, he sat up straight as a bolt and cupped his hands to his mouth. At the top of his lungs, Hickox yelled, "Turn'em, turn'em thar, Porch!"

To calm Hickox, Porch bellered, "Gee! Gee thar!" which to a team of horses or mules means turn to the right. In his mind's eye, Hickox saw the team turn right just as Porch commanded, which took them over the edge of the cut bank. Seeing that, Bill gave a big groan. "There you played hell, Porch," Hickox said. "You turned 'em the wrong way, you blamed fool!" At that, Porch could not restrain himself from a hearty laugh. To which Hickox grumbled, "It's a damn funny thing to laugh about having smashed Whitfield's outfit all to pieces."

Bill Hickox was a hard worker, and that suited George just fine. The two quickly became good friends. It was not long before they decided to become partners in the cattle business. George sold his horses to Whitfield and bought some cattle. He and Hickox threw their few cattle together, and squatted on an abandoned homestead claim a mile and half up river from Whitfield's place but on the north side of the river.

Putting first things first, they started building a log house. They were working on the house when word reached them that the Pierre Livestock Company wanted to sell all of its cattle. Hickox and Porch rode into Pierre to look into the deal. They borrowed six thousand dollars from the First National Bank in Fort Pierre and stocked their ranch with 400 head of cattle.

Fall came, and it was followed by winter. The log house they set out to build still didn't have a roof. So Porch and Hickox slept in the haystack that winter and cooked out in the open on a small iron stove. Being short of supplies, they borrowed a four-horse team and wagon from Hank Scovel, a rancher who lived farther down White River, and went into Pierre to get a winter's supply of grub. After buying what they needed, George said they should get started for home and camp out on the prairie as it would be cheaper than staying in town. They no more than got camp pitched that evening than Bill remembered he needed some rope. "I'm going back to Fort Pierre for that rope," Hickox announced. If George had put two and two together, he would have realized that Bill was not going to town to buy rope. After all, Fort Pierre rolled up its sidewalks when the sun went down. Only the saloons would be open.

Not long after Hickox left, Hank Scovel and his herder came down the trail with a band of sheep bound for the Chicago market. They camped nearby. Before George turned in for the night, he set out a box a little ways from the camp and put their newly purchased kerosene lantern on it to guide Hickox back to camp. It wasn't long and the wind came up and it started snowing heavily. Porch crawled out of his bedroll to help Scovel's herder find the sheep some shelter. As Porch left camp, the wind blew the lantern over. It exploded in a blaze, but the heavy snow immediately extinguished the fire. It was two hours before the herder and Porch got the sheep bedded in the shelter of some brush. When George got back to camp, he found that the wind had blown the tent flat. Lifting the canvas, Porch saw Bill laying there with the tent pole lying across this belly. Bill was dead drunk, having spent all their remaining money on whiskey.

The storm passed during the night; but in the morning, snow covered the prairie. They didn't have the makings for a fire, so they each ate a sandwich, fed the horses oats, hitched up, and drove to White Creek Lake. There, they ate the last of the sandwiches and camped for the night. In the morning, it started to snow again. The wind blew hard out of the northwest, and it got a lot colder. They pulled out for Dry Creek in the makings of a blizzard. As they drove, the snow increased and temperature plunged. There wasn't a house between Fort Pierre and White River. Finding one solitary green cottonwood, George cut it down. With quite a bit of fussing, he got a little fire going; but it didn't give off much heat. That night, Hickox and Porch huddled together, trying to keep warm. In the morning, they pulled out for Scovel's ranch, which they reached near sundown after traveling for three days and enduring frigid temperatures on two sandwiches apiece.

Woman Problems

In the fall of 1893, Porch left Hickox in charge of the ranch while he drove some marketable cattle to Cody, Nebraska. There, the cattle would be put on the Fremont, Elkhorn & Missouri Valley Railroad and shipped to Omaha. Whitfield asked if he could throw a few of his cattle in with the herd. Porch agreed to it. Whitfield had a pair of three-year-old horses that had been hitched to a wagon only a couple of times. Whitfield told Porch that he'd trail after the cattle if Porch would handle his green-broke team. Porch agreed, and the cattle were driven to Cody without incident.

On the way home, Porch and Whitfield stopped at McCorkle's place. McCorkle, who was a Boss Farmer on the Rosebud Reservation, gave them some nice watermelons. From McCorkle's place, Porch and Whitfield went to the home of the Tripp family on Black Pipe Creek. Whitfield knew the Tripp family well, and he wanted to stop and say hello. Mrs. Tripp got the two bachelors' attention when she told them that two young women from Carlisle, Pennsylvania had come to teach in the Indian day school on Corn Creek.

On the way back to White River, Whitfield and Porch just happened to pass right by the Corn Creek Day School. "Why don't we drive up an' give 'em a nice melon?" Porch suggested. Whitfield, who considered himself a Southern gentlemen, said, "Do you think I'd go up there with the likes of you, Sir?"

"Well then, Porch replied, "I guess ya can hold yer colts while I takes a melon to da girls." But Whitfield insisted on going alone. "All right," Porch conceded, "You go." Whitfield picked out a big melon and started for the door of the little house that served as the residence for the schools' teachers. Just as Whitfield put his hand on the gate leading to the house, Porch slapped the reins and called out, "Goodbye, Mr. Whitfield. When ya git your melon delivered, come on home!"

"Wait! Whitfield called out. Porch pulled back on the reins. But he pulled back only hard enough to slow the horses, forcing Whitfield run hard to catch the wagon and jump into it.

"I heered ya talkin' with Mrs. Tripp," George railed before Whitfield could lodge a protest, "and I knowed you'd break yer neck tryin' ta keep me from seein' dem girls. Now ya go right ahead an' break yourself in two to git one o' dem girls, and I'll cut yuh out if it's the last thing I ever do."

A week later, Bill Hickox went down to Whitfield's to borrow a tool. When Bill came back to the ranch, he told Porch that Whitfield had on a white shirt with a paper collar, and he was wearing his vest. He had even on polished shoes. "But he didn't say where he was going!"

"Ain't necessary," George replied. "He's goin' to spark one o' dem school teachers over on Corn Crick."

Two weeks later, Porch drove 450 head of cattle to drive to Cody, Nebraska and shipped them to Omaha, where they would be sold. Whitfield had four steers in the lot, so he went with Porch as far as Cody. At Cody, Whitfield bought supplies, charging his purchases with the proviso that George Porch would pay for them when he came back through Cody after selling Whitfield's steers. Soon, Porch was back in Cody. As agreed, Porch went into Cole's General Store and then to Reeds' Store and paid for what Whitfield had charged. Porch got an itemized statement from each store. Reed's itemized bill listed three baskets of grapes. George knew the grapes were for the school teachers.

On his way home, George stopped at Tripp's place on Black Pipe Creek for supper. They asked him to stay the night; but he declined, saying, "I'm gonna stop at the Corn Crick School an' git acquainted with teachers."

"There's only one now," Mrs. Tripp responded, "And I wouldn't stop if I was you. You see, she's Mr. Whitfield's girl and he might not like it."

"I don't see how that would make it a crime fer me to git acquainted wit' her," George responded testily.

"Well," Mrs. Tripp replied, "maybe not. But I feel responsible. You see, I talked Mr. Whitfield up to her."

"An' I suppose ya couldn't say a good word fer me!" George snapped back.

""Why should I? Mr. Whitfield brought me a nice basket of grapes from Cody," she said, smiling. "He gave one to Mrs. McCorkle, and he also gave one to the school teacher, Miss Sieh. You've never given any of us anything!"

With that exchange ringing in his ears, George turned on his heel and went to the corral to saddle his horse. Mr. Tripp followed him outside. "George," he said. "I sure wish you'd stay the night with us and give up the idea of stopping at the Corn Creek School."

"You're all concerned about me stoppin' at the Corn Creek School, are ya?" George snapped.

"George, you are a friend of mine. And I hate to have Miss Sieh get the wrong idea of you if you were to stop by to see her at this time of the evening. She might think you were a pretty forward fellow – the kind that barges in on a woman not knowing whether or not he's welcome."

"Thank yuh fur ya concerns about me," George replied, stepping up on his horse. Just then an Indian policeman rode up and gave Mr. Tripp a letter. Mr. Tripp looked at the letter and handed it to Porch. "Since you're going to the Corn Creek School despite my advice, you might as well have an excuse for stopping," he said, handing George a letter for Miss Sieh.

So George rode to the Corn Creek School. Upon handing Miss Sieh her letter, George asked, "Did Mr. Whitfield bring ya the grapes that I bought for ya in Cody?"

"Grapes?" She asked.

"Ya. When we took a herd of cattle into Cody to load on cattle cars, I had to go with 'em to Omaha. But the Tripps had told us 'bout two ladies comin' out here to teach. Knowing what lonesome country it is, I thought it might help yuh to know you got good neighbors. So I asked Whitfield to bring ya ladies three baskets of grapes."

Giving a puzzled look, Miss Sieh said, "He left one here and . . ."

"And what?" George asked

"And he gave one to Mrs. Tripp and one to Mrs. McCorkle."

Seeing that Miss Sieh's face was getting red, George had the feeling that she didn't believe a word he said. "I don't think ya believe what I told ya. I am kind of sorry I mentioned it. Yuh see, Mr. Whitfield and me is neighbors. But now it's been said, so let me show you I ain't no liar." Digging into his pocket, George pulled out the itemized statement from Reed's store showing three baskets of grapes with the notion PAID BY GEORGE PORCH. "Well," George said, "It's gettin' dark. I'd better be ridin' if I 'expect to git home."

Miss Sieh bit down lightly on the corner of lip as she searched for words. George waited for her to find them. "I'd like to talk to you a little. Stay. You can sleep in the school house tonight and get an early start in the morning."

George put his horse in the barn, fed him some oats, and walked over to the school teacher's house. He and Miss Sieh talked until near midnight, a lot of it was about Whitfield. Miss Sieh told George that Mr. Whitfield had knocked on her door late one night. "He introduced himself," she said, "and explained that he was trailing some horse thieves and not knowing the country too well, he got confused. Seeing the light, he rode up and was surprised that it was the Corn Creek School. Of course," Miss Sieh said, "this sounded perfectly plausible to me."

"Was he carrying a gun?" George asked, knowing full well that Whitfield never carried a gun.

"Why now that you asked, he wasn't," she replied.

"Do yuh really think a man in this country would trail after horse thieves without havin' a gun? And would he be dressed up in his best clothes with a white shirt with wearing a paper collar and freshly polished shoes?"

"Why, he told me an untruth!"

"That he did!" George confirmed.

"But there is something you have to explain," Miss Sieh said. Then she related the watermelon incident, stating that it looked to her like Mr. Whitfield was intending to bring her a watermelon and George started to drive off and leave him. Having told one big lie, George felt he had no choice but to add another to it. George claimed that he was the one who wanted to bring a watermelon to the two teachers, and he asked Whitfield to hold horses. "After all, they were his horses," George pointed out. "But Whitfield wouldn't even hold his own horses and insisted that I do it. But the horses were green broke and the rustling from the back of the wagon spooked them, and they bolted. "It was all I could do ta get them slowed up a mite."

In the morning, Miss Sieh handed George a letter to deliver to Whitfield. "I'll read it to you," she said. "It says, 'Mr. Whitfield: Don't put yourself out any more on my account. I am glad that I found out about you before it was too late. I don't care to have anything to do with you.'"

"I'm sorry I spoiled what yuh been thinkin' about Mr. Whitfield. But he's my nearest neighbor and neighbors ain't too plentiful in this country," George said, handing back the letter.

"I understand you how feel," Miss Sieh replied. "I'll mail the letter."

That was the end of Whitfield's romance of the school teacher.

Painting the Town Red

The summer of 1894 was dry. That winter, the cattle drifted considerable distances to find grass. This necessitated a large roundup in the spring of 1895. The roundup covered the range from the Standing Rock Reservation in North Dakota south to the Nebraska border, and from the Missouri River west to Wyoming. Virtually every mile of the range was covered. Fortunately, the winter had been mild and there was less than half of one percent loss. Jack Whipple was the wagon boss for the outfit that worked the area from the mouth of the Cheyenne River south to White River and from the Missouri River west to the headwaters of Bad River. George Porch attached himself to Whipple's wagon to look after the cattle bearing Harpole's triangle brand, the cattle wearing W.F. Bartlett's B brand, and his own cattle. Whipple's roundup crew started at the mouth of the Cheyenne River and worked its way back and forth from east to west, gradually moving south. Several weeks into the trip, they were not far from White River. The cowboys camped for the night eight miles west of Oacoma. Their work was nearly complete. They had gathered, sorted, and branded a lot of cattle; they had choked down an a lot of trail dust; and they had developed a thirst that could not quenched by water. To prime the pump, an entrepreneurial saloon owner in Oacoma sent a keg of beer and two gallons of whiskey out to the roundup crew. Soon, the boys were raring to go into Oacoma. Reluctantly, Whipple gave in. "If you boys can get George to go with you, you can go."

George agreed, but on his terms. "Boys," he said, "If yuh'll agree to foller my lead and not start nothin' less I say so, we'll go." They all so promised.

As they started down the main street of Oacoma, someone shouted, "Here come the cowboys!" Everyone ran to look. George spurred his horse. Galloping down the street at top speed, he pulled his gun and fired it into air. The boys followed, yelling at the top of their lungs and firing their guns off like popcorn. George galloped up to the saloon. At the door, he didn't tie his horse to the hitching rail. Instead, George rode his horse into the saloon. The other cowboys did the same, nudging their horses up to the bar to order drinks. A crowd gathered at the door, and George called for them to come into the saloon and have a drink. Meanwhile, the cowboys rode around the pool table, drinking and shooting up at the ceiling or down at the floor. There was a cellar under the full length of the saloon. But somehow the weight of the all the horses didn't collapse the floor.

Before long, George said, "Boys, since we're come this far, we might as well go over to Chamberlain." But word that the cowboys were coming preceded them. The bridge man had fastened chains across the pontoon bridge and half the men in Chamberlain had come down to keep the cowboys from coming across the river. Every townsman was armed with some kind of weapon from pitch forks to mowing sighs.

"You ain't coming across," the bridge man said.

"We won't make you a mite of trouble, Mister." George assured the bridge man as he touched a spur to his horse. His horse cleared the chains with one jump. There was a yell, and the boys followed Porch across the pontoon bridge. Upon reaching the east bank of the river, the boys put up their guns and rode into Chamberlain like they were going to church. But they weren't going to church. The cowboys were headed for the Blind Pig Saloon.

A fellow in the saloon had a fiddle. George set up a beer keg on the pool table and told the man to get up on the keg and fiddle. While the man fiddled, some of the boys waltzed their horses around the pool table. A crowd gathered at the door and looked in. George pushed the crowd inside and closed the door. The cowboys made the spectators dance among their horses. Then someone started shooting, and all hell broke loose. The lights were shot out. Hoping that all of the bullets were going up, George pushed his way to the door. He opened it, and some light came in. Porch saw that some of the spectators were lying under the pool table and others were scrunched tight against the wall. He wondered if any of them were dead. But seeing light, all of them jumped up and ran for door. George hold the cowboys that it was time to head for camp. All of cowboys left the saloon except Hank Randall and Bob Mattheison. They stood on the opposite side of the pool table with their hands on their guns. "Are yuh wantin' some trouble outta us," Randall defiantly sneered. But George had already drawn his gun, and he pointed it at them. "Thar ain't gonna be no trouble at all. You git goin.' I'll be right behind yuh. If yuh pull yer guns, I'll kill yuh." They went.

Dissolving the Partnership

After a few years of partnership, George proposed that Bill buy him out. "I'll sell ya my half of the cattle and whatever interest I have in the place for three thousand dollars," he said. Hickox thought the price was more than fair, but he had no idea where he'd get that kind of money. "I know whar," George said. "Missouri John will lend it to yuh." Sure enough, Missouri John went into his bedroom and came back with a tin box. Opening it, he counted three thousand dollars in cash and handed it to Bill.

Porch moved a short distance upriver, about where Highway 73 now crosses White River. He immediately started on a house – a one-room cabin built of cottonwood logs. It had a dirt roof. The floor was lub-lally, which is gumpo worked up in water and spread across the floor like wet cement and smoothed with a board. When it dries, a lub-lally floor is as hard as cement and the color of slate. As long it is dry, you could sweep the lub-lally floor just like a linoleum one. The house had a doorway, but no door. A cow hide hung over the opening. There was one square window hole, but no window glass. Porch could not afford an iron stove. So he dug a hole the corner of the room, laid the top of a broken kitchen stove over it, and ran the bottom end of the stove pipe into an open hole in the kitchen grate.

To get into the livestock business, George bought a few scrawny steers here and few emaciated cows there until he had a small herd. When his grass gave out that fall, George slowly – very slowly – drove his cattle 126 miles to Chamberlain, allowing them to graze and put on pounds on the way to market. When winter came, George was fourteen hundred dollars to the good.

A Joke that Wasn't

Mrs. Risor was a fine-looking widow who lived in Rapid City. George believed that Mrs. Risor was looking for a man with a candy mountain, and she found one in John Massengale. If Missouri John took a trip west, he always stopped at her place coming and going, and he always stopped late enough in the day that it was convenient to stay until morning. Mrs. Risor frequently came down to the Fifteen Ranch to see John even though it was a trip of nearly a hundred miles and the only transportation was a horse and buggy.

The so-called joke took place in the spring of 1895. In preparation for the spring roundup that year, George gathered his remuda of horses and took them west to Grassy Pass, where he expected to meet with Dude Rounds and accompany him to the roundup camp on Big Buffalo Creek, not far from the Fifteen Ranch's horse pens. However, the tracks showed that Dude had gotten there earlier and had gone on. It was near dinner time. George realized that if he went on to the roundup, he'd arrive too late to get dinner. So he rode down to the Fifteen Ranch where he could expect a meal. George put his horses in the corral and went over the bunk house. Looking in, he saw that Missouri John was taking a nap. So George went up to the house. Mrs. Petersen, the housekeeper, beckoned him in. Looking to see she wasn't being overheard, Mrs. Petersen whispered to George that Dude Rounds had been to Rapid City a few days back; and that while there, he had stayed the night at Mrs. Risor's place. Mrs. Risor sent Dude back with two oranges for Mrs. Petersen's little girl.

"If you'll back me up, Mrs. Petersen," George said, "we can have a lot o' fun with ol' John and Dude on this. I'll tell John that I seen Dude up on the wall, an' Dude told' me the widow gave him a couple of oranges to take ta John. But Dude didn't give 'em to John. He gave the oranges to your little girl instead. An' I'll tell Missouri John how Dude laughed at that thought of John missing out on those oranges. Now yuh don't need to do nothin.' But when John asks yuh if it's so, yuh say that's right, Dude gave two oranges to my little girl."

After Missouri John woke up, he and George talked a little. During the conversation, George mentioned that he had seen Dude over on the wall. In the course of their talking, Dude laughingly told him that Mrs. Risor had sent him back from Rapid City with two oranges for Missouri John, but he gave the oranges to Mrs. Petersen's little girl instead. Concluding the story, George said, "John, ya know ole Dude. He just can't help gettin' a joke on someone. I s'pose he done it just for the fun o' it." Massengale sat on the bed without saying a word, and George went to corral to give his horse some hay.

A little while later George slipped back to the house to check with Mrs. Petersen. "Like you said would happen, Mr. Massengale came asked me about the oranges," Mrs. Peterson reported. "I acted surprised that you were here, pretending I hadn't seen you. And I told Mr. Massengale that Dude did give my little girl two oranges. He looked awful blue. I'm kind of sorry I told him."

All through dinner, John didn't say much. When George went to the corral to saddle his horse, Missouri John accompanied him. Leaning against the corral gate, John gave a deep sigh. "George," he said, "that freckled faced son of a bitch has stepped right in between me and Mrs. Risor. Yes, that's what he's done."

Three weeks later, the spring roundup finished at Allen Spaur's place. Each rep collected his cattle and dispersed. Porch had not gone far with his cattle when he saw someone riding toward him like he was possessed. It was Dude Rounds. Rounds was madder than a hornet. His freckles were standin' out like he'd been splashed with tobacco juice. Greeting him, Porch asked, "What's the matter, Dude?"

"What's the matter," Dude snorted. "You've raised hell down at the Fifteen. I never come so near quitting in my life!" Actually Dude did not get a chance to quit. After confronting Dude about staying the night with Mrs. Risnor, Missouri

John told Dude that he had worked at the Fifteen Ranch long enough. The two men would have come to blows had not Mrs. Petersen stepped between them and told them that George Porch had stirred up the whole mess.

For a good many years after that, Dude did not talk to George Porch. Missouri John sent word to Porch that he wasn't to stop at the ranch anymore. For George's part, he couldn't understand why Rounds and Massengale got so upset over a joke about a couple of oranges.

The Porch Family Comes West

George went back to Missouri in the fall of 1895 and he stayed there all winter. When he returned to the Badlands in the spring of 1896, he set out to get his house fixed up. After all, he was getting married. "I had kinda arranged to marry a girl from Omaha that I'd met at my aunt's house." Among other improvements, George hauled a load of lumber back from Fort Pierre so the house would have a real floor. He even hung a door in the door opening and put glass in the window.

Then on April 6th, Charley Smalley and Fred Sears rode up on gallop. Fred yelled out, "George, pull out. The water's coming down the river ten feet deep over the river bottom. You got get out of here!"

At the time, George had 125 head of cattle gathered around a hay wagon. "Cut the fence and let the cattle out to the north," George replied. I and (Homer) Goodson (a trapper that occasionally stayed with George) will put this lumber on top of the house."

A few days later, George's entire family – his mother and father; his brother, Ab; and three sisters, Phobe, Edie, and Amanda – arrived in Cody, Nebraska. They came across the Rosebud Reservation by buggy. Upon reaching Philip Wells' place (which was where Whitfield lived when George put up hay for him in 1892), the Porch family could not go any farther. White River was running bank full. His siblings stayed with the Philip Wells family, and his parents stayed with the Pecks while they waited for the river to go down. The woman that George *had kinda arranged to marry* was supposed to join the Porch family when the train went through Council Bluffs; but she didn't meet them at the train depot, and no more was heard from George's intended bride.

That summer, Edie, Phobe, and Ab worked on the 15 Ranch. There, Edie met Johnny Livingston, the young man who had come from Wyoming with Missouri John in 1891. The couple hit it off, and they soon got married.

George spent the summer of 1896 building fence. Phoebe drove the team while George set the posts. One day Phoebe went into the house a little before noon to prepare dinner. Edie came up from the house, and she volunteered to drive the team while George set posts. George didn't want her to drive the team because one horse was not well broke, and the other horse was ornery. But Edie insisted. Feeling new, unsure hands on the reins, the bronc lunged. The horses broke the wagon tongue and jerked Edie, who had death gripe on the reins, over the front of the wagon. She was hurt, but no one realized how badly hurt until toward morning. Edie, who was pregnant, started having contractions. She became terribly sick.

Cursing himself for allowing Edie to drive a cankerous team of horses, George set out early in the morning with a team and wagon for the Rosebud Agency, where there was a doctor. There were no bridges and few trails, and it was a hundred miles away. The sun was setting when he reached the Agency. Not to be deterred, George pressed Dr. Compton into accompanying him back to the Badlands. They immediately set out to repeat the hundred mile trip, using the same horses. When they reached Corn Creek, it was raining. But they pressed on. As they headed down Pass Creek, it was pouring. Water was standing on the flats and running down every ditch and gully. George knew that Pass Creek would be bank-full of water, and there was no way to cross it in the dark. So they drove up to an old Indian's log house on a hill. The house belonged to Sitting Up. A group of Indians had taken refuge in the house, and they were as wet and as cold as Porch and Dr. Compton. There was only one place that the roof didn't leak, and that was where Sitting Up and wife were sleeping in bed. Nonetheless, Mr. and Mrs. Sitting Up gave their bed to Dr. Compton and Porch. It was two in the morning, and the rain wasn't letting up a bit.

Just before sunup, Sitting Up woke Porch and informed him that the rain had stopped. Porch hitched up the team, and he and Dr. Compton left immediately. When they got to Pass Creek, it was a mile wide, running from one bluff to the other. There was no use trying to cross it. George pressed on. When they got to White River, it was running water bank to bank. The raging water was sixteen feet deep. "There's no chance of crossing that river, Porch!" The doctor exclaimed. "It looks awful deep."

"It's not so deep as it looks," George replied. "The banks are low right here. Get your medicine bag in both hands so yuh can keep it dry." With that advice, Porch plunged the team and wagon into the river. The wagon momentarily went completely underwater, but the horses were good swimmers. They pulled the wagon across. When the buggy hit the north bank of the river, it turned over, flinging Dr. Compton and Porch out of the wagon. As Dr. Compton got on his feet, he called Porch some choice words, and concluded by saying, "I'll wipe the earth with you."

"I ain't got no time fer fighin,' Doc. Thar's a sick woman waitin' fer yuh. Now git in the buggy and let's get goin.'"

Doc Compton saved Edie's life, but she was never as strong as before. In George's opinion, Edie worked too hard on the ranch that she and Johnny Livingston started near Midland. Edie died when she was twenty-seven.

Whipping a Prize Fighter

George Porch, Jack Whipple, George Saunders, and six other neighboring ranchers marketed their cattle in Sioux City in the fall of 1898. When they boarded the train for the ride back to Cody, there was a husky, hard-faced man in the passenger car. They sat three rows behind him. Before long, three of the cowboys started singing terribly off key. Saunders rolled up a newspaper and jokingly flung it the trio of singers. The paper missed the singers, but it hit the tough-looking guy in several seats ahead of Jack Whipple. The man jumped up. "Which one of you damned son-of-bitches throwed that paper?" He demanded to know. No one said anything.

At the next stop, the passengers got off for a stretch. As the passengers retook their seats, the tough guy walked pass the cowboys and again called them a bunch of son-of-bitches. George walked up to the man's seat and said, "Are yuh suggestin' that I'm one o' them yuh is talkin' about?"

"You are!" He snapped. "And when we get off this train, I'll show you just how much of one you are."

"Make that a promise, will yuh?"

"It's made!" The man said.

After a while, a man in the front of the passenger car came back. Passing by George, he whispered, "I wouldn't push that fellow. He's a bad man with his fists-mean. He's a trained fighter."

"Thanks," George said.

At Norfork, Nebraska George got off the train to stretch his legs. When the prize fighter and his manager got off of the train, George fell in right behind them. A greeting went up from a group of men who had gathered to meet them. As the manager shook hands with the greeting party, George poked a finger into the prize fighter's shoulder. "Don't go off fergettin' yer promise," George said.

Whirling like lightning, the prize figher swung at George. The blow glanced off George's shoulder. George hit the prize fighter, and he hit him good. The prize fighter went down on his elbow, but he immediately got up. George hit him again. This time the fighter didn't get up. Someone yelled for the police, and one happened to be nearby. Swinging his billy club, he said to Porch, "Come with me!" Ignoring the policeman, George turned to get on the train. But two men grabbed Porch, and started dragging him away from the train.

With a loud yell, the cowboys flew off of the train. A tall man in crowd called out, "That's a bunch of shooting cowboys. For God's sake, let him go or there'll be bloodshed." The fellows holding Porch let him go, and George got back on the train.

Chasing Horse Thieves

Three young men stopped by Porch's place in the fall of 1899, saying they were looking for work. They stayed a couple of nights. Then two of them went on; but the third one, a young homesteader that George knew, stayed another night. That night, the homesteader started talking in his sleep. What he said about his two companions got George's attention. In the morning, George rode out to check his horse herd. Four of his horses were missing.

George rode to Fort Pierre and swore out an arrest warrant for the two fellows. The sheriff deputized George so he could go after the horse thieves. Porch picked up the horse thieves' trail and followed them west to the Cheyenne River. There, the horse thieves forded the river and went into the little town of Wasta. In Wasta, a man told George that a couple of days earlier he saw two men driving a bunch of horses. While George was talking to this informant, another man made it a point to get close enough to listen in on the conversation. When the man had an earful, he got on a horse and headed west in the direction that the horse thieves had gone when they departed Wasta. George mounted up and started west, too. The rider could see that Porch was not far behind him, and he put distance between himself and Porch by kicking his horse into a lope every time he got out of sight.

Reaching Piedmont, Porch saw this same man talking with a bunch of men commonly known as the Dirty Dozen. When the man saw Porch, he again slipped away. The Dirty Dozen gave Porch lots of information about which way the horse thieves had gone and advice about how to catch them. Porch pretended to take it all in. But instead of following their advice, George went up Elk Creek Road. In a short distance, Porch came across a well-kept place. The owner told Porch that two men had passed the day before driving a herd of fourteen horses. Several horses in the herd matched the description that George gave of his stolen horses. The man thought the horse thieves were headed for the Roubaix [B]. On the way to Roubaix (pronounced Row-bay), Porch came across several miners who had seen his horses the day before, even remembering their brands.

At Roubaix, the few rooms in the town's small hotel were taken. However, the town barber offered that he had a good bed in his shack, and he would share it with George. In the morning, George went down to the livery barn to give his horse a good feed of oats. The big, red-whiskered Irishman who ran the hotel came charging up to George. "Who in the hell told you to feed that horse oats," he bellered?

"I'm paying fer oats and I 'expect to git oats," George answered. Just then the man's young stepdaughter came up and asked her stepdad something. The big Irishman hit the girl hard enough to almost knock her down. Then he came at Porch, crowding him against the grain bin. George grabbed the big man by his red whiskers, pulled the man's head forward, and slammed his fist into the man's face. The man would have gone down, but George held him up by his whiskers so that he could throw the man into the creek.

From Roubaix, Porch went to Sturgis to see Jesse Brown, the sheriff. At the sheriff's suggestion, Porch printed fifty posters describing his stolen horses and giving their brands. Brown sent the posters to sheriffs in Wyoming, Montana, North Dakota, and South Dakota. That done, Porch went home.

It was not long before the sheriff in Glasgow, Montana contacted Porch, wanting him to come there and identify two suspects who had horses bearing the brands given on the poster. Sure enough, it was the two men who had stayed with him several days. George's testimony sent each of them to prison for several years.

Temporarily Dead

During the spring roundup of 1899, Porch and a group of riders worked the clay buttes north of present-day Murdo. George was riding a horse called Pizen Pup (pizen being a term used back then to describe someone who had drank enough whiskey to feel no pain). Pizen Pup was a tough horse who could stand almost any amount of running. But he wasn't much of a cow horse, and he was ornery. On this particular day, Porch roped a big steer that was running full tilt. When the rope settled around the steer's horns, the Pizen Pup never slowed, and he ran over the rope before it tightened. When the rope tightened, it came up under the horse's belly, flipping the horse on its side. George landed on a flat rock the size of the top of a cook stove, and Pizen Pup came over backward on top of him. George lay unconscious. Sometime later, a cowboy saw Pizen Pup and a steer connected to each other by a lariat, and he rode over to investigate. Finding George unconscious, the cowboy yelled out for help. They found no signs of life in George, not even a pulse. Someone took a shutter off of an abandoned house and brought it to the scene. They strapped George's body to the shutter, and dragged it behind a horse to Durkin's ranch. Leaving George there for dead, they continued the roundup. Seeing Johnny Livingston, George's brother-in-law, a rider told Livingston about George's death.

Livingston immediately rode to Durkin's house, where George's body was lying. Livingston tried to get a pulse, but couldn't. He felt for a heart beat, but couldn't find one. Livingston opened Porch's closed eye lids, but found the eyes lifeless. He felt Porch's body, and found it cold. Livingston got on his horse and started out for home to tell Edie, Porch's sister, that George was dead. But Livingston rode only a little way when he remembered that George's hands weren't stiff, only kind of limp. So he went back to Durkin's ranch, and he moved Porch's arms and legs. In deed, they weren't stiff. Jumping on his horse, Livingston rode out to where the men were working cattle. "Porch ain't dead," he told them. "He can't be. He ain't stiff. I'm goin' to Pierre to get a doctor."

Livingston galloped his horse all the way to Pete Biever's place. There, Livingston told Biever the nature of his urgent mission, Biever said, "Your horse is tired down. He'll never make it. I'll go." When Biever got to George Mattheison's place, they were getting ready to go on a big circle ride in search of cattle. "George Porch is hurt real bad," Biever told the riders. I'm going for a doctor, but my horse is played out. Could one of you boys lend me a horse?" Mattheison was riding a horse that was special to him and he never let anyone else ride him, but he instantly jumped off the horse. Holding out the reins, Mattheison said, "Take mine. Kill him if you have to, but get help for Porch."

Biever sought out Doc Lavery. But Lavery had other patients, and he wasn't able to leave until later that night. Biever and Doc Lavery arrived at Durkin's ranch at dawn in pouring rain. Porch was still unconscious and appeared to be dead, except he wasn't getting stiff. Doc Lavery shook his head, suggesting that Porch's condition was hopeless. But he gave George of a shot of strychnine in his arm. He also put a small amount of strychnine as far back as possible on George's tongue and worked it down Porch's throat by massaging the patients' neck with his fingers. "If that don't do it," Doc Lavery said, "nothing else will."

Doc Lavery stayed until afternoon, but Porch was still unconscious. George had now been unconscious for twenty-four hours without moving a muscle, raising an eyelid, or, as best anyone could tell, breathing. The strychnine did not stimulate Porch's heart into producing detectable beats. Doc Lavery gave Porch a spoonful of water, but it did not elicit even the slightest swallowing reflex. "There isn't a thing more that I can do," Doc Lavery said, "If he comes out if, he'll do it on what I've already given him. If doesn't, he never will." With that pronouncement, Doc Lavery returned to Fort Pierre.

Two days later, George opened his eyes. He didn't know anyone, but he was alive. Porch stayed in bed for another four days, and then got to his feet. When he did, his memory came back. But all of the rest of the summer Porch didn't do much work and mostly rode around in a buggy.

Epilog

George Porch died in 1949 at the age of 87. Today, he lies in an unmarked grave in the Kadoka cemetery.

Notes

[A] Bill's name is variously spelled "Hickox" and "Hicox." The Census data of 1910 spells it Hickox, as does the ledger kept by Missouri John Massengale. However, a map of early ranchers spelled it Hicox, as does several entries in the *Jackson and Washabaugh* Counties, grassroots history spearheaded by Lois Prokop.

[B] Roubaix was located 16 miles south of Deadwood. It existed because of the nearby Uncle Sam Gold Mine. The gold mine caved in 1905. Shortly thereafter a flash flood washed the town away. In the 1930s, the WPA built a dam on the stream. Roubaix Lake now covers the old town of Roubaix.

CHAPTER 9

Denizens of the Badlands: 1890–1896

An assortment of humanity came to the Badlands when it opened for white settlement in 1890. A few were old fur traders who wanted to live out the last years of their lives in one of the last places in the West that still afforded solitude. Others were men who came west with the U.S. Army, found they had no stomach for killing Indians, and instead married Lakota woman. Many were irascible old codgers like Missouri John Massengale and George Porch who liked to be a law unto themselves. All those who came to the Badlands had one thing in common – they liked elbow room.

The Agreement of 1889 between the Lakota Indians and U.S. Government opened 11 million acres between White River and the Cheyenne River to white settlement. Legal title to 160 acres could be obtained by living on the land for five years and cultivating ten acres. However, the land was too arid and too isolated to attract many homesteaders. Instead, the area was regarded as open range. It belonged to whoever used it. Cattlemen laid claim by right of occupancy to thousands of acres and delineated their range by watersheds. An unwritten code mandated that others respect their land, and move on.

One white family and one bachelor came to the Badlands just prior to 1890 on the rumor that the land would soon be opened to public domain. A few settlers came in 1890, but the Indian uprising that year kept their numbers to a minimum. The bulk of the settlers came in 1891 and 1892; and as best as can be determined, these were the denizens of the Badlands during the years of 1890 to 1896.

Back row: Mandy, Ada, and Pearl. Front row: Frank, Hulda and Jack Turner.

Stearns

Stearns was a store at the eastern edge of the Badlands. It was built by **Smokey Stearns** and his father, an elderly widower who once worked for a fur trading company. Exactly when the store or trading post was built is not known, but it became a post office on June 20, 1890 with **David S. Johnson** as the first postmaster.[1] **J.W. Garret** bought the store in 1892. **L.D. "Jack" Turner,** his wife and four children came from Colorado in 1892 with a hundred head of horses.[2] Turner tried to graze his horses south of White River on the Rosebud Reservation, but the Indians quickly ran them off their land.

Turner pooled with **Frank Swartz** in 1893 to buy the Stearns store. Mrs. Turner sorted mail and sold general goods in one room while her husband and Mr. Swartz sold whiskey in the other. The bar was not fancy. The cowboys put their glass under the keg's spigot and filled their own.[3]

Most cattlemen lost more livestock to wolves than to rustlers, so they had a standing order for their men to kill every wolf they came across. The cowboys considered it unsporting to shoot a wolf. If circumstances permitted they let down their lariat and put a spur to their horse. Frank Turner, L.D. Turner's son, probably holds the world record in this sport. One foggy, wet morning in the spring of 1903, he, Erdley Ham, and Will Hughs were riding along Antelope Draw when they spotted five wolves gorging on a freshly-killed cow. They waited until the wolves had eaten their fill and then rode down on them. Ham and Hughs each came back dragging a wolf at the end of their rope. Turner came back with one wolf tied on his pommel, one tied behind the cantle and a dragging a third wolf on the end of his rope.[4]

Divine Albert Whipple, better known as "Jack," was a full-blooded Irishman. He was born in Carasagas County, New York on May 14, 1850. He ran away from home and ended up in Texas before he was 11 years old. Whipple first came to Dakota Territory at the age of 18 with a cattle drive, and he drove cattle herds to the Spotted Tail Agency for the next six years. Following the discovery of gold in the Black Hills, he freighted on the Sidney-Black Hills Trail.[5] In 1881 Whipple married Sally Kelly, a part-Indian woman. She taught him to speak fluent Lakota. They moved to the Stearns area in 1892, taking up residence in a cabin whose former tenant had died under strange circumstances. Mrs. Whipple white-washed the walls of the house, and she periodically induced Jack to go outside at night and fire shots to scare away ghosts. Sally was the first person in the community to raise cats and chickens.[6]

Bert Gorum settled in the Stearns area in 1890 and ran about 25 head of cattle.[7]

Hugh Caton was born in Binghamton, New York in 1872. In 1880, his parents came to Salem, Dakota Territory. Caton located west of Stearns with a small herd of cattle in 1891. He married a teacher, Mabel Jane Towne, from Valentine, Nebraska in 1902.[8]

Ester Lawrence Currier and her two young sons, Oscar and Osmer, came from Dundee, Michigan to Ainsworth, Nebraska by train in 1882. There, Mrs. Lawrence homesteaded, ran a few milk cows, and married a man by the name of Currier. The family moved to the Badlands in 1886, well before the area was opened to white settlement. Mrs. Currier was the only white woman in the Badlands. The nearest towns were Pierre and Chamberlain, each over 100 miles away. The family went to town twice a year and then they stayed only long enough to get supplies. They moved into Buffalo Gap during the Indian uprising of 1890, but returned to the Badlands in the spring of 1891.

About this time Mr. Currier died. Mrs. Currier stuck it out.[9] Neighbors gave her their orphan calves, enabling her to build a small herd of cattle. She met the trials and tribulations of ranching head on, spending many days in the saddle looking after her stock. She was riding south of White River one spring day looking for cows when the river ice went out. She was stranded on the Rosebud Reservation for three days. Each day, her sons put some sandwiches in a box and threw the box into the river. Mrs. Currier followed the box downstream until she could retrieve it. The sandwiches were soggy, but they were still food.

Oscar, the oldest boy, took a homestead one mile north of Stearns when he came of age in 1892. Osmer was the first mail carrier between Westover and Stearns when the route was established in 1891.[10]

Charley Smith came to Dakota Territory from Iowa at the age of 20 and filed on a homestead near Pukwana in 1879. He trailed 80 head of cattle from Pukwana to the Stearns area in the spring of 1890 and lived in a tent while he built a one-room log cabin. Smith married Mary Scovel in 1902.[11]

W.F. Bartlett, a man known for his prodigious strength, located his place a few miles west of Stearns.[12]

Whitfield

Robert Peebles Whitfield was born in Smithfield, Virginia in 1856. He came to the Badlands sometime prior to 1886 to serve as a Boss Farmer for Chief Lip's band of Brule Sioux. At the time, Lip's band was living near the mouth of Pass Creek.[13] Whitfield lived in a small cabin two miles farther upriver at the base of heavily timbered river breaks from whose sides trickled the most beautiful springs in the entire Badlands. Whitfield was one of the few boss farmers who successfully persuaded the Sioux to give up their nomadic ways. Under Whitfield's tutelage and because of his willingness to work right alongside them, the Indians in Chief Lip's camp built log cabins, raised livestock, put up hay for the winter, and gardened extensively. Chief Lip made three visits to Washington on behalf of his band. In particular, Chief Lip wanted a school so that the children in his band could become educated. In response, a school was built at Lip's camp and it commenced serving children in September 1885. An Episcopalian Church was built the following year.[14]

When Short Bull, the medicine man for Chief Lip's band, became an ardent advocate of the Ghost Dance in 1890, Whitfield met with Chief Lip and his headmen to dissuade them from embracing the ceremony. As a result, Short Bull and his followers were ordered out of Chief Lip's village. Short Bull and his followers retaliated by breaking into Whitfield's cabin, demolishing his furniture, and stealing his entire winter supply of food.[15]

When Richard Pettigrew was elected to U.S. Senate in 1890 and took his seat on the Indian Affairs Committee, he brought political patronage to bear in full force on the federal jobs on the South Dakota reservations. Simply put, only loyal Republicans were allowed to hold jobs on the reservations. Despite his proven success with the Indian people, Robert Whitfield, a staunch Democrat, was removed from his position. As a result, Whitfield was forced to move off the Reservation. He re-located a few miles downstream on the north bank of White River at the mouth of the long drainage that flows south-southeast from the present-day town of Kadoka. Starting in June 30, 1891, Whitfield's place was designated a post office [A]. However, the *town* of Whitfield did not last long. The post office was discontinued the following year on July 10, 1892.[16] In about 1901, Whitfield left the Badlands and returned to Virginia.[17]

George Porch and **Bill Hickox** were partners in the cattle business in 1893 (see Chapter 8). Their place was on the north bank of White River, two miles downstream from the mouth of Pass Creek. By 1895, the partnership has been dissolved. George Porch located on a place about where present-day Highway 73 crosses the White River.

Abner (Ab) Porch, was born in Iowa in 1868. Ab was the younger brother of the infamous George Porch; but Ab was cut from a different cloth. He was always a gentleman. Ab and the entire Porch family (see Chapter 8) came to the Badlands in the spring of 1894 to visit George Porch. Ab worked for Missouri John Massengale that year; but in 1895, he located on his own place, just above William Hickox's ranch. During the winter of 1898, Ab returned to Missouri to visit his parents. When he returned to the Badlands in March of 1899, he had a bride, Rose Batt Porch.[18] The newlyweds arrived in Cody in a blizzard. The town was full of drunken and brawling Indians and cowboys. Despite the weather, the couple set out in a jolting lumber wagon pulled by a team of half-broke broncs for "home." The first night they got as far as Ed Amiotte's place. As Mrs. Amiotte, a full-blood Lakota, showed Rose her room, she said, "You poor little thing. You don't know what you're letting yourself in for." When the Porch's woke the next morning, Mrs. Amiotte was preparing them breakfast.

After they ate, Mrs. Amiotte showed them her baby that been born during the night. By the next night, the newly weds went as far as Jack Whipple's. His wife Sally was also part-Indian and, in Mrs. Porch's words, "nobody could have been kinder."

Rose Porch found "the country awfully bleak and lonely, but she fell in love with the beautiful Badland vistas and the wild, untamed West. Soon, she got on her first horse, riding side saddle. A few years later, side saddles went out of fashion and Rose got a regular saddle and wore divided skirts. "Then I was a real cowgirl, and I enjoyed my freedom." Part of that freedom included socializing. "We would ride 40 miles to a dance at someone's place, dance all night, and come home the next day or maybe the day after that." Soon, Rose was the mother of two boys – Bill and Cy Porch. But there was no school or no church. So Rose taught the children to read and to do arithmetic, and she dressed them up every Sunday morning and held Sunday school for them.

In 1906, the Ab Porch family moved to the former Philip Wells place just west of the mouth of Pass Creek. But in 1910, they bought 320 acres of deeded land on the Pine Ridge Indian Reservation from Frank Randall near where the little hamlet of Hisle was once located. There, the Porch's ran a post office called Porch and a small general store, freighting the groceries in from Interior in a four-horse team.

J.P. White, Darwin Collins, and **Frank P. Gannaway,** all three men were from the South, all were Democrats, and all were terminated as part of Sena-

Rose Porch, Charley Price, Ab Porch, Meda Porch, Charles Price, Jr., taken at Porch ranch on Bear-In-the-Lodge Creek in 1934.
Photo courtesy of Peggy (Schoon) Porch.

tor Pettigrew's political patronage system that insisted on awarding all of the jobs every reservation in the State to South Dakota Republicans. When these three men were terminated in 1890 at the Crow Creek Agency, they went to the Badlands to start the Shovel Ranch. J.P. White was born in Virginia. Frank Gannaway was born in Hardinsburg, Kentucky in 1859. He was appointed Boss Farmer for the Lower Brule Reservation in 1886. In addition to his interest in the Shovel Ranch, Gannaway ran a general store at Lower Brule until 1896. [19]

Philip Faribault Wells was one-fourth Sioux.[20] Philip Wells was born in northern Minnesota to a fur trader, James "Bully" Wells, and Jane Wells, who was half Santee Sioux and spoke only Dakota. Philip Wells arrived in Sioux City, Dakota Territory in 1875. There, he was able to sell his services as a guide to parties destined for the Black Hills largely because his brother, William "Wallace" Wells, was the chief scout for the Army patrols that ranged out of Fort Randall to intercept parties attempting to trespass into the Black Hills. Philip Wells successfully guided four parties to the Hills that summer. All other parties who tried to reach the Hills that summer via the eastern corridor were captured by the U.S. Army.

On one of these trips to the Hills, Wells' party spotted a dapple-gray horse apparently loose on the prairie. Wells noticed that when the dapple-gray tried to look to one side, it couldn't. Suspecting that someone was leading the horse as a decoy, Wells hung back. Another member of the party, greedy to claim the animal, loped toward the horse; and he was shot dead by an Indian who lay hidden in the grass.

The next morning, Wells reconnoitered the area. He spotted a troop of cavalry from Fort Bennett who were searching for them. One of the men of the party who was familiar with the area suggested that they turn south, toward White River, and go to the mouth of Pass Creek where there was a spring, timber to hide the horses, and good grazing. Wells liked the setting and decided that some day he'd live there. This is site where Robert Whitfield lived during his tenure as Boss Farmer. But no one was living there in 1894 and being on the Rosebud Reservation, no whites were permitted to live on this ideal location. However, an enrolled member of the Santee Tribe, Wells was permitted to move there in 1894. Wells' wife, Mary, taught the Pass Creek Day School.

Philip Wells was then nearing the end of a long and colorful career on the plains. He served as a scout for the U.S. Army in 1876 and then worked for the Indian Service. On the morning of December 29, 1890, Wells was serving as an interpreter for Colonel James W. Forsyth when the Army attempted to disarm Big Foot's band. Wells noticed that an Indian medicine man, Yellow Bird, was haranguing a group of young warriors, exhorting them to stand firm against the white soldiers. Wells approached an honorable and intelligent-looking Minneconjou man and, in Lakota, asked him to quiet the medicine man because he was making trouble. The Indian scoffed at Wells. While they talked, a powerfully built man stepped out of the circle of young braves and slowly walked behind Wells. At this instant and elsewhere in the camp, a soldier pulled back an Indian's blanket to reveal a gun. According to both Indian and white witnesses, the gun accidentally discharged. Its shell went harmlessly up into the air; but upon hearing the gunshot, a dozen Indians pulled guns from beneath their blankets. A sergeant yelled to Wells, "Look out! Look out!"

Wells wheeled around. The Indian who had been stalking him was slicing down at him with a huge knife. Dropping to one knee with the agility of a cat, Wells threw up his rifle. The Indians' wrist struck the gun's stock, but the long knife sliced through Well's nose. The Indian thrust again, using all of his weight in an effort to break down Wells' guard. But he could not. Wells smashed the butt of his rifle into the Indian's stomach, sprang back, and leveled his rifle at the Indian's breast. The Indian, anticipating the blast from Wells' gun, dropped to his hands and knees. Wells fired. The Indian pitched forward on his face, dead.

Wells started to pull off the bloody end of this nose, which dangled by two stripes of skin over his mouth. "My God, man! Don't do that," Lt. Guy H. Preston shouted at Wells. "That can be saved." Wells was led from the battle.

David Lincoln McLane came to the Reservation in 1892 and settled along Cottonwood Creek. He married a part-Indian woman, Louise Giroux. At the time of her marriage to McLane, Louise Giroux had four children and a section of land along Cottonwood Creek. McLane had a college education. He did his best to maintain a small library, and read widely. McLane served as a clerk at the Rosebud Agency, and he was assigned on checking off cattle as the cowboys took their livestock across White River. During the roundup of 1902, McLane checked off 11,000 head of cattle brought across the river at Westover at $1.00 a head.[21]

John Massengale, best known as "Missouri John" and **James Ross** lived farther up White River at the mouth of a creek now known as 15 Creek (See Chapter 7).

Wanblee

Wanblee was established in 1891 by the federal government in an effort to locate the nomadic Lakota in permanent villages. Officials told the various Indian bands that if they located in one spot, the government would establish an issue station there and a day school. The day school enabled the Indians to keep their children at home instead of sending them to the dreaded boarding school in Pine Ridge.

The name Wanblee was derived from the Lakota words *Wanblee Hokpiln,* meaning "Eagles' Nest Butte"—a stone-capped mesa southwest of the village. The Indians who settled in Wanblee were under Chief Lip, whose Indian name was Pute' (pronounced Poo'-te').[22]

Dick Thyer was married to an Indian woman, and they had a small ranch on Eagle Nest Creek. Dick was a self-taught musician. If anyone stopped at the Thyer Ranch and stayed for any length of time, Dick treated them by playing the banjo or the guitar while his children sang the verses. Thyer went to Gordon, Nebraska in 1901 to sell cattle. He never returned. It is not known whether he met with foul play, had a fatal accident, or abandoned his family.[23]

M.P. Ganow was also a Democrat who had a government job on the Crow Creek Reservation, but was terminated in 1890. He started a ranch two miles upriver from the mouth of the creek that is today known as Craven Creek.[24]

Lodge

Lodge was a trading post established by **Edward A. Asay Jr.** on the north bank of the White River, across from the mouth of Eagle Nest Creek. It is presumed that Ed Asay was related to James Asay, who was the licensed Indian trader for the Pine Ridge Reservation and had a store at Pine Ridge. Even though Lodge was not on a U.S. Government mail route, it became a designated post office on December 8, 1890 – something that begs for an explanation. The explanation is that Ed Asay when went to Pine Ridge to get supplies for his store, he brought back the mail for settlers living near Lodge. If Asay did not need supplies, anyone who stopped by Lodge and was heading to Pine Ridge was given the mailbag.[25] Operating a post office out of the store was good for business. Anyone coming in for mail was a potential customer. Lodge was discontinued as a post office on July 20, 1893.[26]

W.W. Anderson was a staunch Democrat from Kentucky. In 1886, he was appointed the Indian Agent at Crow Creek and, as such, had the honorary title of Major. In 1890, Senator Richard Pettigrew used his position on the Indian Affairs Committee to remove Anderson and virtually every Democrat who held a job on the Crow Creek Indian Reservation. Anderson moved to the Badlands and started the Rake Ranch at the mouth of creek that is now called Rake Creek. After John Massengale sold out in 1896, **Dude Rounds** became a co-partner with Anderson. Anderson and Rounds sold the Rake Ranch in 1898 and moved their ranching operation to northwest Nebraska in 1898. However, when Anderson got a government job in Washington, D.C., Rounds returned to the Badlands.[27]

Frank Linn lived a half mile upriver from the mouth of Rake Creek. His first year in the Badlands, Linn shot and killed a grizzly bear.[28]

According to a survey made in 1894, the **Nelson Brothers** (Carl, Olaf, Nels and Albert) were then living along White River, directly across from the mouth of Bear-In-The-Lodge Creek.[29] However, it is likely that they were only transient residents because they were sheepmen and cattle thieves. Missouri John Massengale would not have tolerated them as permanent residents. The Nelson brothers ranged their sheep from Stearns east to the Missouri River and stole cattle from farmers living along the Missouri River. Their place in the Badlands was a refuge when things got too hot for them along the Missouri River.[30]

Henry and **Ben Smith** came from Murfreesboro, Tennessee in 1890 to a establish a ranch on the north bank of White River one mile upriver from the mouth of Bear-In-The-Lodge Creek. They called their place the Oar Lock Ranch.[31]

Above the Wall

Warren Young, a former officer in the Confederate Army, came to the Badlands in 1894 with his wife and nine children. He established a sheep ranch east of Martin Johnson's place and not far from the present-day town of Kadoka.[32]

Martin Johnson (no relation to Oliver Johnson) was born in Norway in 1866. In 1890 he settled along White River south of the present-day town of Draper, where he raised sheep.[33] He trailed 3,000 sheep from Colorado to the

The Warren Young ranch.
Photo courtesy of Muriel Kjos.

Badlands in 1894 and tended them for Oliver Johnson. The cattlemen in the Badlands would not tolerate sheep grazing on their range, so the sheep had to be run north of the Badlands wall, beyond Cedar Pass. There, Martin Johnson homesteaded in a dugout.

Charley Thompson and his wife Ida lived on Big Buffalo Creek with their seven children. Ida was the postmistress, and their cabin became known as the post office town of Recluse[34] (See Chapter 7). While it was legal to file a homestead and fence off your 160 acres, the cattlemen did not like homesteaders, and for more than a decade they did not tolerate them. A man by the name of Brown attempted to homestead a few miles west of Recluse, and he was told to get out. But he didn't. Before long, a bunch of cowboys came by Brown's place about sunup. They threw ropes around the small lumber shack where Brown lay sleeping and dragged him and his house across the prairie. Brown wasn't seen after that.

The cattlemen also did not like sheep. There was not a single sheepman in the Badlands. Those who tried to raise sheep had to do so north of the Badland Wall, over in the Bad River drainage. But even there, the sheepmen were not always tolerated. Joe Hall and J.W. Jones, who would eventually become brothers-in-laws, came West in 1892 from the Crow Creek Reservation. There, Joe Hall's mother was a teacher and J.W. Jones served as a Boss Farmer for his uncle, Major Anderson, the Indian Agent. Hall and Jones built a crude cabin along the north fork of Bad River and put in a set of corrals.[35] There were good rains in the summer of 1894, allowing them to put a good deal of hay. That fall, J.W. Jones rode horseback to Nebraska to buy 1,000 sheep. Driving them back, he stopped one night to bed down his sheep on a particularly green Badland flat. When he woke in the morning, 500 of his sheep were dead. They had eaten the cockleburs, which in the two-leaf stage are as poisonous as strychnine. To make matters worse, when Jones got back to his place on Bad River, he found that his hay stacks had been torched. Our respective families, meaning the Hall family and the Jones family, always suspected that it was Charley Thompson who set the hay stacks on fire.[36]

Henry E. Farnham, generally known as John, was born in Hannibal,

John and Ellen Farnham.
Photo courtesy of Hallie (Trimble) Young.

New York on July 17, 1850. Lying about his age, Henry enrolled in Company E of the 4th Infantry Regiment in February 1866. Farnham was immediately sent to Fort Laramie and served there until October 9th. He was then dispatched to Fort Fetterman. At the age of 18, Farnham took a full-blood Oglala woman for his wife, giving her father several horses. His wife's Indian name was Wacante Wastewin (Makes People Happy); her white name was Sophie Goodheart. Farnham was honorably discharged from the U.S. Army in February 1869.[37]

At Fort Laramie, Farnham served for a time as the post interpreter.[38] Louise and Nellie were born there in 1871 and 1874, respectively. The couple moved to Fort Robinson in 1875. Bessie and Lizzie were born at Fort Robinson in 1876 and 1878. After serving as a scout for General George Crook during his summer campaign against the Sioux in 1876, Farnham worked as a wagon boss freighting on the Sidney-Black Hills Trail. The job required that he be gone from home for long periods of time. He found that Wacante Wastewin, who had been born in a tepee, could not provide his daughters with the training he desired for them. He sent her back to her father and brought Ellen Tashnatowin (Blue Shawl), the daughter of Eh Tonka (Chief Big Mouth) and Kawingewin, into his home in 1877. Ellen Tashnatowin was then 22 years old.[39] The couple

Henry (John) and Ellen Farnham with their grandchildren. Their son Ulysses is at the left.
Photo courtesy of Hallie Trimble Young.

ran a road house called Willow Springs on the Sidney-Deadwood Trail where, as one traveler related, "Everything a worthy pilgrim desires can be secured."[40]

Episcopal Bishop P.C. Wolcott married John Farnham and Ellen Tashnatowin on December 23, 1880 at Pine Ridge. The couple continued to run the road house until 1884. They briefly settled in Montana Territory near the present-day town of Ekalaka.[41] The Farnhams later adopted an Indian boy, Ulysses, who was born in 1889.

John Farnham and his family were living on the east bank of the Cheyenne River, across from the town of Creston, during the Indian uprising of 1890. Farnham and his wife went to Cole's place on December 18, 1890 to bury a young Indian that Cole had killed and who was still laying in the corral, right where he had been shot. Mrs. Farnham identified the young brave as her cousin, Dead Arm. They dug a grave for Dead Arm in Cole's corral. While John Farnham recited from memory an appropriate passage from the Bible, Dead Arm was buried.[42]

Because of the obvious sympathy the couple bore for the slain warrior, Colonel Carr concluded that they were giving refuge to hostile Indians who raided the ranches west of the Cheyenne River, Carr also suspected the Farnhams were giving the Indian warriors information about the troops' movements. The next day, Carr dispatched a detail of soldiers to arrest John Farnham and remove him from his place for the duration of the conflict. Farnham was irate. When he was brought to Colonel Carr, Farnham demanded to know what authority the military had to arrest him and evict his family from their home. "I stand on my rights as an American citizen," the old frontiersman informed Carr. Farnham was allowed to stay on his place while soldiers camped in his front yard.[43]

John Farnham and his family moved farther into the Badlands in 1892. They first located at Potato Creek. A few years later, they moved two miles up from the mouth of Lost Dog Creek and built a home above a nice spring. By using a ram pump, Farnham supplied the buildings with water from the spring.

Henry Farnham was an uncommonly intelligent man who had a prodigious memory. At special occasions like funerals or weddings, he quoted from memory long passages from the Bible or from Shakespeare.[44]

Black/Interior

Interior was begun by two Norwegian brothers, **George** and **Louis Johnson** (See Chapter 6). They managed a way station there from 1883 to 1886 for the independent freighters hauling between Chamberlain and the Black Hills. George and Louis Johnson returned to the way station in the spring of 1890. Their sister, **Mary**, and her husband, **Oliver Johnson**, moved to the area in 1890. The Johnson brothers formed a partnership with their brother-in-law, Oliver, to start

166   *Philip S. Hall*

a general store. George's twin sisters, Tina and Christina, came out in the fall of 1891 to keep house for their brothers. The twins were electively mute, but they understood each other so well that they seemed telepathic. George and Louis' parents, Nels and Margaret, moved out from Chamberlain the following year. The settlement became a post office in 1891 called Black. The town's name was changed to Interior in 1894.[45]

Louis lived to the ripe old age of 90. George died in 1915. Modesty killed him. George took his wife and another woman on a long buggy trip that summer. Rather than embarrass the women, George suffered for hour and after hour with a full bladder. When they finally reached their destination, George's bladder was so swollen and distended that he could not urinate. A few hours later his bladder burst, and he died.[46]

C.A. Dibble located in the vicinity in 1891. He married Guy Trimble's sister, Ethel.[47]

Guy Trimble came from Iowa with his parents when he was 15 to homestead in the southeast corner of Dakota Territory. He moved to the Interior area in 1890. Trimble married John Farnham's daughter, Bessie, in 1898. The couple had three children: a daughter, Eloise, born in 1899; a daughter, Hallie, born in 1901; and a son, Henry, born in 1903. Bessie died of tuberculosis in 1905 at the age of 29, and the children went to live with their grandparents, John and Ellen Farnham.[48]

Bessie Farnham Trimble.
Photo courtesy of Hallie Trimble Young.

Guy Trimble and family, Hallie, Henry, Guy and Eloise.
Photo courtesy of Hallie Young.

Potato Creek

Potato Creek was an Indian village established in 1891 as part of the government's effort to locate the nomadic Sioux in permanent villages. Many of the Indians in this village were survivors of the Wounded Knee Massacre. **Amos Ross,** a Lakota Indian, was the minister in Potato Creek. Hunts-His-Horse was the Indian policeman stationed there.[49]

John Linn started teaching school at Potato Creek in January 1892. He was 38 years old and had been married for four years. He and his wife Olive, had a three-year-old daughter, Pauline. Mr. Linn taught school that winter in a three-room log cabin. Man Above, the local chief, lived in one room; his horses occupied the second room; and class was held in the third room. The Lakota dubbed John Linn "Chanlee Tanka" – Big Tobacco. They called his wife "Hustah Wea" – Lame Woman.[50]

Langburn Fisher was born in West Virginia in 1846, and he came to the Pine Ridge area sometime prior to 1880. In 1880, Langburn married Julia Harvey Wilde, a part-Indian woman born in 1859 along the upper White River. At the time of their marriage, Julia had a four-year old son, Jim Wilde. The Fishers ranched at the mouth of Porcupine Creek prior to 1890. They abandoned the ranch during the Indian trouble of 1890. After the Indian unrest subsided, Langburn Fisher moved his wife and four children to the mouth of Potato Creek. There, three more children were born.[51]

Nellie Farnham Gallagher.
Photo courtesy of Hallie Young.

Charley Gallagher.
Photo courtesy of Hallie Young.

Charles Gallagher came to the Badlands in 1889 and squatted on a parcel of land three quarters of a mile upriver from the mouth of Potato Creek but on the north side of White River.[52] Charles' father was Hugh Gallagher, a Colonel in the Civil War and the Indian agent for the Pine Ridge Reservation from 1886 to 1890. Charley had a few years of college education, and his neighbors regarded Charley as a highly educated man. Later, Charley married Nellie Farnham. The couple had one son, Paul.

John Black and his two adult sons, Phil and Barney, settled a mile and a half upriver from the mouth of Potato Creek. Phil worked as a bronc buster from 1891 to 1894 for Missouri John Massengale.[53] Phil Black likely trained the horses by riding between Massengale's place and his father's place, 21 miles up-river., delivering the mail to settlers living between the 15 Ranch and his father's place west of present-day Interior. The settlers in the area probably had their letters addressed as *In Care of Black*. Hence, the reason Mary Johnson's post office was initially called Black. Phil Black worked for one rancher or another all of his life and served as the cook on roundups. Barney Black could not tell time. If asked what time it was, Barney surreptitiously took the sun's bearing while he pointedly studied his watch. He then announced the time—always accurate within ten minutes.[54]

Henry Hurley and his adult son Charley came to the Badlands in 1889. They stayed with Charley Gallagher their first winter. In the spring, Hurley located ten miles west of Interior. Charley Hurley courted one of P.C. Woods' twin daughters, but the courtship was broken off. Charley later married Grace Fisher. Henry Hurley died in 1894 and was buried at the graveyard in Interior.[55]

Ben Tibbitts was born in Philadelphia in 1840 [B]. When the Civil War broke out, Tibbitts enlisted in the Union Army and was assigned as a freighter. Tibbitts soon acquired the reputation as being the best mule skinner in the Union Army. He stayed with the Army after the Civil War and served under Lt. Col. George A. Custer in the Washita campaign.

Tibbitts was hired in 1868 to move Spotted Tail's band of Brule Sioux from Fort Laramie to Whet-

Ben Tibbetts.
Photo courtesy Minnilusa Pioneer Museum.

stone on the Missouri River. The band made it only part-way that year when winter struck, forcing them to encamp until spring at the forks of the White River. Tibbitts, as the only white man on the scene, was essentially the Acting Indian Agent that winter.

In the 1870s, Tibbitts worked as a butcher at Fort Robinson. Nick Janis, a widely known early-day fur trader, was living White Clay Creek. At the time, he was living with a full-blooded Oglala woman named Wah-tela. In a trade that could only happen in the old West, Ben Tibbitts obtained Wah-tela from Nick Janis in exchange for an unknown number of horses. At the time, Wah-tela had an 18-year-old, part-Indian daughter, Alice. Alice's father was Jules Eccoffy. Everyone knowledgeable about the situation believed Ben Tibbitts bought Wah-tela in order to be near her attractive daughter.[56]

Ben Tibbitts returned to Philadelphia a few years later to visit his mother. Shortly after his return to the Pine Ridge Reservation, Alice married George White, a clerk in the commissary in Pine Ridge, and Ben Tibbitts married Emily Janis. The first few months of their marriage were tumultuous. But to understand why, one has to know become acquainted with Emily.

Emily was the daughter of Nick Janis and full-blood Oglala woman. In her youth, Emily was a firebrand. Her first husband was John Richard (pronounced Reeshaw) Jr., a mixed-blood. In 1868, Richard killed Corporal Francis Conrad at Fort Fetterman. A warrant was issued for Richard's arrest. To avoid being tried for murder, Richard hid out with Red Cloud's band, and he took Emily with him. While with Red Cloud's band, Richard participated in several Indian attacks against the soldiers guarding the Bozeman Trail. He also accompanied a war party to search the Black Hills for gold prospectors. They found seven miners and killed five of them.

Emily was Richards's sixth wife, and his last. On May 17, 1872 Richards stabbed Yellow Bear, an Oglala sub-chief. An unknown Indian who was member of Yellow Bear's band immediately shot and killed Richard.[57]

Emily went back home to live with her father, Nick Janis. At the time, Nick Janis was running a trading post on the North Platte River. A tragedy occurred there on Christmas Day, 1872. William and Pete Janis, sons of Antoine Janis and nephews of Nick Janis, were killed in a drunken brawl. The boys were part-Indian; and as such, they could not legally buy whiskey. A lame fellow by the name of Palladay had supplied the liquor for the party. Feeling guilty about his role in the Janis' deaths, Palladay stopped by Nick Janis' house, where the bodies had been brought, to apologize for his part in the tragedy. As Palladay walked away, Emily grabbed a gun, shot him dead, and cut out his heart.[58]

Emily Janis later married Bob Pugh, but theirs was a short-lived relationship.[59]

On May 22, 1881, five months after her marriage to George White, Alice gave birth to a son. George White deserted Alice and the baby that June, and he left the reservation. Ben Tibbitts brought Alice and her baby into his home. But Emily harbored such anger toward the infant that Alice hid her son in the bushes for several days. Alice and her son then went to live with Alice's mother, Wah-tela. However, when Ben Tibbitts died, the court awarded a portion of Ben's estate to his biological but estranged son.[60]

As early as 1882, Ben and Emily Tibbitts were living near a spring just below the top of the bluff overlooking the mouth of Cain Creek, making them the first permanent residents of the Badlands. They were living there when the Indian unrest of 1890 broke out. A good number of people living in the area gathered at the Ben Tibbitts' home for protection.[61]

Emily Janis Tibbetts.
Photo courtesy Minnilusa Pioneer Museum.

The Tibbitts relocated a few years later to an isolated place south of White River and a few miles up from the mouth of Red Water Creek. By then, Emily was well known as a skilled dispenser of herbs to relieve various afflictions. Many Indians came to her seeking treatment. Ben Tibbitts died in 1911 at the age of 71. Emily Tibbitts died in 1912 at the age of 62. They are buried side by side in the Fairview Cemetery in Interior.

Will S. Hughs came from Maine to Rushville, Nebraska in June 1889. He set out the next day by stage for Pine Ridge dressed like an Easterner—a seersucker suit, white shirt, a brightly colored cravat, and a derby. Hughs worked for his uncle, W.C. Smoot, and he quickly learned the skills of a cowboy. In 1892, H.A. Dawson, who ran a store in Pine Ridge and had $20,000 to invest in cattle, asked the 19-year-old Hughs to manage a ranch for him in the Badlands. The ranch, was two-and-a-half miles down-river from the mouth of Cain Creek. The ranch buildings consisted of a 14 foot by 16 foot log structure with a dirt floor, some good corrals, and nothing else. The grazing along White River was taken, so Dawson's cattle ranged in the Badlands basin northwest of Sage Creek Pass.

Hughs got his mail at Black. One fall day in 1893 George Johnson asked Hughs to deliver a letter to P.C. Woods. Woods, who had just moved to the Badlands, was frantically working on his house when Hughs arrived with the letter. He asked Hughs to help him get a roof over his family before the snow flew. Thus began a three-year courtship between Will Hughs and one of P.C. Woods' twin daughters, Maude. The couple married in 1896, and they moved to a small ranch west of Hermosa.[62]

P.C. Woods, his wife, sons and twin daughters moved to the Badlands from Nebraska in 1893. They built a small ranch on White River, near the mouth of Cain Creek.[63]

Algernon "Bud" Holcomb was born in Carthage, New York in 1849. He moved with his parents to Dubuque, Iowa. While living in Dubuque, Bud married in 1876. The couple and two of Holcomb's brothers came to the Black Hills in 1877 with a herd of milk cows. In time, each of the three brothers became wealthy cattlemen in their own right, and they dissolved their partnership. Bud, his wife, and two sons moved to the mouth of Cain Creek in 1890 and established the 6L Ranch.[64]

Bud's hired man was Jake Herman, an Indian who later gained notoriety as a rodeo clown. On October 10, 1891, Bud and Jake were cutting out steers for market when one steer broke away. Bud, who was riding a horse called Buck, took after it. The steer made a sudden turn. Buck also made the turn; but he lost his footing and fell, knocking his rider unconscious. The horse frantically

Lunch at the 6L.
Photo courtesy of the South Dakota State Historical Society.

rose to his feet and ran away. Bud Holcomb was dragged a considerable distance before his foot came loose from the stirrup. A rider was immediately dispatched for Dr. Flick in Rapid City, but Holcomb lived only four hours after the accident.[65]

The horse, Buck, was lethal. Buck was part of the deal when Corb Morse bought the 6L in 1896. A 6L cowboy by the name of Pancheka was riding Buck while working cattle. A steer took out, and Pancheka and Buck were right on top of him. The steer stumbled and fell, and Buck rolled over the steer. Pancheka was killed instantly. He was buried then and there beside a clump of willow trees along White River.

Buck was later traded to Charley Gallagher. After a big snow storm, Charley saddled up Buck in order to search for his drifted cattle. The snow was deep. Buck stepped in a badger hole and fell. Charley did not get up with the horse, and his foot was caught in the stirrup. Buck ran away, all the time kicking at the lump dragging behind his heels. He would have kicked Charley to death had it not been for his heavy, buffalo-hide coat. Fortunately, Gallagher's body wedged in a deep rut and his foot came loose from the stirrup.

Charley traded Buck to an Indian named Coyote Belly. Coyote Belly later came afoul of the law, and an Indian policeman was detailed to bring him in. Coyote Belly lit out for the Badlands.[66] He was tracked down. While attempting to flee on Buck, Coyote Belly was shot and killed.

Mrs. Holcomb moved to Rapid City after her husband's death, but she continued to run the 6L with the help of her Mexican foreman, Manuel Coy. Manuel Coy was born in old Mexico and came north after he reputedly killed a man. Coy always wore a six shooter and knew how to use it.[67]

A survey in 1896 found that the 6L headquarters was two miles inside the Pine Ridge Indian Reservation. Mrs. Holcomb sold out to Corb Morse, and Manuel Coy went to work for Narcisse Narcelle.[68] Isam Brown, better known by his initials – I.J.M. – was Corb Morse's foreman of the 6L. Charles Smalley was Isam Brown's right hand man on the 6L.[69]

Henry Lange left his boyhood home in Iowa and arrived in Chadron, Nebraska in 1886 at the age of 25. He initially worked as a laborer in a lumber yard in Chadron. In 1888, Lange

Wedding Photo of Henry and Annie Lange.
Photo courtesy of Mabel Lange Swanson.

worked for a large cattle outfit in the southern Black Hills. In 1890 Lange took up occupancy in a dugout along Cain Creek, about a mile and a half below the present-day, ghost-town of Imlay.[70] The dugout had been occupied just a few months earlier by Frank Lally.[71] But Lally, better known as a mining claim jumper than a rancher, and he was soon back in the Hills.[72]

Lange established a partnership with Bill Hargrave. Although Hargrave's legs had been amputated below the knees, his spirit was undaunted. He looked after the cattle while Lange freighted supplies between Gordon, Nebraska and Kyle for Jack O'Rourke, who ran a store in Kyle. O'Rourke was married to a part-Indian woman and had six children. In 1896 Lange sold out to Corb Morse and married one of O'Rourke's daughters, Annie. The groom was 36 years old and the bride was 18.

Lange took his new wife back to Iowa to live; but Annie was a child of the prairie. She missed the Badlands. Before a year passed, the couple was back on Cain Creek living in Hargrave's place. In 1898 a fire burned the cabin with all of their belongings to the ground. They moved a few miles down Cain Creek.[73]

Casey

Casey was a one-room, stone building that served as a general store and saloon. John Roth, the proprietor, lived at Run-a-way Springs, a mile east of the general store.[74] The general store and saloon were located just outside of the north border of the Pine Ridge Reservation, and wagons ruts that are still visible indicate that a lot of store's customers came from the Reservation. Casey was designated as a post office on June 3, 1891, but it was discontinued as a post office in 1893.[75]

In 1898 **C.A. Dibble** and his wife began running the store at Casey, and the post office was re-established.[76] Both the store and the post office were discontinued in 1907. However, Casey was a town that refused to stay put and it died reluctantly. A later survey located Casey north of Conata (when it existed) and near the base of Badland wall.[77] However, potable water is difficult if not impossible to find in that area of the Badlands. Casey did not last long at its second location.

Kyle

Kyle was established as a permanent Indian village in 1891 at a site occupied by Little Wound's band of Oglala Sioux. Initially, the location was merely a place for distributing rations. Later, William Bird Head opened a trading post about three miles south of the present-day town and soon thereafter Charles Turning Hawk started a small store near the present-day site of Kyle. Besides Turning Hawk's store, the town also included a government commissary and a few scattered buildings. Turning Hawk later visited Washington as a representative of the Oglala tribe and met U.S. Senator James Kyle. Senator Kyle later visited Turning Hawk at his store. Turning Hawk was so honored that he named his store after the Senator, and the settlement eventually became known as Kyle.[78] James Smalley was the Boss Farmer for the Medicine Root District, and he and his family lived in Kyle from 1894 to 1907.[79]

Medicine Root

Henry Clay "Hank" Clifford and **Mortimer Clifford,** brothers, were born in 1839 and 1842, respectively. After the Civil War, they moved to Nebraska City, Nebraska and then to the upper North Platte River. There, the Cliffords lived as fur traders among the Whistler's band of Lakota Sioux. Both men married Oglala women. Little is known about Hank Clifford's Indian wife, Maggie. "Morty" married Julia Lucia, a mixed-blood, in 1869. Julia was born in 1851 at Fort Laramie to an Oglala woman and Augustine Lucia, a French trapper and post interpreter who was killed at the Grattan Massacre. When Julia married Morty Clifford in 1869 she could not speak or read English. However, in exchange for eggs and butter, the neighboring white women taught her English and helped her to learn to read. In 1886, a branch of the B&M Railroad was built through Frontier County, Nebraska. Morty contracted to build a portion of the railroad, but he underbid the expenses and went broke.

Hank Clifford left Frontier County shortly thereafter and moved to Fort Laramie. He next moved to the Niobrara River, south of Fort Robinson. There, Hank Clifford he had a ranch and ran a stage station from 1876–1882. During this time, Hank Clifford was also a fossil collector for O.C. Marsh, a professor at Yale University who amassed a world-renown collection of vertebrate fossils.

In approximately 1886, Hank and Morty moved to the mouth of Clifford Creek in the southwest corner of the Badlands. They started what was probably the first ranch in the Badlands. Phil and Barney Black, former laborers on Morty's railroad construction project, accompanied the Cliffords to the Badlands.

The Cliffords had barely begun to establish a ranch near the mouth of Medicine Root Creek when the 1890 Indian unrest began. They abandoned their ranch and stayed with Ben Tibbitts on Cane Creek until the spring of 1891. The Cliffords then returned to Medicine Root Creek. In time, the Cliffords built a large, two-story log house, smoke houses, barns, corrals, feed lots, and even strung a few fences. In 1894, they hired a surveyor and engaged 18 men with teams and fresnos to build an elaborate irrigation system using spring-fed Medicine Root Creek. Mortimer died in 1904. Running the ranch and looking after the large extended family fell to Julia. An innately intelligent woman, she was up to the task. Her mother, Titokonlati Win (Moves Camp Woman), trained Julia and empowered her as a medicine woman. Her grandchildren recalled her considerable powers. When Julia wanted her cattle and horses, she filled her long-stemmed Redstone pipe with a mixture of tobacco and dried red willow bark, and lit it. At day break she would sit on the ground in front of the house and, as she smoked her pipe, would point to the four winds while she sang her Indian song to her livestock. Between 10 and 11 o'clock, all of her stock would come from all directions and assemble on the creek bottom east of the house.

Julia Clifford also understood the howl of the coyotes, which allowed her to predict the arrival of company several days in advance, and the hooting of owls which told of births and deaths in the surrounding area.[80]

Pumpkinseed, an Indian family, lived just up-river from Medicine Root Creek at a place with a good set of corrals.[81] Pumpkinseed had been a sergeant in the Indian Police during V.T. McGillycuddy's tenure as the Indian agent at Pine Ridge.[82]

John Palmer and his part-Indian wife, Maggie, ranched on Palmer Creek near a spring at the base of the south Badlands Wall.[83]

Harvey, a mixed blood, and his Indian family lived on Spring Creek about a half mile from its confluence with White River. **Martin Shangreau,** a mixed blood and the son of Louis Shangreau, an early fur trader, lived across the creek.[84]

Richard Stirk came to Fort Laramie in 1872 with a cattle drive from Kansas. In 1873, Stirk married Emma, a part-Indian woman, by Indian rites – that is to say he gave three horses for her. Emma's biological father was Henry Smith, a Captain in the U.S. Army. Emma's mother died when Emma was two years old, and Emma was raised by her maternal aunt, Mary Bordeaux.

Stirk moved to Red Cloud Agency in 1874, where he worked as a government herder until the fall of 1875. Then he and five other men went to the Hills to prospect for gold. Stirk had no luck at finding gold and was soon back at Red Cloud Agency. The others went to robbing stages.

Stirk was recruited by General George Crook during his summer campaign of 1876 to relay dispatches, which Stirk and a companion did under the cover of darkness. Once, they came upon ten warriors who shot Stirk's horse out from under him, but Stirk and his partner escaped into the night.

Stirk then turned to freighting over the Sidney-Black Hills Trail, but he moved his operation in 1883 to Valentine, Nebraska, the temporary terminus of the Fremont, Elkhorn & Missouri Valley Railroad.

When the Ghost Dance uprising came in 1890, the Stirk family was living near the mouth of Porcupine Creek. On December 1, 1890, Two Strike's band of Brule Sioux stole six of Stirk's horses and ransacked his abandoned house as they pillaged their way to the mouth of Wounded Knee Creek. Dick Stirk witnessed the Wounded Knee massacre and delivered dispatches about the battle to the telegraph office in Rushville at $100 each for the reporters of the *Chicago Herald,* the *Omaha Bee,* and the *Kansas City Star.*

Dick Stirk returned to his 115 Ranch at the mouth of Porcupine Creek and near present-day Stirk Table after the situation settled down. He lived there, at the south edge of the Badlands, for the remainder of his life.[85]

Red Shirt

Red Shirt was located in 1891 along the Cheyenne River near the northeastern corner of the reservation. Originally known as Red Shirt's Village, after the local chief, it was established as a permanent Indian encampment, complete with an issue station and a day school.

Grant lived along the Cheyenne River just north of the reservation line. According to a survey in 1894, Gandy lived a mile farther up-river. Grant and Gandy were partners in a horse ranch based west of Hermosa, along Battle Creek.[86] They took out homesteads on the east side of the Cheyenne River so that they could run their horses in the Badlands basin north of present-day Cuny Table.

George Bale was born in 1867 in Norfolk, England. His oldest brother, Robert, immigrated to America in 1884. George, the next oldest child in the family, came to America in the spring of 1885. The two brothers met in Watertown, Dakota Territory and headed for the Black Hills. They liked what they

Left to right: Georgiana, Henry, Arthur, and Robert Bale.
Photo courtesy of Marvin Bale.

found and sent literature advertising the Black Hills back to their parents in England. Meanwhile, an agricultural depression in England during 1886–1887 drove their parents into bankruptcy. Mrs. Bale's sisters decided that a grand solution to the family's worsening economic woes would be to finance their trip to the Dakota Territory. The Bale family presented a pathetic picture as they stepped off the train at Buffalo Gap in 1887—an abjectly poor, 50-year-old man; his 48-year-old wife; girls of 18, 16 and 11; and little boys of seven and eight. The entire reunited family of nine moved into a two-room log cabin. Water had to be carried to the house, and it was bitter and scarce. The two oldest girls died within a decade. George acquired a preemption claim along the divide between Battle Creek and French Creek. He moved to the Cheyenne River in 1891, where he earned a modest living dealing in horses.[87]

A survey in 1897 placed **John Doherty, Littledale, Pap Thompson, Phil Miller, Denn,** and **Clarence Smith** along the Cheyenne River between Indian Creek and Kube Table. They presumably were located there in 1895. Little can be learned about these men, but it is known that John "Doherty" (the surveyor's phonetic spelling) was none other than Captain John Daugherty, the former freighting magnet (See Chapter 3). Daugherty still resided primarily in Yankton, South Dakota; but in 1891 he developed extensive ranching interests along both sides of the Cheyenne River. When one of his employees, Adolph Fiesler, took a fancy to his daughter, Kitty, Daugherty sent Fiesler to the Badlands to manage his ranching interests.[88]

According to a survey, **John H. Hart** had a place on Spring Creek, at the base of what is now known as Hart Table. John Hart was born in 1847 in Indiana and moved with his parents to Iowa when he was a small boy. At the age of 17, Hart joined Company A of the 147th Iowa Infantry and served in the Civil War. In 1876 Hart started west with a freight train from Nebraska City, Nebraska headed for Salt Lake City. He came to the Black Hills in 1877 and freighted on the Fort Pierre-Deadwood Trail, and later over the Chamberlain-Rapid City Trail[89] (See Chapter 3). Hart's main headquarters was a ranch he started south of Rapid City in 1897. During Hart's freighting days, he was traveling back and forth between Chamberlain and Rapid City, making it convenient to have one wife and family in Chamberlain and another wife and family in Rapid City.[90]

Frank Hart, John Hart's son, was one of the Badlands' real characters. Even though Frank Hart only stood five foot four inches, he did not know the meaning of the word fear. During the Indian uprising of 1890, an Indian slipped into the 6th Cavalry's horse herd that ranged near the mouth of Rapid Creek and stole two horses assigned to Colonel Eugene Carr. Carr announced that he would give $25 apiece to anyone who could retrieve his horses. Frank Hart set out that evening for the area of present-day Stronghold Table, where the hostile Indians were encamped. Under the cover of darkness, Frank Hart rode into the

Indian's horse herd. He put a rope around Carr's horses and slipped them out right under the Indians' noses. When Carr woke the next morning, Frank Hart was waiting outside the Colonel's tent to collect his reward.[91]

In 1895, Frank married Tenny Jones, a Methodist preacher's daughter. The couple moved into the Hart cabin on the west side of Spring Creek Valley where a nice spring flowed out of the hillside. The couple had two children – Clayton and Iva. But Frank spent a lot of time away from home performing with Buffalo Bill's Wild West Show and later, riding the rodeo circuit. Although he rode broncs before Kings and Kaisers and twice won the world championship saddle bronc riding, his far-flung exploits came at a price. Tenny divorced him.[92]

Freed from the obligations of being a husband, Frank added to his lore. A story underscores Frank Hart's toughness. According to the story, a bronc once threw Frank onto the frozen ground while he was riding in a blizzard. Frank hit the flinty ground so hard it apparently killed him. The cowboys covered him with a tarp and loaded him on a buckboard to haul him into Rapid City and the undertaker. Some kind soul noticed that Frank still wore his spurs and out of consideration started to remove them. The boys turned ghost-white when an unmistakable voice rumbled beneath the canvas tarp, "Don't touch those spurs. Just tell me where that damn horse is. I'm gonna bust him wide open!"[93]

Frank liked to ride wild broncs atop precipitous Badlands tables not much larger than a corral. He figured that a horse with any sense wouldn't buck over the side. It usually worked, but once an unbroken horse took him over the side of a 200-foot Badlands table located between Medicine Root Creek and Palmer Creek. According to Hart, it was a well-trained saddle horse by the time they reached the bottom.

The **Herman Kube** family came to the Badlands in the late fall of 1890. As they came across the Badlands, a small band of Indian warriors took after them. Kube told his family to lie down in the bottom of the wagon. He whipped his horses into a gallop and raced the Indians to the top of a large table. There, the Indians broke off the chase. Kube settled beside a good spring near the northwest corner of the table, which is now known as Kube Table.[94]

Americus Thompson was born in Plymouth, Indiana. On January 19, 1876 he and a group of 13 others set out from Fort Randall for the Black Hills. They arrived at Rapid City on February 7, 1876. He was in Custer that summer for the town's big Independence Day celebration wearing buckskin, a broad-rimmed white hat and two ivory-handled six shooters. A month later he was at the blockhouse in Rapid City fending off Indian attacks.

By 1878 Americus Thompson had moved 18 miles down Rapid Creek, near the present-day town of Farmington and within sight of a high prominence now called Thompson Butte (See Chapter 3). Thompson lived there as an affable recluse who spent weeks roaming the country on hunting trips, often in the company of Indians. Indians visited him so frequently that the valley running southeast from his place toward the reservation became known as Indian Trail Draw. One fall day in 1880 Americus Thompson returned from an extended absence to find that a small band of Indians had visited him. The Indians had eaten part of the beef hanging in his root cellar. Thompson grabbed a bucket of lard and lit out immediately on the Indians' trail. He found them camped but a short distance away and forced the Indians to eat the lard. He thus saved the Indians' lives. The beef had been laced with strychnine so it could serve as wolf bait.[95]

Thompson got caught up in the Ghost Dance uprising of 1890. Among other duties, he piloted Col. Eugene Carr into the Badlands on December 24, in search of Big Foot (See Chapter 4). Thompson guided the soldiers up the Fort Laramie-Fort Pierre Trail to Sage Creek, where the troops pitched camp and passed a miserably cold Christmas Eve. Americus Thompson knew that in the morning Carr would ask him where Big Foot might be. It was probably a question that Thompson did not want to answer, so he deserted that night.[96]

Thompson moved from his place on Rapid Creek in 1892 to the place east of the Cheyenne River at the base of a bluff. The site had formerly been occupied by John Farnham in 1890.

Creston

Creston was a store and post office located near the mouth of Rapid Creek in 1884 to serve the cluster of settlers located on the west bank of the Cheyenne River.[97]

Link

Link was ten miles down-river from Creston at the mouth of Box Elder Creek and across from the mouth of Sage Creek. It originally was a "store" that **Joe Buck** operated out of his claim shack. Many of Joe Buck's customers were Indians, so he compiled a little dictionary of the Lakota words he needed for conducting business with them. Whereas others abandoned their places during the Indian uprising, Joe Buck felt he got along well enough with the Indians that he was in no danger. One morning, he was awakened at daybreak by his dog's barking. Looking out his loft window, Buck saw several Indians in war paint and regalia. He asked them what they wanted. They replied that they needed flour, coffee, and bacon. Buck told them to stack their weapons beside a tree and he would let them in. The Indians got their groceries and peaceably left.[98]

A post office was started adjacent to Buck's store on June 10, 1886 with **Joe J. Pitts** as the postmaster.[99] It was named Link after the Chain Link brand. Pitts was succeeded on August 22, 1887 by **Elmer Crow**. Joe Buck became the postmaster on July 5, 1891. The name of the post office was changed in 1891 from Link to the more auspicious sounding name of Dakota City. Frank Morris bought out Buck in 1898. Charley Belnap took over the post office in 1905, but Dakota City became just another ranch when the railroad passed it by in 1907.[100]

Wild and Untamed

The Badlands had few takers after 1896. The United States had bankrupted itself by insisting on maintaining the Silver Standard. When Grover Cleveland abandoned the Silver Standard, the citizens realized the hopelessness of the silver illusion. To make matters worse, America's gold reserves fell 100 million dollars. Panic swept across the country. By 1894, Washington was under siege by Cox's Army of the Unemployed. America slid into a deep depression that lasted for four years. Arid, isolated land considered to be part of the Great American Desert was of no value. Few new settlers came to stake a claim in the Badlands and the population along White River remained static for the next 15 years. When the nineteenth century came to a close, there were but three, one-room schools in the recently ceded 11 million acres and not a single church – and that was just how the denizens of the Badlands liked it.

Towns, People, & Brands: 1890–1896

(refer to the accompanying maps)

Family	Brand	Location
STEARNS		
1. Smokey Stearns		
David Johnson		
J.W. Garret		
Jack Turner and wife		
Frank Swartz		
Jack and Sally Whipple		
Bert Gorum	HOT	right side
Hugh Caton	KTN	
Ester Lawrence Currier	$\frac{6}{6}$	right side
Osmer Lawrence	$\frac{O}{L}$	left hip
Oscar Lawrence	XIV	left side
Charley Smith		
2. W.F. Bartlett	⌒	left hip

WHIFIELD
　　Robert Whitfield　　　　　　　22　　　left hip, horses
　　　　　　　　　　　　　　　　　　　　　　left shoulder, horses
　3. William Hickox　　　　　　　 ▽
　　Ab Porch

LIP'S CAMP
　　Philip Wells
　　J.B. White　　　　　　　　　　S▢　　left side
　　Frank P. Gannaway
　　Darwin Collins
　　George Porch
　4. David Lincoln McLane
　5. John Massengale & John Ross　15　　　left hip

LODGE
　6. Dick Thyer
　　M.B. Ganow　　　　　　　　　1C　　left shoulder
　　　　　　　　　　　　　　　　　U　　 left hip
　7. W.W. Anderson　　　　　　　　⌐╫　 (rake) left side, cattle
　　　　　　　　　　　　　　　　　　　　　left shoulder, horses

ABOVE THE WALL
　9. Warren Young
　10. Martin Johnson
　11. Charlie Thompson　　　　　　CT　　left side

LODGE
　12. Nelson Bros.
　13 Henry & Ben Smith
　14. Henry Farnham

BLACK/INTERIOR
　　Johnson Bros.　　　　　　　　　⌐▷　(hammer) right side
　　Oliver Johnson　　　　　　　　　　　 left side
　15. C.A. Dibble
　　Guy Trimble
　16. William Challis

182 *Philip S. Hall*

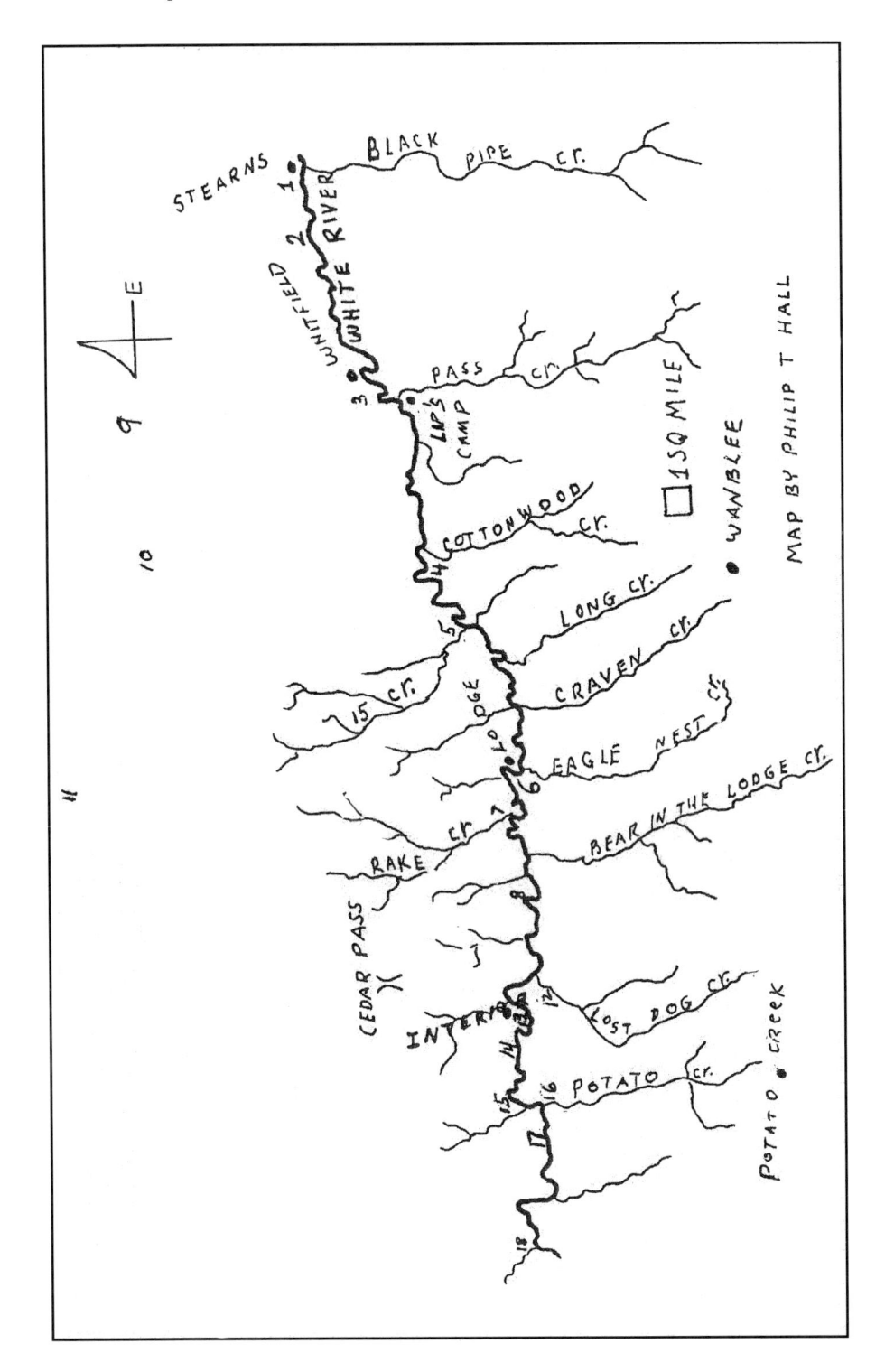

Denizens of the Badlands: 1890-1896 183

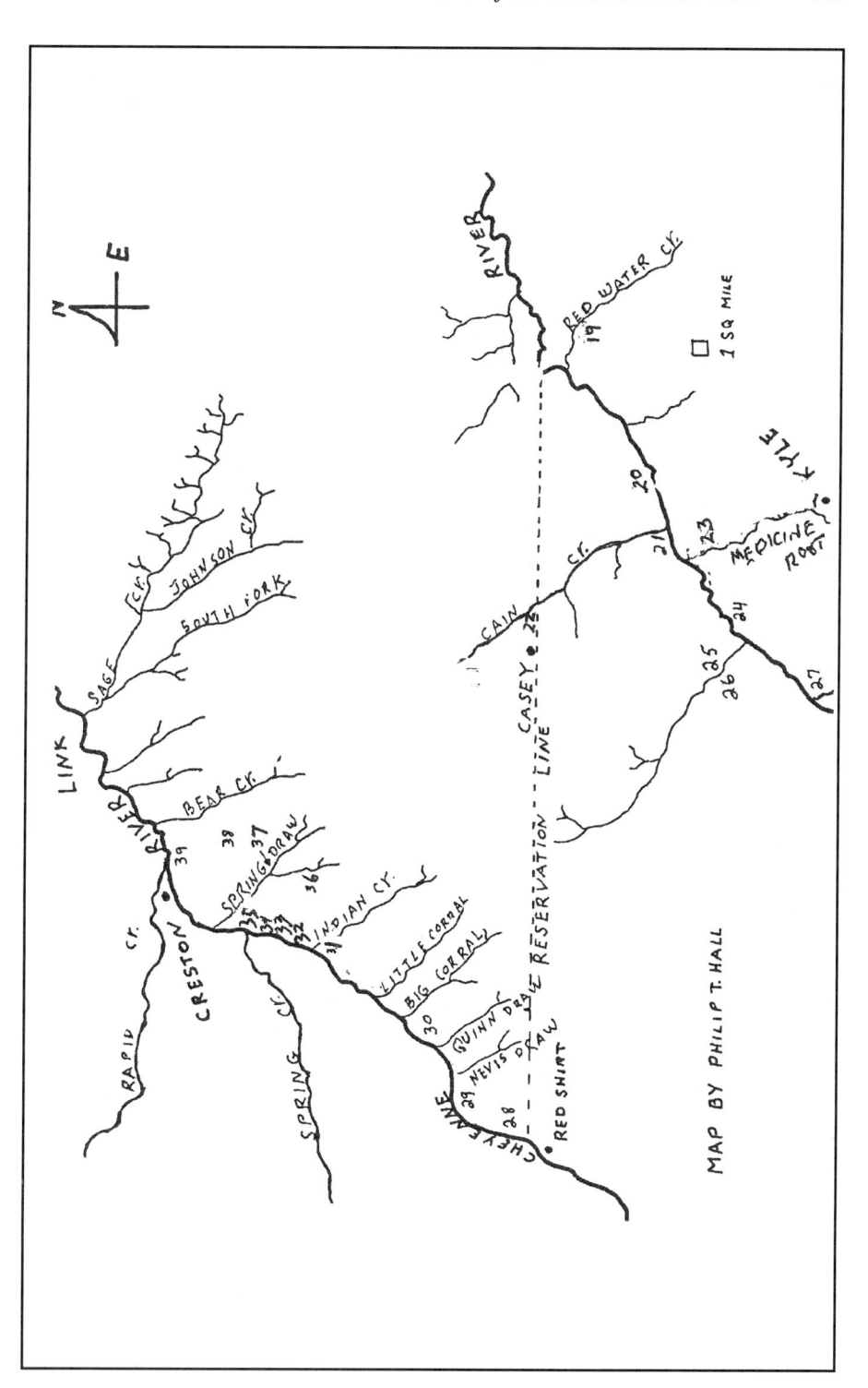

POTATO CREEK
- 17. Langburn Fisher
  Charlie Gallagher
- 18. John Black
  Henry Hurley
- 19. Ben Tibbitts
- 20. Will Hughs
- 21. P.C. Woods
- 22. Bud Holcomb   6L
  Henry Lange

CASEY
- John Roth

KYLE/MEDICINE ROOT
- 23. Mortimer and Hank Clifford   MHC
  Pumpkinseed
- 24. John Palmer
- 25. Harvey
- 26. Martin Shangreau
- 27. Richard Stirk   115

RED SHIRT
- 28. Grant
- 29. Gandy
- 30. George Bale
- 31. John Daughterty   JD
- 32. Littledale
- 33. Pap Thompson
- 34. Clarence Smith
- 35. Denn
- 36. Frank Hart
- 37. Phil Miller
- 38. Herman Kube
- 39. Americus Thompson

Notes

[A] During the drought of the 1930s, my grandfather Joe Hall leased a ranch along White River. My dad spent the winters of 1932 and 1933 looking after the family's cattle. He stayed "at a log cabin that had once been a post office. It was so cold in that cabin that I could sit with my back to the wood stove feeling its nice warm heat while my fingers holding a book darn near got frost bit." Dad did not know the name of the former post office. However, I am certain it was Robert Whitfield's place.

[B] There are several spellings of Tibbitts. The name is variously spelled Tibbetts, Tibbits, and Tibbets. The name used here (Tibbitts) is as it appears on the headstone of Benjamin Tibbitts, who died in 1911, and Emily Tibbitts, who died the following year. However, Tibbetts is the commonly used spelling in many historical works.

CHAPTER 10

The Last Years of the Open Range

The Badlands was a cattlemen's paradise in 1896. The government owned it, but no one ever came to collect the rent. Thousands of cattle grazed between the Badlands walls and grew fat on the protein-rich buffalo grass. There was not a barbed wire fence from Stearns west to the Cheyenne River. When Frank Lynn tried to string one up in 1905, he was shot ten times with a 30-30 Winchester.[1] The murderer, Frank Turner, rode to Pierre and informed the law of the incident. No charges were brought [A]. The Badlands were the cattlemen's exclusive domain, and in those days they ruled it to suit themselves.

Frank Edwin Turner.
Photo courtesy of Jerry Smalley.

A preacher left Chamberlain early in the spring of 1894 armed with a wagon load of Bibles and bound for this unchurched wasteland. The reverend wound his way up the White River valley selling Bibles, baptizing heathens, preaching an occasional sermon, and giving the last rites over any departed soul he was lucky enough to come upon at the auspicious moment. The trip progressed in accordance with the preacher's best expectations. He was warmly received at most ranches and always put up for the night. The trail along White River was marked by cottonwood trees that sheltered him from the hot sun.

The preacher was as far west as Stearns (the first settlement in the Badlands) by July. Fortified by the fruits of his labor, he continued on. At the end of his first day in the Badlands, he came upon the slovenly abode of two heathens obviously in need of salvation.

George Porch and Bill Hickox welcomed the man of God, and sat him down to as fine a meal as they could prepare. After supper the men propped their chairs against the west cabin wall to witness the sunset and to enjoy the evening's freshness. The confab began. Each had his story to tell. The preacher started first. He informed the two heathens about the Ten Commandments, original sin, purgatory, the road to hell and damnation, and all those other good Christian things.

At some point George Porch interrupted the preacher. He felt obliged to prepare the man for the earthly miles ahead. George began by telling the preacher that there was no such thing as Sunday in these parts. There was no God over the next ridge, and there were no Christian burials. If a man died in the Badlands, it was the coyotes' good luck. As George acquired the preacher's attention, he warmed to the task. George told the preacher of the painted women in Rapid City, the Indian torture of anyone who strayed too close to the reservation, the cowboys who came into town at the end of a roundup to shoot up the place, a saloon in Deadwood aptly called the Bucket of Blood, and more. Bill Hickox quietly listened to each story, and at its conclusion gravely shook his head and said, "Amen." The sky was starting to lighten in the east when George reached the end of his good advice. The preacher had lost interest in sleep. He went to the corral, hitched up his horse, and headed east—back the way he had come.[2]

W.F. Bartlett, who lived 15 miles down-river, rode into George Porch's ranch later that afternoon. Bartlett told them that the preacher had stopped at his place that morning, but he had stayed only long enough to water his heavily-lathered horse. The reverend seemed mighty anxious, Bartlett related, to get out of the Badlands. "I rode up here," Bartlett informed Porch, "to find out what kind of stories you fed that preacher."[3]

In running the preacher out, George Porch had acted in accordance with an unwritten code that governed the Badlands. The Badlands were ruled in the 1890s by a tightly knit group of men who were bound together by a common desire to keep out the law, local government, and anyone who might be carrying the seeds of structure and conformity. This group was held together by the big operators—men who grazed thousands of head of cattle in the Badlands. Corbin Morse was the biggest operator of them all.

Corb Morse came to the West River country from New York in 1882 as a youth of 16. He settled on an 80 acre homestead east of Rapid City while he worked as a 40-dollar-a-month cowhand. But Corb managed to save most of what he earned, and most of what he saved went to buy a cattle. Once Corb Morse had a few cattle, he became a wheeler-dealer. If you wanted to sell, he would buy. If you wanted to buy, he had something to sell.

Corb Morse and his silent partner, the Denver Livestock and Loan Company, were soon buying entire ranches. In 1896, Morse bought the 15 Ranch from Massengale and Ross, paying $55,000 in cash and giving them a note for the remaining $20,000 (See Chapter 7). He also bought the 6L from Bud Holcomb's widow; Will Hughs' adjacent ranch, and Henry Lange's place on Cain Creek.[4] Morse abandoned the buildings on the Holcomb place when a survey disclosed the ranch headquarters was on the Reservation, and he moved the 6L to Lange's place on Cain Creek. There, Corb Morse built the first frame house in the Badlands. The house was also the first residence in the Badlands equipped with running water and a flush commode, both made possible by a spring located above the site. An elderly woman, called "Aunt Bell," tended the house. A full-time groundskeeper maintained the flowers and manicured the lawn. The groundskeeper carefully trimmed the trees and painted the first five feet of their trunks white. I.J.M. Brown was the foreman of this spread.

However, the place on Cain Creek was not Corb Morse's main headquarters. He lived in a large, two-story frame house on his original homestead five miles

Corb Morse (seated).
Photo courtesy of the Arvada Center.

east of Rapid City. It was a show place. The original 80 acres had expanded to 5,000, and not a fence marred the view. The house was richly furnished. Paintings by Remington and Russell hung on the walls. Silver candlesticks that had once belonged to Martha Washington adorned his mantle. A Mexican saddle, a gift from Poncho Villa, hung from a peg. Outside, he installed a swimming pool. The basement had a well-stocked wine cellar. A French chef prepared the meals. Corb Morse, an inveterate bachelor, wore diamond stickpins, drank the most expensive whiskey, and entertained in grand style everyone from cattle buyers to opera stars, railroad presidents to important politicians. People such as Theodore Roosevelt, Mark Twain, William Jennings Bryan, Jim Colbert, Lillian Russell, and Diamond Jim Brady were his guests.[5]

Corb Morse and the Denver Livestock and Loan Company soon owned more than 120 brands. In 1900, Corb bought out the big operation jointly owned by Peter Duhamel, Alex Duhamel, and Mike Babue, paying them $185,000 in cash. Corb Morse never marketed fewer than 10,000 head of cattle a year. One year he shipped 36,000 head.[6]

Cornelius Augustus (Gus) Craven ran the largest, non-syndicated ranch in the Badlands during the last years of the open range.[7] Reared in Indiana, he set out as a young man to please his Irish parents by studying for the priesthood at the University of Notre Dame. The calling was not for him. Instead, the lure of the West compelled him in 1875 to take a train to Abilene, Kansas. There, cattle drovers offered him passage to Wyoming in exchange for cooking and night herding. Craven, who had never before ridden a horse, signed on. By the time they reached Cheyenne, Wyoming, Gus Craven desperately wanted to go back home – but he was broke.

In 1876, Cheyenne was full of men headed to the Black Hills in search of gold. Craven joined a group of them. He ran a butcher shop in Custer City until word came of the Custer massacre and Indians started killing people on the edge of town. Craven returned to the safety of Cheyenne.[8]

Craven was in route to Cheyenne when he spotted three maverick cows. He branded them with the cinch buckle from his saddle. This started him in the cattle business, and it was the beginning of the Open Buckle Ranch.

Craven and a partner, Mike Dunn, started a ranch on Hat Creek. They delivered most of their beef to the Pine Ridge Indian Reservation. While there, Gus Craven met Jessie McGaa, a young lady who was one – fourth Sioux. They married on November 11, 1881. She was 15. The groom was 31.

The Cravens initially lived just south of the Pine Ridge Reservation, where Gus worked for V.T. McGillycuddy as a government herder. Homesteaders soon moved in—too many to suit Gus. The Cravens moved to the mouth of Indian Creek in about 1887. There, they established a ranch; it was possibly the second ranch in the Badlands.

The Cravens paid little attention to the rumors of Indian unrest that circulated across the frontier in the spring of 1890. Gus was in Hermosa buying lumber on December 1st when Two Strikes' large band pillaged and plundered their way down Wounded Knee Creek. Mrs. Craven had washed the laundry that day. Even though it was dark, she was hanging the last two sheets out to dry when the evening quiet was broken by the sound of horse hooves on the frozen ground. Thinking it was a hostile Indian, she stood motionless in the dark. When the rider came closer, she saw that he was a white man. "What are you doing here?" She asked.

"What in the hell are YOU doing here?" He retorted. The rider, George Gosgrove, told Mrs. Craven to immediately put her three children and few personal effects in a wagon while he hitched up a team. Jessie and the children stayed at the John Hart home near Hermosa during the rest of the winter.[9]

Gus served as a scout for Colonel E.A. Carr during the Indian uprising. He was returning to Carr's camp on Rapid Creek on the afternoon of December 17th when two hostile Indians jumped him. Unfortunately, he was leading his fastest horse, a mare named Bird. The Indians quickly gained on him. Bullets whizzed by his head. He let go of Bird so he could draw his pistol and defend himself. Just as he did, the Indians reined in their horses. Looking up, Craven saw Pete Lemley and Frank Hart riding to his rescue. "Boy, am I glad to see you fellows," he told them. "I thought I was a goner."[10]

Soldiers used Craven's ranch as an outpost during the last month of the unrest – December. When the Indian uprising was over there was little left of the ranch. Indians had run off most of Craven's cattle; soldiers had butchered the rest. Most of their pigs were gone. Their winter supply of food was gone. A clock was the only moveable thing left in the house. In despair, the Cravens abandoned the ranch.

As reward for his service to Colonel Carr, Gus Craven was given a job as the Boss Farmer for the Medicine Root District of the Pine Ridge Reservation. By his own wife's admission, Gus was a green Boss Farmer. Gus also served as postmaster for the newly-established community of Kyle. The postal department requested a report of his first quarter's business. Craven's report was brief: "Never received a letter, nor sent one."

Mrs. Craven and Mrs. Andrew Chips, an Indian woman, taught at the school in Kyle. Members of Little Wound's band were the primary occupants of the village. They had been ardent ghost dancers during the uprising. Young warriors in the band had raided the ranches west of the Cheyenne River, and some of them had been killed by cowboys defending their property. Little Wound's band was reluctant to send their children to school. Only four children initially attended.

Gus Craven eventually built his herd back to the point where he needed more range, He loaded Jessie and the five children into a wagon in the summer of 1898 and took them on an extended camping trip while he looked for a ranch site. About 30 miles down-river he found a ranch site that pleased him. But where Gus saw lush grass and natural protection from winter storms, his wife saw perpendicular Badlands canyons, bare crags, and wind-swept tables. Their nearest white neighbor was miles away; and, worse, there was no school. Jessie reluctantly agreed to make her home in the God-forsaken Badlands on the condition that in five years they would sell out and move to Denver.

Gus built a log cabin entirely out of cottonwoods for his family, which soon grew to seven children. Then, he then turned his attention to building a ranch, It was good cattle country, and he prospered. Craven eventually had 5,000 head of cattle and 300 horses ranging from Bear-In-The-Lodge Creek to Cottonwood Creek on a ranch that covered 360 square miles.[11]

The tens of thousands of cattle that grazed on the open range necessitated an operation that became the hallmark of the West – the roundup. The ranchers usually held two roundups a year. One roundup was held in the spring and a second roundup, the beef roundup, was held in the fall. During the beef roundup the cattlemen gathered their marketable animals, generally four-year-old steers, for shipping. A nickel a pound was top money. The price was not much, but when the grass was free, fortunes could be made at those prices.

The spring roundup was larger and more colorful than the beef roundup. It was necessitated by the strong northwest winds that swept the prairie during the winter and drifted the cattle before it. By spring, cattle had drifted as much as 200 miles from their home range. It was not unusual for cattle from as far away

Craven's Open Buckle Ranch. The women are Jessie McGaa Craven and her daughter.
Photo courtesy of the South Dakota State Historical Society.

as Montana to drift clear to the Pine Ridge or Rosebud Indian Reservations – a distance of 400 miles.

The winter drift was not the cattleman's curse – it was their boon. The drifting pushed the cattle onto the Pine Ridge and Rosebud Indian Reservations where winters were typically mild, flowing springs were numerous, and grass was abundant. The ranchers along the way sanded the ice and pushed congregated cattle across the various rivers that tended to block this natural migration. In the spring, the cattlemen came onto the Reservations to gather their cattle. For years, no fee was collected. Then, in 1897, the Indian Service imposed a fee of a dollar for every head of livestock found on the reservation. The *Rapid City Journal* pleaded the case of the indignant cattlemen. "It can readily be seen how unjust," the Journal reported, "it would be to cattle owners to be forced to pay a tribute of a dollar a head for every head of stock found on the Reservation when it is no fault of the owners."[12] Appeals to Washington were to no avail. The grazing fee stuck.

Cattlemen from western South Dakota, parts of Wyoming, and eastern Montana gathered at the Harney Hotel in Rapid City each spring to organize the roundup. The cowboys took time from their work to stage horse races, roping contests, and bronc riding events. Most of the activities were held in the center of town – right in front of the Harney Hotel. Tom Sweeney, who ran a big general store a block down from the Harney, once bet "a barrel of money" that Frank Hart could ride the worst bronc that could be located while "slick-heeled" (no spurs) and with both hands in the air – and he did.[13]

Branding a calf on a spring roundup.
Photo courtesy of the South Dakota State Historical Society.

The first spring roundup in the Badlands was held in 1881, and one was held every year thereafter for over two decades. The biggest roundup was held in 1902.

The summer of 1901 was dry.[14] Grass was short. By fall, the grazing land north of the While River was depleted. Winter came early with a 14-inch snowfall in November. The cattle started drifting south in search of grass and shelter. The prairie was soon laced with thousands of cattle trails winding southward through the snow. The tough winter persisted to the very end. A heavy, wet snow came in on April 1, 1902 with gale-force winds that pushed the cattle even farther south. By spring, over 100,000 cattle had drifted onto the Rosebud and Pine Ridge Indian Reservations.

Captain LeRoy Brown, Acting Agent for the Pine Ridge Indian Reservation, decided in 1894 that the Oglala Indians would manage the roundup on their Reservation. Each of the five districts on the Reservation supplied its own roundup wagon and crew to cover its designated area. The Indian crews were not paid cash. Instead, they were authorized to divide the slicks (unbranded cattle) between them. In addition, the cattlemen had to pay the Oglala Tribe one dollar a head for the cattle that trespassed onto the Reservation. Captain Brown appointed John Darr, the government herder, to be in charge of the overall Pine Ridge roundup. The cattlemen selected Dude Rounds to meet the Indian crews at the north edge of the Reservation and receive livestock that were to go back north; Ben Harrison was selected to manage the cattle dispersed to ranchers to the west; and Ed Ross was selected to represent interests of the Nebraska ranchers.

On the Rosebud Reservation, Agent Charles McChesney allowed the cattlemen to come onto the Reservation and collect their livestock under the general supervision of his government herder, John Neiss. The cattlemen selected Henry Hudson, foreman of the 73 Ranch, as the overall boss.

The 1902 roundup commenced on May 25th. Thirteen roundup wagons worked the area from the North Dakota line south the northern border of the Pine Ridge and Rosebud Reservations. There was the Indian wagon, the TL wagon (Hans Thode), Flying V wagon, Limekiln wagon, 73 wagon (Scotty Philip and Steube), the WM wagon, (Tom Jones and Dick Mattheison), the Lower Bad River wagon, the Turkey Track wagon, the Hart wagon, Williams from Philip and a partner on the Cheyenne River had a wagon, Matador wagon, the Rake wagon (Rounds and Anderson, and Louie Johnson, and the Three Rails wagon from the Hermosa, Buffalo Gap, Rapid Creek, and Box Elder Creek area. The roundup wagons set out to cover every bit of South Dakota west of the Missouri River. Each roundup wagon was really two wagons: a cook's wagon and bedroll wagon. The crew for each roundup wagon consisted of the foreman, the cook, a horse wrangler, a night hawk, and the "reps." The reps were sent

A typical roundup scene on the Cheyenne River.
Photo courtesy of the South Dakota State Historical Society.

by any cattleman who thought that some of his cattle might have drifted into the area being worked by that particular wagon. The large outfits sent a rep with every wagon. Each rep showed up with his horse hobbles, a few personal effects in his "war bag," a bedroll, and a string of six to ten horses – all geldings. He wore a six shooter, had a lariat hanging from his saddle, and carried a slicker across the back of his saddle. These were the tools of his trade.

A roundup day began at the crack of dawn with the cook's call. The nighthawk had the horses in a rope corral by the time breakfast was finished. A man who was handy with a rope entered the corral and roped the horse requested by each cowboy. The men then went over to the wagon boss for orders.

The foreman first picked the men to relieve the hands guarding the herd. These men would hold the animals until noon. The boss then told the cook where to make the next camp and designated the place for the forenoon roundup.

Two men well acquainted with that particular range were chosen as circle leaders. Each man took half of the riders and went in opposite directions around the area to be worked. The circle leader dropped off a man or two every mile and ordered them to work certain draws. As the range was worked, every critter was pushed toward the center of the circle. Initially, there were only a few head of cattle; but their numbers grew as the circle tightened. Hundreds of bellering cattle were soon on the move. When the herd was gathered, a few men held them while the rest went to the wagon to eat lunch and to change horses. The herd was then worked.

Three or four good ropers rode into the cow herd, put a rope on a calf, dragged it to the branding fire, and announced the mother's brand. The calf was scorched with the same brand its mother bore and castrated if it bore the equipment. It was then time for supper. After the evening meal, two or three cowboys caught their night horses and relieved the men guarding the cattle herd. The nighthawk took over the saddle horses from the horse wrangler. Three shifts of night guards for the herd were announced. The nighthawk started the cook's breakfast in the early morning hours and woke the cook. All too soon the cook was yelling, "Come and get it or I'll throw it out," and it started over again.

Sixteen roundup wagons worked the Rosebud Reservation in 1902. Eight wagons began along the border with Pine Ridge and worked east under the direction of Jack Whipple. The rest started at the east end of Rosebud and worked west. They converged at the forks of the White River, just above the town of Westover, on June 25th. Throwback wagons from as far away as North Dakota and Montana were there to meet them and to collect their stock. D.L. McLane, who was clerking for the Rosebud Agency, was on hand to check the cattle across White River and assess each owner a dollar a head. The reps at this encampment covered all the West River country clear to the Yellowstone River. There were roughly 500 cowboys, 4,000 horses, and 50,000 cattle. The 20-mile-wide encampment stretched for 30 miles along the Little White River, earning its place in western history for being the biggest roundup the world has ever seen. The disaster that was about to strike only added to its lore.

A line of black clouds rolled up in the northwest on June 26th. By 4:00 p.m. it was almost dark. The cowboys knew they were in for a heavy rain. Tent stakes were driven in deeper. Wagons were tied down. A double guard was put on the cattle. The storm struck about 8:00 p.m. It began as a terrible wind. The tents were sucked into the air and blown away. Richard Jones, who was with the White River Pool, was able to get under a bed wagon. The wind blew the tied-down wagon as high as the ropes would let it. Over the nearly deafening din of the storm, Jones could hear a young cowboy in the wagon praying for all he was worth. The men on horseback were blown, saddles and all, over the horses' head. Anyone who couldn't find shelter was blown across the prairie like a tumbleweed.

Then as suddenly as it struck, the wind ceased. It was followed by a torrent of rain laced with hail the size of turkey eggs. Bill Bigelow, a man known to stretch the truth to make a point, claimed that a hailstone glanced off his head and struck a full grown steer between the eyes, knocking the animal to the ground. Every cowboy who couldn't find protection, and there were lots of them, was beaten black and blue.

The hail and rain no more than let up when lightning crashed and thunder rolled over the prairie. It seemed as if the whole earth was on fire. Fifty thousand head of cattle and 4,000 horses stampeded. Albert Walker, a hand with the Native Cattle Company, was killed by a lightning strike. The same bolt killed his horse and two steers. Will Hughs was riding by a knoll when lightning struck it. The bolt killed a cow and knocked down his horse. Elsewhere, Dick Wickert was killed by a lightning strike.

The full extent of the disaster was not comprehended until morning. The camp was in chaos. The wind had rolled many of the wagons into the river, where they were washed away. Other wagons had been blown into the bottom of a nearby canyon and wrecked beyond repair. Most of the 500 cowboys were on foot. Their horses and the cattle were scattered over 50 miles.

The men were two days in retrieving their horses and getting their roundup outfits into working shape. The cowboys milled in the mud and forded the swollen river and creeks to re-gather the cattle. However, the roundup was completed on schedule – the fourth of July.

After the 1902 roundup, the Indian Service fenced the northern boundaries of the Rosebud and Pine Ridge Reservations. A combination of native red cedar and steel posts were placed every rod along the boundary. Five strands of barbed wire were tightly stretched from post to post. Indians were hired as fence riders to repair broken fence, to make sure the gates onto the Reservation were kept shut, and to drive off cattle that congregated next to the fence. The five-strand barbed wire fence along the north border of the Rosebud and the Pine Ridge reservations was the death knell for the big roundups, and it signaled that the day of the open range was about over. It ended in 1905.

In 1905, spring came early. The livestock had shed their winter coats by April and were chasing green grass. Cattle prices were strong. Corb Morse had shipped in 3,600 two-year-old, white-face steers, distributing them in four bunches from Smithville on the Cheyenne River to present-day Kadoka. Everywhere, the range was heavily stocked.

A warm spring rain began on the evening of May 2nd. The ranchers saw the moisture as yet another sign of a good year in the cattle business. By morning, everything was drenched. It was getting colder. The wind had picked up. The rain turned to snow. The cattle's matted, wet hair froze on their backs. The temperature continued to drop, the winds got progressively stronger, and the snowfall increased. The next day, May 4th, the snow began to drift. The prairie was enveloped in a white-out. On May 5th, the storm became a howling blizzard so with visibility reduced to near zero. The snow was blown into drifts 17-feet deep.

The cattle started moving before the wind. As their numbers grew, their pace quickened. The drifting became a stampede.[15] Baldy Williams of the Triangle Ranch saddled a horse and followed the herd for a few miles, trying to get ahead of them, but his horse played out plunging through the deep snow, and

Williams went home. George Porch was above the wall checking on his stock when the winds brought him the sound of the stampede. He rode to a location ahead of the herd and did his best to turn them. But even singeing the cattle's' noses with pistol shots could not turn the herd into the biting wind. The stampeding cattle almost ran over Porch and his horse. Driven by the wind and the biting cold, the entire herd ran headlong over the Badlands wall and plunged 200 feet to their deaths.[16]

Every rancher lost cattle in the blizzard of May 5, 1905. Gus Craven, who had his stock in well-sheltered, timbered draws below the south Badlands wall lost only 50 head. Others were not so fortunate. Ranchers who grazed their stock north of the Badlands wall lost heavily. Martin Johnson lost 5,000 sheep and a herder. Warren Young had 3,000 lambs and 65 horses plunge to their death. Corb Morse lost 6,000 head over the Badlands wall, and elsewhere he lost another 5,000 head. Livestock that did not go over the wall died less mercifully. Thousands of cattle drifted into swollen creeks and the raging White River. Unable to get up the slippery banks, the cattle either drowned or froze to death. White River was so choked with dead cattle that their carcasses formed a dam that had to be dynamited to lower the building flood waters. After the storm was over and the temperature rose to a seasonable level, the stench of rotting cattle and horses was unbearable.

The sun rose on May 6th to a crystal-clear sky and a temperature of 20 below zero. Isam Brown, foreman of the 6L on Cain Creek, rolled his clothes into a few blankets and rode east. When he reached Dude Rounds' place, he put his horse in the barn. Brown walked into Rounds' house and without so much as a greeting went to the cupboard and took down a bottle of whiskey. Sitting down to the table he poured himself a drink. "I'll be leaving these parts, Dude. Corb Morse won't be needin' a foreman for some time. He's completely wiped out."

A few days later a 6L rider reached Rapid City. He found Corb Morse in the Harney Hotel. The crestfallen cowboy reluctantly informed Corb Morse that he had lost over 10,000 head of cattle. Morse merely commented, "Easy come, easy go."

The blizzard of 1905 proved once again and for the final time that cattle cannot be profitably raised on the open range. Nineteen winters out of 20 in the Dakotas are reasonably open. The snow depths remain light. The January thaw comes on schedule, and cattle can survive. But experience had shown that a killer blizzard, the kind that devastates entire herds, can be expected once every two decades.

When the homesteaders arrived in mass in 1907 they met little resistance from the cattle barons. The day of the open range had already come to an end.

Notes

[A] There are two stories about how it came that Frank Turner shot Frank Lynn. One version has it that Frank Lynn strung up a barb wire fence to keep the cattlemen's livestock from a watering hole. The sheepmen, meaning Doll Johnson, tell that story. The other version is told by the descendants of cattlemen. According to the cattlemen's version, Frank Turner hauled firewood to Frank Lynn and his wife. However, Frank Lynn and his wife did not have a cordial relationship. While Lynn was out herding sheep for months on end, the sheepherder became obsessed with the idea that Frank Turner was sparking Mrs. Lynn. Believing that, Frank Lynn borrowed a six-shooter from Dude Rounds, got liquored up, and went looking for Frank Turner. He found Frank Turner on Dude Rounds' ranch building a pole barn. Lynn pulled his borrowed six-shooter and started blazing away at Turner. However, Lynn was a sheepherder and a drunk one at that. He missed. Frank Turner grabbed his 30-30 Winchester, and he shot Lynn in self-defense. Frank Turner rode to Pierre and informed the law of the incident. No charges were brought.

CHAPTER 11
Starvation Claims

The Milwaukee Railroad pushed through the Badlands in 1907 and down its tracks came the dispossessed and the disappointed naively believing they could make a living off 160 acres of barren Badlands. By 1910 a homesteader's shack could be found on almost every quarter section. "The Government bet the homesteaders," as a local wag put it, "160 acres against their $14 filing fee that within five years the homesteader would either freeze to death or starve. It was a pretty safe bet – safe, that is, for the government."[1]

A "farm" in the Badlands.
Photo courtesy of the Department of Interior, Badlands National Park.

The Chicago, Milwaukee & St. Paul Railroad entered into negotiations in 1890 with the U.S. Government pursuant to laying tracks from Chamberlain to Rapid City. A deal was struck. The government would give the Milwaukee Railroad 20 acres for station ground every ten miles along the route, 640 acres of land on the west bank of the Missouri River, and 188 acres along the north edge of Chamberlain if they would build the railroad.[2] However, it was not until 1905 that the Milwaukee Railroad put a pontoon bridge over the Missouri at Chamberlain and began laying track west.[3]

Wanting freight for its trains and buyers for the town lots in its station yards, the railroad advertised widely that homesteaders could acquire 160 acres of *prime* farm ground in the White River valley merely by staking a claim. People flocked to the Badlands by the thousands expecting to grow lush crops, to become prosperous farmers, and to own land. In accordance with the Homestead Act of 1862, all they had to do was pay a $14 filing fee, put ten acres under cultivation, and live on the land for five years. Once they "proved up" and paid an additional $14, the land was theirs. Alternatively, the homesteader could live on the land for fourteen months and then buy the land for the price of $1.25 per acres. In 1907, few of the would-be homesteaders had the $200 it took to buy the land. So most of the homesteaders in the Badlands acquired their 160 acres the hard way – they lived on the land for five years.

Lured by these advertisements for "free land," a few homesteaders came to the Badlands ahead of the tracks. Frank and Pearl Andrews, newlyweds, were one such couple.[4] They started west from Mitchell on a cold blustery day in early November 1905 with all of their belongings and a winter's supply of food packed in a horse-drawn wagon. Three days later they reached Chamberlain and lodged in the Musman Hotel.

The next day, they crossed the river on the ferry and headed west. Their team could not pull the heavily loaded wagon up the Seven Mile Hill. To lighten the load, the hillside soon was strewn with potatoes, flour, coffee, and other precious food. Cresting the hill, they followed the grass-filled ruts laid down two decades earlier by freighters and traveled for two days without seeing man nor beast.

On the third day they saw in the distance great herds of cattle milling around water holes and roaming the prairie in search of grass. A light snow was falling. It melted upon hitting on the ground. Gumbo rolled up on the wheels so thick the horses could not pull the wagon. Grabbing a spade, Frank scraped six inches of gumbo off the wheels and urged the horses on, but the team pulled the wagon only a short distance before the wheels again balled up. Frank had to walk beside the wagon, continuously going from wheel to wheel cleaning off the gumbo. The couple grew thirsty from their labors, but they had used all of their water. At last, they caught the sun's reflection off a tin can perched on a post. Beside it was a spring.

After a hundred miles they came to some dilapidated log buildings that, in the West, represented civilization and passed for a roadhouse. It wasn't a pretty picture. They told Ernie Place, the proprietor, that they were on their way to Little Buffalo Creek to homestead.

"You had better see Charlie Thompson when you get there," Place solemnly advised. "He's a hunter and a scout. If he likes you, it will be all right. You'll be safe. But if Thompson doesn't like you, you had better turn around and go back. These are bad times. Watch your step. There is no law here – only the gun."

The Andrews rose early the next morning. Disgusted by their lodging and apprehensive about what lay ahead, they harnessed their team in silence and pulled out. They drove all day without letup. Just before dusk, they pulled to the top of a hill. To the southwest, the setting sun cast shadows on the Badlands making them look, as the earliest travelers had noticed, like the ruins of an ancient city. To the north and west lay rolling prairie as far as the eye could reach. Below them ran Little Buffalo Creek and their potential homestead.

The next day, the Andrews went four miles down the creek to Charley Thompson's place, which had become known as "Recluse" in 1898 when Ida became the postmistress. Even though it was a cold November day, several of Thompson's seven children were playing outdoors barefoot.

The oldest child (John Lloyd) was 17, and he had never seen a town nor attended school.

Charley Thompson sold the Andrews logs that were intended for his children's school house and helped drag the logs to Andrews' claim so they could build a cabin. The young couple interpreted Thompson's actions as a welcome and concluded that it was safe for them to stay.

Not all of the early homesteaders were similarly received. Tony Flynn, a settler in the Interior area, told the Andrews that it would not be long before they got an insatiable craving for the taste of butter, chicken, eggs, milk, or fresh meat – all unavailable to a homesteader. He admonished them against succumbing to the temptation of shooting one of the plentiful cows which grazed all around them. Flynn told the Andrews that some so-stricken homesteaders occasionally went out at night and shot a "jackrabbit" – really a calf. One such poacher had recently died of what was euphemistically called "lead poisoning." The shooting wasn't investigated. "The only law," Flynn informed them, "is in Fort Pierre. It takes a week to get there, and it is another week before anyone comes out to investigate. By then, a lot of evidence gets lost and memories grow dim."

Ida Thompson's health began to fail in 1905, and she died in 1907. Taking up the duties of the postmaster, Charley threw the homesteaders' mail into an apple crate. Any honyocker, as the cowboys called them, who came by for mail was told, "If ya kin find any in thar with yur name on 'er, I reckon ya can have it." No one complained about the service. Every homesteader within a radius of 20 miles knew that Charley Thompson ended each day by using a hammer to start a few nails into a dead cottonwood tree, and he began each day by driving the nails into the tree by shooting at them with his pistol – just to keep the touch.[5]

Despite the reception that many honyockers received from Charley Thompson and other old-timers like him, the homesteaders kept coming. By 1911, Charley Thompson could not stand them any more. He sold out and moved to Forsyth, Montana. But if the prospective homesteaders had only known what the Badlands had in store for them, Charley Thompson could have stayed on Little Buffalo Creek and the open range would have lasted forever.

The hardships endured by the Charles Fetch family were a case in point.[6] The Fetch family left Presho in January of 1906 in a covered wagon. The temperature was well below zero and a cold wind drove falling snow at them. Mrs. Fetch and her six small children huddled, nearly frozen, in the bottom of the wagon. Just before dark, they came to a roadhouse operated by the Devine family. There, the Fetch family got a hot supper in front of a warm fire and a good night's rest.

Recluse.
Photo courtesy of South Dakota State Historical Society.

The second day was still cold and stormy. They jolted, jostled, and shivered from dawn until dusk. It was well after dark when they came to Ernie Place's roadhouse. Supper was stale bread, fried potatoes, a small piece of unidentifiable meat. After supper, the Fetches were taken to a sod shanty without heat and shown three bunks made of boards. There were no mattresses. The bedding was a stiff horse-hide.

In the morning, the Fetchs set out on the third and last day of their journey. It was still snowing and bitter cold; but the wind had quit, which was a good thing. If it had been blowing it would have whipped the several feet of snow on the prairie into a ground blizzard and the family would have perished. After what seemed an eternity, they reached their new home – a one-room shanty with a dirt floor that Mr. Fetch had previously built out of whatever material he could find. The only furnishings were three bunks and an old broken stove. The damper didn't work on the stove. The wind either sucked the heat up the chimney or blew the smoke into the house. The only fuel was cow chips that the children walked about the prairie to collect. They had brought a supply of staples with them, but they rarely had fresh meat or vegetables. Their water came from melted snow. Soap was a luxury they couldn't afford. Mrs. Fetch was expected to make the shanty into a home for eight people, feed them, and keep their clothes clean.

Kadoka

The first train arrived in Kadoka on December 21, 1906.[7] It was crowded with would-be homesteaders. It seemed that half of Iowa, eastern South Dakota and eastern Nebraska were coming out to homestead. Amongst the newcomers could be found people of every work, business, or profession: preachers, teachers, barkeepers, gamblers, grass widows, old maids, bachelors, cooks, clerks, street-car conductors, bakers, stonemasons, farmers, fiddlers, doctors, dressmakers, and prostitutes. Many of them paid a "locater" to find them 160 acres to homestead. Some locators guided the homesteaders to 160 acres plots in the Badlands where an ant would have starved to death.

The Milwaukee Railroad temporarily terminated for the winter of 1906–1907 above the "Hodoka," which in Lakota means hole in the (Badlands) wall. As a temporary railroad terminus, Kadoka had an influx of fly-by-night businesses, hastily started by people who thought they could make a few dollars off of the town's short, but lively surge. Queenie and Georgia Parker, two sisters, followed the track down from Presho to establish a notorious rooming house. Scott Wellman and Ike Wilfang ran a restaurant out of a tent. Ernie Place ran a saloon called the Cowboys' Home out of a tar-paper shack. The Black Pipe, another saloon, was just down the street. The seeds of social order were also planted in Kadoka. Miss Lenora McCarthy became the postmistress in 1906. In the fall of 1907, Miss Ethel Jewett started a tuition school. A 30-foot well was hand dug in 1908 right in the middle of the main street. The town was off to an auspicious beginning.

Most businesses that planned to make a go of it in Kadoka were operating by 1909. They were:

General Merchandise
Chastka and Co.

Clothing and Shoes
R.W. Gross, proprietor

Hardware and Mechanic Tools
J.T. Doty, proprietor

Confectionery, Cigars & Fruits
Otto C. Sharon, proprietor

Kadoka Machine Shop
F.L. Edwards, proprietor

Hardware and Machinery
A.C. Zemanek

Pool Hall
F.E. Reidinger, owner

F.E. Reidinger Land Agency

Livery Barn
Rohan brothers

General Merchandise
Chamie and Beraney

Lumber, Coal, Wire & Salt
Jas. A. Smith

Furniture Making
R.G. Skove

Hats & Millinery
Mrs. F.E. Reidinger

Harnesses, Saddles & Tack
J.A. Fraser

Methodist Church

Skrove Bros. Land Company

Fullerton Lumber Co.

General Merchandise
Johnson & Moore

The Bank of Kadoka
Martin Johnson, president
O.E. Stuart, cashier

Kadoka State Bank
W.T. McConnell, president
W.C. Meyer, cashier

Fresh & Cured Meats
Rogers & Eddy

Kadoka Drug Store
Mr. Doren, proprietor

General Merchandise
G.G. Skrove

Hanford Produce Co.
(butter, eggs & cream)

Dacotah Hotel
Martin Johnson, proprietor

Kadoka House (hotel)
C.B. Gilchrist, owner

Volunteer Fire Department

Presbyterian Church

Catholic Church

Kadoka Grain Co.

208   *Philip S. Hall*

The First School in Kadoka.
Photo courtesy of Lois Prokop.

Kadoka became a trade center not only for the homesteaders but also for the Indians from the nearby Rosebud Reservation. The Indian trade was welcomed, but it occasionally created uncertainties among businessmen who were unfamiliar with the Indian people. Mr. McConnell, the President of the Kadoka State Bank, was a case in point.

During the fall of 1911 Silas Breast, a full-blood Sioux Indian, came into McConnell's bank wanting to borrow $100 so he could buy his family's winter food supply.[8] McConnell wanted the business, but being uncertain about loaning a hundred dollars to an unknown Indian, he asked Silas what he could give as collateral.

"Collateral?" Silas asked. "What is collateral?"

"Collateral," the bank president explained, "is something that you own which is worth a hundred dollars. Something the bank could have if you were unable pay back the loan. Do you have any cattle, any sheep, or any horses?"

"Oh, me got a hundred ponies," Silas replied.

The answer came too quickly and was too exact to satisfy the cagey banker. McConnell decided to put the Indian off until he could find someone who knew Silas Breast and could verify whether he had a hundred ponies.

Pettyjohn crew building railroad track from Murdo to Rapid City.
Photo courtesy of South Dakota State Historical Society.

The banker searched the town during the noon hour for someone who might know Silas. Luckily, he found Philip Wells, the interpreter at Pine Ridge during the Wounded Knee massacre who now ranched south of Kadoka. Wells told McConnell that Silas Breast did not have ponies; rather, Silas had a hundred, top-quality horses and Wells knew that Silas had a contract to sell the horses in the spring to the U.S. Army. Satisfied, McConnell loaned Silas the $100 that afternoon in exchange for a mortgage on a hundred horses.

When spring came, Silas walked into the Kadoka State Bank with a check from the U.S. Government for $3,000. The lady at the teller's window was reluctant to cash such a large check, even if it was from the U.S. Government. She took the check into McConnell. He told the teller to cash the check with the proviso that Silas pay off his loan. Silas paid the note, pocketed the remaining cash, and walked out the door.

Having observed the transaction, McConnell was beside himself seeing that much money leave the bank's vault and go down the street. "Mr. Breast, Mr. Breast," McConnell called as he ran down the street after Silas, "Why don't you leave that money with the bank?" Silas stared at the banker in disbelief. "Oh, of course we'll give you interest," McConnell added.

"Interest?" Silas asked, "What is interest?"

"Remember when you borrowed a hundred dollars last fall," McConnell reminded him, "and now you paid back a hundred dollars plus seven more. Well, the seven dollars was interest. You leave your money with the bank and we'll pay you interest."

First train penetrating the Badlands, April 14, 1907.

The Indian studied the banker from his leather shoes up to his wire rimmed glasses. Perplexed by what he saw, Silas asked the banker, "How many ponies you got?"

When the railroad grade was extended past Kadoka, Elroy Pettyjohn got the subcontract to build the grade. The grade work was done with teams of horses and mules, pulling Fresno scrappers and graders. A lot of men were required. The men had to be fed, and they liked to eat meat. George Porch got a contract to supply the beef at eight and a half cents a pound. He made good money delivering a quarter of a beef to Pettyjohn's construction camp every day.[9]

Elroy Pettyjohn had a sister, Maude. Maude had been married twice, and she had three daughters and a son from the previous marriages. Maude showed an interest in George. Looking back on it, George realized that she was interested in him only because he was pretty well fixed. "And that means somethin' to a woman who's got to work fer a livin.'"

George Porch married Maude Dee Peu in 1913. He was 51. After a while, "we knowed we was gonna have a baby. I prayed to God it would be a son. I started workin' extra hard at the ranch, all the time think' how I'd fix it up fer him and make ever' cent I could. Of course, I didn't know a damn thing 'bout gettin' ready fer a baby, and I left it all up to her. She resented it, and made up her mind to leave me. We wasn't very good company fer awhile."

The baby was a son. He was named Parley-George's mother's maiden name. George loved that baby more than anything in the world. But the baby was weak. When Parley was two-years-old, he caught measles and died. As George stood over his son's grave and the dirt clattered down on the little coffin, tears flowed down George's hardened face. "I'll be joinin' yuh soon, Parley," he whimpered.

When the railroad construction was finished, George Porch started a butcher shop in Kadoka. He rode up from his ranch several times a week to check on it. On one such trip, Porch stayed in town after the butcher shop closed because his brother Ab was coming back from visiting their parents in Missouri. The train arrived at 2:30 in the morning, but Ab wasn't on it. George started for home. He usually went home by way of a well-worn trail, but it was a cold, dark night laced with wind-blown snow. Feeling chilled, George wanted to get home as soon as possible and crawl into his warm bed. There was a place along the trail where a little distance could be saved by leaving the path. George took the shortcut, and he kicked his horse Smokey into a lope. All at once the horse struck fence that a homesteader had built right across the trail. Smokey hit the fence hard, tearing loose for two or three posts. The panicked horse ran along barbed wire fence, and barbed wire sawed its way into the lower part of Porch's right leg. When George finally got the horse away from the fence, he felt blood pouring out of his leg. He knew his leg was cut to pieces, and that he'd never live long enough to make it home. So George turned the horse into the wind-blown snow and whipped his horse all the way back to Kadoka. Seeing a light on in the pool hall, George reined his horse to a stop right at the door. The horse died on the spot. George somehow made it to the pool hall door, opened it, and fell inside.

The patrons laid George on pool table. His pulsating blood spurted to the ceiling. Someone tied a clean dish towel tight over the cut, and they carried George over to the Martin Johnson hotel. In the morning, Susie Barr looked in on Porch. She found him in pool of blood and unconscious. Susie called for help. They put him on the next train to Chamberlain, and Susie Barr stayed with Porch all the way to the hospital in Chamberlain.

George was in the Chamberlain hospital for a long time. No one, not the doctors or even George, thought he'd live. George directed that all of his cattle be sold, and he also sold his ranch to Elroy Pettyjohn. George eventually got out of the hospital. However, he never again rode anything but a gentle horse. His leg healed, but only partially. A cavity remained where most of the calf muscle had been torn away. Skin grew over the hole. But for the rest of Porch's life, the wound occasionally became infected and oozed puss. When it did, George drained the pus and backed the cavity with a little strychnine, which he believed cut down on the poison.

George and Maude had another baby in 1916 – girl whom they named Mary Elsie. But things came to head in the family in 1928. Maude left George, forcing George and Mary Elsie to go it alone.

Weta

Weta was ten miles to farther west and below the Hodoka (hole in the wall).[10] The town was established near a reservoir built by the railroad to provide water for their steam-powered locomotives. Weta, the Lakota word for island, referred to a small island formed by the reservoir.

Anise Mills, a widow woman with four small children, was one of the first to take up residence in Weta. The Milwaukee Railroad rented her the section house with the stipulation that she board the section foreman, Charley Davis, and his crew of eight men. When the track was finished in 1907. Most of the railroad crew was laid off. Mrs. Mills was out of a job and out of a way to pay the rent; and Charley Davis was out of a place to live. Be it love or convenience, Anise Mills and Charley Davis solved their respective problems by getting married.

A school was started in Weta with Mrs. Bill Gilchrist and Mrs. Russell as the first teachers. They taught classes in their claim shacks until a school house was built in the fall of 1908. Ed Freemole and his wife Emma came to Weta in 1908. They built the town's only general store. It also served as the post office. Fred was the postmaster. The mail destined for Wanblee, the Indian village south of White River, was dropped off in Weta and given to anyone in town, white or Indian, going to Wanblee. When Wanblee became an official post office in 1916, Blake Fiske got the contract to carry the mail there. Blake hauled the mail in a wagon pulled by four small horses. Fiske had to ford White River and then cross Buckle Creek (now often called Craven Creek) 18 times to get to Wanblee. Fiske's team and wagon once got bogged down in the sands of White River. He took the wagon apart and carried it, a piece at a time, to the other side. There, he reassembled the wagon and went on his way. Another time, the wagon tipped over while Fiske was swimming the team across the swollen river. He left his son on the drifting wagon while he swam for shore holding the mail out of the water.

Money was hard to come by for the homesteaders. They did what they could to earn a little cash. The homesteaders in the Weta area were particularly enterprising. Herman Barber grew broom corn on his claim and set up a factory in his house so his wife and children could make brooms. When the corn crop failed, he shipped in a supply of corn tassels. The family traded the brooms to Ed Freemole's general store for groceries. Peter Simon homesteaded ten miles out of town, but he came into Weta every day to run his blacksmith shop. John

McHenry and his family came to Weta in 1908 and built the town's only hotel. McHenry brought in 20 thoroughbreds thinking that he could capitalize on the cowboys' infatuation with tall, fast horses. Failing to appreciate the harshness of a Badlands winter, McHenry did not provide them any shelter. That winter, all but four mares froze to death.

What little cash the homesteaders earned came from cows—dead ones and live ones. A fertilizer company back East paid two dollars a ton for bones. Homesteaders in the Badlands brought in bleached-white cattle bones, remnants of the blizzard of 1905, by the wagon load. Live cows, or rather the cream they produced, was the homesteaders' only reliable source of cash. But 160 acres of Badlands would not support more than the requisite team of horses and a couple of cows. The typical homesteader sold five gallons of cream a week, which brought in three dollars—barely enough money to get by.

For a while, Weta thrived. A high school was started in 1911. Miss Soule was the instructor of its five children. Awakened from her sleep in McHenry's hotel on the night of May 15, 1912 by the smell of smoke, Miss Soule raced into the hall to rouse the other hotel guests and to help them get out of the building. As people gathered to watch the fire, Miss Soule remembered an eight-year-old child who had been sleeping in an adjoining room. She dashed into the inferno, but found that the child had escaped through a small window. As Miss Soule fled the burning building, the stairs gave way under her. Miss Soule somehow fought her way outside and collapsed on the street. She was taken to the hospital in Chamberlain where she was several months recovering.

Interior

Ten miles away, Interior sat along the north bank of White River waiting for the railroad. But the railroad passed two miles to the north of the original town, and the town had to move. Clet Hight built the first house in the new town. C. Allen Moore established the new town's first business – a newspaper. The first edition of the *Interior Index* was printed on May 10, 1907 in a ten foot by twelve foot tar paper shack. Moore and his family lived nearby in a tent. Like most businesses in the Badlands, the paper was dependent on the one-time flash of activity from homesteaders. The *Interior Index* printed the legally required notice that John Q. Homesteader had "proved up" on his claim and was ready to apply for a patent deed.

Interior was already an established trade center, and the new town grew quickly. By 1910, the following businesses had been established:

| The Home Cafe | Eagle Livery Barn |
| *Mrs. Hatti Swett, owner* | *Charlie Smalley, proprietor* |

214 *Philip S. Hall*

**Interior of the Johnson brothers' store, circa 1910.
Left to right: George Johnson, Sam Petit and John Ellingson.**
Photo courtesy Department of Interior, Badlands National Park.

Bank
initially owned by the Bullard brothers, soon sold to O.E. & Harlan Snodgrass

Saloon
Jim Six, proprietor

Blacksmith Shop
John Cotant, owner

Confectionery Store & Hotel
W.R. Burkholder, owner

Hotel
Mr. Swartz, proprietor

General Store
James Smalley, proprietor

Drug Store
Earl Roberts, owner
Clet Hight, manager

Lumber Yard
J.F. Sigrist, owner

Ranchers' Supply
Louis & George Johnson, owners

Hardware Store
Ed Sauders, proprietor

Presbyterian Church

Methodist Church

James Smalley's General Store in Interior. James Smalley is behind the left counter. Charles Smalley is behind the right counter.
Photo courtesy of Jerry Smalley.

Interior was haunted from the beginning by fires. Swartz's hotel, merely a tar paper shack, burned to the ground in 1908, and it was not rebuilt. George & Louis Johnsons' two-story general store and several adjacent buildings went up in flames the next fall. But with the determination characteristic of those that "made it" in the Badlands, the Johnson brothers rebuilt.

Fires were hard to bring under control because the town lacked water. The Milwaukee Railroad dug a cistern at the depot and kept it filled with water hauled from Rapid City. But at 50 cents a barrel, the water was used only for drinking. The citizens put in a dam across a draw west of town to water livestock. James Smalley attempted to dig a well; but after digging 100 feet down into a dry hole, he gave up. The Milwaukee engineers drew up a plan in 1910 to get water from the river for an estimated cost of $5,000. The townspeople passed a bond to cover the expenses, but the railroad decided that it had plenty of water elsewhere and cancelled the project. Bert White, head of the water supply department for the railroad, agreed to contract independently with the town to put in a water system. A ditch was dug by hand, a two-inch line was laid, a water tank was built, and a pump was installed. The town finally had an adequate supply of water.[11]

To draw even more homesteaders to the Badlands, the Milwaukee Railroad brought out a steam-powered tractor that pulled a six-bottom plow, and it was used to break hundreds of acres of sod.[12] The freshly plowed ground laid fallow for the rest the summer, and it absorbed the fall rains and the melt from the winter snow. The first crop of corn thrived on the precious moisture and the nutrients from the decaying prairie grass, and it produced. But "sod corn" was nature's ruse to lure more homesteaders to the Badlands. The second crop, lacking both the nutrients and the moisture, withered away when struck by the first hot winds of July. The Badlands had taught the homesteaders yet another lesson.

Discouraged but not yet defeated, the homesteaders continued searching for a way to eke a living out of the harsh land. Bill Hickox, who by then had married a homesteader's daughter, knew that in some select places along White River the ground was relatively fertile. He thought that if the land was given water it could produce. Hickox bought a Fairbanks & Morse Irrigation Pump and used it to suck water from White River to irrigate a hundred acres, He raised a lush crop of alfalfa.[13]

Hickox's irrigation system was so successful that the Stock Grower's Bank in Pierre bought 320 acres along White River from Corb Morse. They installed an irrigation pump and induced Charley Carlbom, Roy Norby, Dave Bull, Nels Emmett, Fred Pengra, Happy Thompson, Roy Oberling, Douglas Canon, and Elsie Woodburn to come out to the Badlands and work the irrigated ground for a share of the crop. The Irrigation Colony was located seven miles west of Interior. The colony raised vegetables, corn, watermelons, and muskmelons by the bushel; and cabbage by the ton. It was a success – to a point. There was no market for the produce. Their potatoes sold for 35 cents a bushel. Cabbage brought only five dollars a ton. The Irrigation Colony soon went out of business.[14]

Conata

Conata, which means skull in Lakota, was next town west of Interior. The town was built near the site of the Milwaukee's second reservoir in the Badlands. Like all of the towns in the Badlands, the railroad was the thread that held the town together. Mrs. Hudspeth was the depot agent. Willie Ness was the section foreman. Two middle-aged, unmarried sisters, Harriet and Bea DeHaan, came from Pella, Iowa to start a general store. Harriet was also the postmistress. Either she or Bea faithfully met the train to pick up the mail in a big-wheeled, platform cart. Most of the town folk followed the cart back to the general store to immediately see if they had received any mail. There was another general store in town. Chris Heuther ran it. Minnie Steel ran a boarding house. It was primarily used by the railroad crew.[15]

Ernest B. Yoast, a cousin of Isam Brown, the foreman of the 6L, came to the Badlands from Iowa.[16] As a young man, he worked for Brown as a bronc buster until a fall from a horse broke his jaw. He bought the livery barn in Conata and married Myrtle Campbell in 1911. Their first two children died as infants and were among the first buried in the Conata Cemetery. Mrs. Yoast was a nurse, and she was much in demand for assistance with health problems and medical emergencies.

The town had a Catholic Church and a Protestant church, a two-story school house, and a dance hall. Conata didn't have a saloon and its population, including every homesteader within sight, never exceeded 50 people.

However, Conata had a mining and manufacturing company. Art Hegemen was convinced that the barren Badlands must be good for something. So he set up a mining operation in an area of the Badlands north of Conata that was rich in volcanic ash. Hegemen also built a processing plant on the edge of town to wash, sift, and package his ore. He marketed the Badlands diggings under the name of the Knife and Fork Brand Metal Polish. Hegemen even induced Henry Warner, the president and treasurer of the Warner Hotel Company in Chicago, to endorse the product.[17]

> We cannot refrain from writing you of our experience with the Knife and Fork Brand Metal Polish. We have tried many polishes for our table silver, plate, brass and copper but two years ago we found what we believed was the best. For the last ninety days we have used the Knife and Fork Brand, testing it against all others and found that your product is far superior. It

Main Street, Conata, South Dakota, 1910.

cleans easier and quicker, and gives a higher polish and the metal stays clean longer. We will need some more in about thirty days.

Citing this endorsement, Hegemen advertised the metal polish far and wide saying that upon receipt of 25 cents a full can of it would be mailed anywhere in the United States or Canada. Only the Milwaukee Railroad bought much of the cleaner, and then only for a short time. The Milwaukee stopped using Knife and Fork metal polish when they began to lay off passenger cars. Hegemen soon went out of the mining business. Shortly thereafter, he became "woman crazy" and was sent to the State Mental Institution in Yankton.

Imlay

The town of Imlay lay ten miles west of Conata.[18] It was named for Imlay Tibbitts, a son of Ben Tibbitts and a nephew of well-known fur trader Nick Janis. The little town consisted of a general store, a post office, a pool hall and a dance hall – all run by W.H. "Harry" Godfrey. Mrs. Winnifred Bright, Frank Bright's wife, ran the post office and sold some groceries. Valentine Bretts was the Milwaukee section foreman stationed at Imlay. Imlay's main reason for existence was the excellent set of corrals and loading chutes located north of the tracks.

A heinous crime occurred in Imlay on Sunday morning July 5, 1908. Frank Bright was murdered. Ernest B. Randall, a homesteader and a part-time hired man for Bright, found Bright dead shortly after noon. Frank Bright was laying in his corn field with two bullet holes in his body.[19]

Only six people were known to have been in the Imlay area that morning. All of them instantly became suspects. Harry Godfrey was a prime suspect. Everyone knew that Godfrey did not like Bright, and the two had exchanged harsh words. However, Harry Godfrey and Hiram Reynolds, a mixed-blood, had attended the Fourth of July celebration in Scenic, and they had been seen in Scenic on the morning of July 5th catching the train to return to Imlay. But someone remembered that Godfrey had a race horse, and someone else recalled that Reynolds had bought a revolver in Scenic. It was theorized that Reynolds galloped over to Frank Bright's corn field, shot him, and raced back to Scenic in time to catch the morning train. But even a fast horse could not have traveled 20 miles that quickly. Deputy Sheriff Tom Hewett decided that Hiram Reynolds did not kill Frank Bright.

Valentine Betts, the section foreman, was another suspect, but he, too, had a good alibi. Betts was manning Godfrey's general store all morning. Taylor Palmer and a young woman companion were in Scenic for the Fourth of July, and they had left for Imlay in a buggy on the morning of July 5th. The young couple did seem preoccupied, but no one believed that it was murder that was on their minds. That left only two suspects: Ernest B. Randall and Mrs. Bright. Of the two, Randall seemed the most likely killer. Deputy Sheriff Hewett concluded that Ernest Randall murdered Frank Bright over jealousy of Bright's young wife. Based on that motive and the lack of a good alibi, Hewett arrested Ernest Randall on suspicion of murder. Randall was quickly brought before a coroner's jury.[20]

At the coroner's jury, Valentine Betts testified that Mrs. Bright had been in to sort the mail between 8:00 and 10:00 a.m., and that she had then left. Brett testified that he heard two shots some time between 10:00 a.m. and 12:00 noon, but hearing shots in that area was not unusual. He gave no heed to the gun fire until Ernest Randall came into the store at 3:00 p.m. to report that he had found Frank Bright in his cornfield shot to death. Betts related that a messenger was dispatched for the sheriff in Rapid City, and he and Ernest Randall stood guard over Bright's body until the sheriff arrived. Betts reported that Randall seemed scared during the night and jumped at any noise, but Betts did not venture an opinion as to who had shot Frank Bright.

Mrs. Bright was called upon to testify, and she did not waste any time implicating Randall of the murder of her husband. She told the corner's jury that her late husband had not liked Randall. But she refused to answer questions about the problems between Bright and Randall.

Ernest Randall was then called to testify in his own defense. His statements were all that the coroner's jury needed to determine that Randall was the likely murderer. When Randall was asked if he had ever been convicted of a crime, he first said "No." Then he refused to answer the question. The 38-caliber revolver that had been used to kill Frank Bright had, by then, been found. The pistol was behind the bed in Bright's homestead. Randall admitted that he occasionally carried that very revolver, but denied that he had worn the gun on the day of the murder. It then came out in court that Ernest Randall had taken a trip that spring with Frank Bright to the West Coast. But again, Randall refused to answer any questions about the events or the circumstances of the trip.

Finally, Dr. H.G. Rose testified. Dr. Rose related that Mr. Randall had been with Mrs. Bright almost constantly since the two came to Rapid City for the inquest. The doctor's testimony established the suspected motive – a love triangle. The corner's jury ordered Randall arrested and remanded to the Pennington County jail until the fall session of court.

While Ernest Randall was sitting in jail, more information came to light.[21] First, it was learned that Mrs. Rosalie Winnifred Bright was not actually Mrs. Frank Bright. She was Winnifred Bartonne from Chamberlain, or at least she went by the name of Bartonne. Really, she was Winnifred Barton; but to Winnifred's ears, Bartonne sounded more aristocratic than Barton. Winnifred's father, also of Chamberlain, had not spoken to his daughter for several years. While

220 *Philip S. Hall*

living in Chamberlain, Winnifred Barton (or was it Bartonne) married a man by the name of Lewis, but they soon separated. In 1907, Winnifred Bartonne Lewis met Frank Bright when he was in Chamberlain on business, and she came to Imlay to live with him. In the Badlands, she introduced herself as Mrs. Frank Bright.

That wasn't the only cat hiding in the bag. It was soon learned that Frank Bright was not really Frank Bright. His wife (the real one) arrived in Rapid City from Snohomish, Washington. Hilda (Bright) Halverson let it be known that the murdered man, Frank Bright, was really Marion Frank Dragoo. He went by four different aliases, and he married her under the name of C.R. Bright in 1892.

It was also learned that Marion Francis Dragoo (alias Frank Bright) had visited his wife (the real one) when he and Ernest Randall made a trip that previous winter to the West Coast. Presumably, Randall had not answered questions about the trip west because he did not want to reveal that the not-really Mrs. Frank Bright had a disputed claim on the not-really Mr. Frank Bright. Furthermore, Hilda Halverson let it be known that Ernest Randall had been convicted of a crime, just as everyone suspected. In 1893, Randall and Frank Bright stole some chickens from Percy Schubert. In the course of stealing the chickens, Mr. Schubert was murdered. Ernest Randall had spent a year in jail awaiting trial on burglary charges; but the case against Randall was dismissed

Bud Dalrymple.
Photo courtesy of the South Dakota State Historical Society.

before it went to trial. Frank Bright was convicted of the murder, and he served time for the crime.

All this information was public knowledge when Ernest Randall went to trial that fall for the murder of Frank Bright. Little new information came out at the trial. The facts of the murder were these: Frank Bright was shot with his own gun, a 38-caliber pistol. Whoever shot Frank Bright did so from atop Frank Bright's own horse. Isam Brown testified that a few months before the murder Frank Bright had produced about $1500 from a sack worn around his neck. No money was found in Bright's homestead. During the inquest, Randall was almost constantly with Winnifred Barton Randall, and Mrs. Winnifred Bright (Bartonne) bought a lot of new clothes while in Rapid City.

After hours of deliberation, the jury was deadlocked. Five believed that Ernest Randall was guilty, but seven felt the evidence was not sufficient. Randall was remanded to the Pennington County jail until a new trial could be held the next spring. Several months later, Winnifred Bartonne confessed that she had murdered Frank Bright. For the second time in his life, Randall was released from jail after serving months for a murder he did not commit.[22]

Scenic

The town of Scenic, another ten miles down the tracks, was the train's last stop before it left the Badlands and went on to Rapid City. The town was named for its picturesque setting in a broad basin surrounded by Badlands formations. Carl Bohling, a homesteader in Quinn Draw, thought that Scenic was a unique town. "It's the only place in the world," he quipped, "where you can walk across main street knee deep in mud and have dust blow in your face."[23]

Ab Jefferson was Scenic's first citizen.[24] Prior to moving to Scenic, Jefferson built a ranch snug up against the southwest base of Sheep Mountain Table. By tapping into a water seep several hundred feet up on the side of the Table and running a pipe down the butte, he had running water. In the early spring of 1905, Jefferson placed his stock on top of Sheep Mountain Table. The May blizzard pushed all of his cattle over the edge and wiped him out.

Ab Jefferson built the first business in Scenic – a saloon; it was a ten foot by twelve foot tar paper shack located south of the railroad track. Ab, who was illiterate, kept his books by scratching a tally on the saloon wall. He also had a propensity to drink too much. When he was drunk, Ab openly sold whiskey to Indians, which was a federal crime. He was arrested in 1910, convicted, and sentenced to prison at Fort Leavenworth. While being held in the Rapid City jail, Jefferson tried to cheat the Judge by drinking a bottle of strychnine; but he involuntarily vomited up the poison before it completed its work.[25]

The Hynes "Mansion" atop Sheep Table.
Photo courtesy of Peg "Dakota" (Hynes) Jurisch.

Ab Jefferson also had a hotel in Scenic. In his absence, his three daughters managed the business, and it became a notorious establishment. With a saloon on one side of the tracks and a boarding establishment of questionable repute on the other, Scenic was off to a raucous beginning. It became widely known as a wide-open town where there was usually a game of chance in progress. A lot of poker was played in the Alamo Pool Hall, Synder's livery barn, and a tar paper shack on the north edge of town belonging to Happy Hines.

Like every town in the Badlands, Scenic had water problems. Connie Hannifan dug a cistern and filled it with water hauled five miles in wooden barrels. He sold the water for ten cents a gallon. Despite the shortage of water, Scenic became a trade center for the surrounding homesteaders. Len Anderson started a grocery store in 1907. Mrs. Bill Fisk ran one of the town's two restaurants. Her husband, Bill, ran a blacksmith shop. Other establishments included a mercantile store and the Alamo Pool Hall. W.B. Lloyd, who also served as the postmaster, ran a drug store. Print Palmer started a paper, *The Scenic Observer*. Henry Snyder had a livery barn with a big hay loft that, in later years, served as a dance hall, theater, town meeting place and a basketball court. H.O. Malby built a grain elevator in 1908. Miss Sherwood, a physician, moved to Scenic. She cared for people afflicted with illness or accident and also gave advice on treating sick animals. Al Wentz had a building on main street. He lived in the back and operated a bank out of the front. There was also a lumber yard and an ice house.[26]

The town of 286 people even acquired a few vestiges of civilization. The Protestants built a Congregational Church in 1911 on Kube Table. They moved it into Scenic in 1914. Father Thomas McNaboe rode the train down from Kadoka once a week to conduct Catholic services in private homes. In 1913, the Catholics decided they should have their own priest.[27] To get one, they had to build a church. Matt Jobgen and Johnny Mulloy went around to the town's faithful Catholics asking for donations. They finally collected $200. Connie Hannifan orchestrated the construction effort. He put a strong young fellow, Clarence Jurisch, to work digging the footings.

Clarence was hard at work the day the new Catholic priest, Father McGonagall, arrived unexpectedly in town. No one had been asked to greet the priest, and he did not announce himself with the traditional black shirt and white collar. The man simply got off the train and inquired as to where the Catholic Church was being built. He found Clarence Jurisch hard at work digging the footings for the new church. The stranger walked around eyeing the work carefully, and then he proceeded to tell the young laborer that some aspects of his work needed improvements. Clarence was not one to take advice. He exploded. "Go to hell" Clarence summarily told the stranger. "I ain't working for you. I'm working for Connie Hannifan." And so that is how Father McGonagall was welcomed to the Badlands.

Upset by how he had been treated, Father McGonagall went looking for Connie Hannifan. When the priest found Hannifan, he asked, "Why do you have a smart aleck digging the footings for our new church?"

"Cuz he can dig more dirt than any ten men." The priest seemed satisfied with the answer.

Every town in the Badlands had its characters, but in Scenic the characters had a town. The colorful Frank Hart lived just west of town. Between gambling and riding unbroken horses down main street, he enlivened the town. Poker players in the livery barn occasionally looked up to see a full-grown wolf stalking down main street. It was Bruno following at the heels of his owner, Bud Dalrymple.[28]

Bud Dalrymple and his wife Nora lived west of Scenic, on Spring Creek. Bud was something of a photographer, gunsmith, and even an author; but Dalrymple was primarily a wolfer. He trapped and hunted wolves all over the Badlands, particularly in the rough canyons and draws between Spring Creek and Cuny Table. By grass-roots study, Dalrymple became an expert on wolves and their habits. He published articles about wolfing in the *Traders-Trappers Magazine* and even wrote a how-to book about wolfing. Whereas Dalrymple understood the necessity of ridding the country of an animal that killed hundreds of head of livestock, he clearly admired the grey wolf.[29]

The Hynes family, the quintessential homesteaders of the Badlands, lived 13 miles south of Scenic.[30] Mrs. Mary Hynes and her husband, William, moved to Murdo, South Dakota when the Milwaukee Railroad arrived in 1906 and the town sprang up. There, she operated a hotel and cafe. Mr. Hynes made boots. According to Mrs. Hynes, Mr. Hynes suffered a case of amnesia in the spring of 1907 and in his confusion wandered off and left his wife and eleven children.

By the time the family realized that Mr. Hynes was not coming back, the track had been laid farther west and the bloom was off Murdo's rose. Few people came by Hynes' hotel seeking lodging and the cafe did not serve many meals. Mrs. Hynes realized that if she stayed in Murdo she would not be able to feed herself and the five children who were still at home. Homesteading seemed the only option.

She rode the train to Scenic to investigate whether there was any good, unclaimed land in the area. At the hotel, Ab Jefferson gave her the sad news that most of the level ground had already been taken. The only land available, Jefferson informed Mrs. Hynes, was on top of Sheep Mountain, and it was inaccessible. The next morning Mrs. Hynes hired Bill Osborn to take her there. Using his pocket knife, Osborn dug handholds in the precipitous side of the table so that Mrs. Hynes could climb to the top. The view that greeted her was spectacular. She looked out upon 1,500 acres of waist-high grass that seemed like it was growing on top of the world. Three hundred feet below, the Badlands stretched in every direction as far as the eye could see. Mary Hynes knew that she had found a home, She paid Mr. Osborn five dollars to stake her claim.

Mrs. Hynes returned to Murdo and sold everything. With the resultant stake of $1,200, she set out to rebuild her life. She bought 20 cows at $10 a head, four horses broke to drive, a wagon and a two-month supply of staples. Mrs.

"Happy" Hynes, Norman Roller, age four, Mary Hynes, and Dakota Hynes, at age twelve.
Photo courtesy of Peg (Hynes) Jurisch.

Hynes loaded the supplies, the family's belongings, and five children (Happy and Dewey and the three girls, Goldie, Minnie, and Peg) in the wagon and set out for Sheep Mountain.

The family lived in a tar paper shack at the base of Sheep Mountain while the boys toiled for weeks with picks and shovels to make a crude path to the top. When it was finished, a sure-footed horse was hitched to a plank sled with wooden runners, and the horse was led and prodded to the top. Everything necessary to build a homestead was loaded onto the sled and hauled, a few pieces at a time, up the side of Sheep Table.

On top, the Hynes family cut blocks of sod three inches thick by 18 inches long by 12 inches wide from the prairie and built a 28 foot by 18 foot sod house. Fortunately, they built close to Ab Jefferson's water seep, 100 feet below the rim of the Table. At first, they lugged water from the seep a bucket at a time; but eventually Happy put in a gas motor that pumped water to the house.

By 1915 the trail up Sheep Mountain was so improved that it appeared possible that a car might be driven to the top of the table. They tried, but the Model T Ford stalled out part way up. The steep incline would not allow the gas to gravity-feed from the tank to the carburetor. They turned the car around, and drove it backwards to the top. Encouraged, the Hynes improved the route from a path to a trail. When cars became equipped with fuel pumps, intrepid sightseers drove up the rough road to enjoy the marvelous view from the top of Sheep Mountain. Happy Hynes put a sign at the bottom of the precarious trail to advise drivers: "Put your car in low. Step on the gas. And don't look back.

Most homesteaders came to the Badlands expecting to grow lush crops, to acquire "free" land, and to become wealthy. But few of them lasted the five years it took to "prove up." The Badlands dealt the remaining homesteaders a particularly bad hand in 1911. It hardly rained. Luckily, most homesteaders proved up that year. They had something to sell, and sell they did. Sorry that they ever came to the Badlands, most homesteaders bought a one-way ticket on an east-bound train. Those that couldn't afford even the price of train ticket, loaded their few possessions in a wagon and headed east-back the way they came. That fall, a nearly endless line of wagons moved down White River Valley passed through Chamberlain.[31] The homesteading era in the Badlands was over. Its duration was not long; but its importance was not its longevity, it was its legacy. Today, most people living in the Badlands are the progeny of the few homesteaders who, despite crop failures, poverty, hardships, and droughts, "made it."

CHAPTER 12

Big Leases, Big Celebrations, and Big Busts

Some people look at a land and immediately hatch a plan to make it do their bidding. They plow the ground to grow crops, re-channel rivers to irrigate deserts, dynamite mountains to carve their images in granite. The Badlands, being a good judge of character, will not tolerate such self-seekers. She shrivels them down to size with her hot summer winds and blows them away with her cold winter blizzards. She teaches that anyone wishing to abide in the Badlands must do so on her terms.

After America entered World War I in 1917, producing beef became an *essential industry*. Accordingly, the Indian Department leased the Rosebud and Pine Ridge Indian Reservations to big cattle companies. The cattlemen put up a bond for five-year leases, paid each year's lease in advance, fenced their leased unit, and developed the necessary wells, springs, and dams to water their cattle.

Tom Arnold moved into the Badlands because homesteaders were crowding him out of Wyoming. He placed a stenographer in the Agency offices in Pine Ridge. The stenographer worked all of 1918 drawing up lease agreements with Indians who owned quarter-section allotments within Arnold's big lease. Several other cattlemen did likewise. By the time they were done, the Reservations were, for all practical purposes, in the hands of cattlemen. Most of them were white.[1]

Starting at the east end of the Badlands, Fred Sears leased everything from Black Pipe Creek east for 18 miles and then south for six miles. He purchased posts and wire in Gordon, Nebraska to fence his 104-square mile pasture; but some Indians burned his posts. After that, Sears bought his posts from the Indians and had no more problems completing his fencing.[2] Moving up White River, successive lease units were held by Gus and Jessie Craven; Dude Rounds; Brown and Weir (A Bar) on the upper part of Bear-In-The-Lodge Creek; and Hank and Morty Clifford at the mouth of Medicine Root Creek. Tommy Ward had a big lease south of Clifford's lease. Tom O'Rourke had big lease to the north of Clifford's lease, and Dick Stirk had a big lease farther up-river. The Newcastle Land and Livestock Company (7L) leased every thing from the upper part of Porcupine Creek to Wounded Knee Creek; and Charley Cuny and Bill Twiss, mixed-bloods, had large lease units southwest of Wounded Knee Creek.[3]

Tom Arnold leased the entire northwest corner of the Pine Ridge Reservation for five cents an acre per year. Arnold's lease ran from the Cheyenne River east to Imlay, and from the Reservation line south to Cuny Table – more than 72 sections. In the middle of his lease, Arnold established the headquarters of the XU outfit on a section of deeded land he bought surrounding Harney Springs. There, he built a house, huge corrals, and a big barn. He also built a house, a hay yard, and lambing sheds near the big spring at the north base of Cuny Table.

Arnold moved into the Badlands in 1919 with 6,000 head of cattle and 15,600 sheep. The Indians did not like to see sheep on their Reservation. Several of them set fire to the grass on Two Bull Table, anticipating that the south wind would send the inferno onto Arnold's lease. Arnold saw the whole thing unfold. He set a back fire and drove his sheep onto the fresh burn; and he held his sheep there while the fire swept around the herd. Afterward, Arnold sought out the two Indians who had set the fire. In no uncertain terms, Arnold told the two Indians that he had witnessed their actions. He told them he would let it go on one condition – it wouldn't happen again.[4]

Maurice Keliher also operated in the Badlands at this time. Operating north of the White River, Keliher ran his cattle from Creston as far east as Interior on land vacated by homesteaders. Some of Keliher's cattle showed up on the tables of the few remaining homesteaders; but as long the homesteaders ate the beef they stole from him, Keliher considered the small loses to be the price of doing business. He often joked that as often as possible he stopped in at a homesteader's place at supper time so he could eat some of his own beef.[5]

With cattle prices on the rise, the big cattle companies brought huge herds onto the reservations in the spring of 1918. All over the two reservations, dams were dug with horse-drawn fresnos, corrals were built, housing for cowboys was established, and fences were strung.

The hundreds of miles of fence needed to enclose the lease units required barbed wire and fence posts by the freight-car load. The tough, weather resistant cedars that grew near the top of the nearly inaccessible Badlands tables were in great demand. Post cutters lugged axes, saws, and 600 feet of smooth No. 9 wire up the sides of these precipitous tables. The cedar trees were felled, trimmed, and cut to eight-foot lengths. The No. 9 wire was anchored to a tree stump and rolled off the table. The lower end of the wire was spliced into a log chain that, in turn, was anchored to a "dead man." The wire was then stretched tight. Each readied post was suspended to the taunt wire by means of a staple at each end, and turned loose. As the post accelerated downward, the staples set the wire singing. When a post was on the wire, the man at the bottom of the table hid behind the wagon because if a staple pulled out the heavy log flew off the mountain like an undirected missile. When it worked right, the wire guided the cedar post to the log chain, and the log chain ripped out the staples and dropped the post next to the waiting wagon.

Al and George McGaa, mixed-bloods, logged off the south end of Sheep Table in 1918 and 1919.[6] In 1920, Louie Blummer helped a crew log off Cedar Butte in the southeast corner of Sage Creek Basin.[7] Elsewhere in the Badlands, nearly every straight cedar tree over eight feet tall was cut and turned into a fence post.

Hay was also in demand. By experience, the cattlemen learned that the flat topped tables that punctuate the Badlands were not good areas to graze cattle, as the beasts often plunged to their death when a storm struck. But the tables made perfect hay ground. Scouting out the most accessible spot along the 300-foot wall, the men filled in gullies and cut away protrusions to carve a path to the top. Then, they took a hay mower apart and hauled it, a piece at a time, up the table. "Finally," as one old-timer put it to underscore the precariousness of the trail, "we took apart the horses and hauled them up a piece at a time."[8] In truth, the ranchers led a sure-footed saddle horse up the trail; and if he made it, the draft horses followed.

Mowing hay on top of Sheep Table.
Photo courtesy of South Dakota State Historical Society.

When the hay was cut and bucked into piles, it was slid off the tall mesa by means of a "hay slide." A hay slide was a wedge-shaped affair five feet wide at the base with wings that spread out and up to a width of eight feet, and it was 600 feet long,

Five hay slides were built in the Badlands.[9] Louie Blummer and Charley Wyant started the idea of hay slides in 1912 when they built one out of smooth wire off the south side of Hay Butte. But the gaps between the wires allowed gusts of air to pick up the hay and scatter it, rendering their wire hay slide useless.[10] In 1915, R.F. Lewis built a wood hay slide off Philip Randoff Table. It worked perfectly. Maurice Keliher built a hay slide off the west side of Sheep Mountain Table that led down to Ab Jefferson's abandoned buildings. Tom

Hay slide off of Sheep Table.
Photo courtesy of South Dakota State Historical Society.

Arnold built a hay slide off the north side of Cuny Table during the winter of 1919–1920, and he put up hay on Cuny Table in the summer of 1920.

One evening at quitting time, Candy Langdale decided that rather than walk down the steep hill to their camp, he'd catch a ride on the last load of hay. With the extra weight, the load of hay gained speed and overshot the wagon. Instead of landing in a bed of soft hay, Langdale hit a milk cow broadside, knocking her flat. Man and beast lay lifeless on the ground. After five minutes, Langdale and the cow came to, looked each other in the eye, and jumped up. Neither man nor beast suffered serious injury.[11]

The fifth hay slide in the Badlands was off the northeast corner of Sheep Mountain Table.[12] On a dare, Frank Hart took a ride down that hay slide. Hart lost most of the hay he was sitting on within the first 50 feet. The bottom of his trousers lasted for another hundred feet, and he made the rest of the ride on bare skin. Like Langdale, he overshot the wagon, but there was no obliging milk cow to cushion his landing. Frank was on crutches for six months.

Traveling the Badlands by car.
Photo courtesy of the Badlands National Park.

Getting enough hay to winter their large herds of cattle was a chore for big operators, but paying for hay that never existed was downright irksome. This occasionally happened because the Indians who continued living on their allotments usually put up enough hay each summer to feed a saddle horse and couple of cows. They strung a few strands of loose wire around the stack. When the snow got deep and the winds grew bitter, the big operators' cattle walked through these flimsy fences and ate the hay. Each spring, the cattlemen got a bill from the Indian agent at Pine Ridge who, on behalf of these Indians, wanted payment.[13]

One fall, Tom Arnold proposed to Henry Tidwell, the Indian Agent, that they go around to the Indian allotments inside his lease and measure the existing hay stacks. Then, if Arnold's cattle got into any of the stacks, they would have a pretty good idea of how much hay Arnold should pay for.

At one point in their work an Indian took Tidwell and Arnold to the base of Squaw Humper Table. A rutted wagon road steeply wound up the table to the alleged hay stack. It was apparent that a car had never been up the trail. The trio were in the agent's Model T Ford; but he declined to be the driver. "Tom," he said, "you've had lots of experience with roads like this. You drive. We'll walk part way up the road and be there in case you need a push."

When his help was in place, Tom Arnold revved the car motor and started up the grade at a good clip. He breezed past the men and without any difficulty made it to the top. Arnold slowed the car, but he did not push in the clutch and the motor quit. Then, he pushed in the clutch! Before Arnold knew what was happening, the car rolled backwards off the 300-foot cliff.

"And then," as Tom Arnold related it, "all at once—crash! The car stopped falling. I looked around and there were cedar boughs all around me. The front of the car was up against the side of the bank and the back end was in the top of a big cedar tree growing out of the side of the Badlands wall. I looked down and, my God, I was looking into eternity."

Arnold was afraid that if he even slightly rocked the car, it would give way. He slowly opened the door and carefully shinnied over the hood. Standing on the radiator, he reached up, grabbed a sagebrush, and pulled himself to the top. Arnold looked over the side of the cliff and saw that there was not another cedar tree within a half mile that could have stopped the car. His knees gave out from under him, and he collapsed to the ground.

The men used barbed wire to anchor the front axle to a big cottonwood tree. Then, they walked down to the Cheyenne River to get a block and tackle. Using it, they were able to get the car back on top.

The big leases, the high cattle prices, and all the activity that the new growth precipitated brought back ranching the likes of which the Badlands had not seen since the days of the open range. It was a situation and a time that called for western-style celebrations.

Since its beginning in 1890, Interior had been the scene of many celebrations. The annual picnics were discontinued when the homesteaders left during the dry year of 1911, but they were revived in 1915 and have been held every August thereafter. Soon, a grandstand with a judge's booth, chutes, and holding pens were built on the south edge of Interior. A baseball park and an outdoor dance pavilion were adjacent to the rodeo grounds. Even a steam-driven merry-go-round was available; rides were a nickel.[14]

In August of 1920, Dude Rounds organized the biggest celebration ever seen in Interior. Even by today's standards, it was spectacular. Six steers were donated to the 500 Indians who came to town to see the events and participate in the activities. Their authentic Indian dances were a special attraction. More than 100 Indian tents, many of them traditional buffalo-hide tepees, were pitched on the west edge of town.

The Milwaukee Railroad brought tourists, some from as far away as Chicago, by the train load. The one, small hotel in town quickly filled. Most of the tourists pitched tents on the school grounds. More people came to the celebration than the town could accommodate. Drinking water could not be replenished fast enough. Gasoline for cars ran out the second day. The grocery stores and restaurants were out of food by the third day. Despite the inconveniences, everyone had a grand time.

At dawn on August 18th, the tourists camping in their tents on the school grounds were startled out of their sleep by 100 Indians in full war attire (loin cloth, painted faces, and eagle feathers in their hair) charging through their camp on 100 thundering horses as they fired rifles in the air and shrieked blood curdling war whoops. One easterner ran out of his tent, looked up at a savage riding down on him with a tomahawk in hand, and passed out. The tourist camp turned into bedlam. Men were yelling for help and women were fainting. Indians were splitting the air with rifle shots. The organizing committee worried that some people might be hurt, but a thorough search revealed no physical casualties.

The Sunrise Charge was followed by the Sioux Indians performing the Omaha Dance. Then it was time for lunch. The Grand Parade began at 1:30, with music by the Presho Marching Band, and the band was followed by a full retinue of the events:

Cowgirl Bareback Horse Riding	$ 300 purse
Cowboy Steer Riding	$ 300 purse
Rooster Catch	$ 10.00 for 1st
	$ 7.50 for 2nd
	$ 5.00 for 3rd
	$ 2.50 for 4th

(the roosters were turned loose in the center of the arena and the cowboys had to catch them by reaching down from their saddle.)

Bull Dogging Contest	$ 300 purse
Clown Contest	$ 200 purse
Cowboy Bareback Horse Riding	$ 400 purse
Cowboy Bucking Contest	$ 2,000 purse
Money on Bucking Horses	$ 645 purse
Trick Riding Contest	$ 200 purse
Steer Roping	$ 500 purse
Cowgirl's Horse Race (1/2 mile)	$ 100 purse
Indians Only Horse Race (1/2 mile)	$ 150 purse
Indian Travois Race	$ 150 purse
Indians Only Horse Race	$ 150 purse
(All riders were dressed in full war dress)	
Wild Horse Race	$ 300 purse

The same agenda was followed each day for three days.[15] The evenings were capped off by big dances in the outdoor pavilion.

At the end of the rodeo, after all of the events had been staged and prizes had been awarded, an old man wearing a white shirt topped off with a colorful, silk bandanna settled down on the meanest, toughest bronc the rodeo stock had to offer. The gate swung open, and the hunched up horse exploded into the arena arching his back and sunfishing through the air. The man, who was far too old to be riding a bronc, calmly puffed on his pipe and nonchalantly visited with friends in the stands as he rode the horse out. It was none other than the grand old man of the Badlands, Frank Hart.[16]

The power of the cattlemen in those days is underscored by a murder that occurred at a

Frank Hart.
Photo courtesy of South Dakota State Historical Society.

dance in Conata in the early summer of 1918. An Indian by the name of Bear stopped by Tom O'Rourke's place to borrow five dollars so he could go to the dance. O'Rourke, a mixed-blood, told Bear that Conata would be full of drunk cowboys looking for trouble. He advised Bear not to go. But seeing Bear's desire to attend the dance, O'Rourke lent him the money and Bear went to Conata expecting to have the time of his life.

A few hours later Bear lay in front of the dance hall with a bullet hole in his stomach. He was immediately rushed to the E.B. Yoast home. Mrs. Yoast, a nurse, opened his bloody shirt to find a small bullet hole directly below his sternum. She knew that Bear was bleeding internally. There was little she could do for him. Four hours later, Bear died.

The next morning, E.B. Yoast, who was a deputy sheriff, rode north of Conata to Joe Keliher's place. Yoast informed Joe Keliher that Bear had died during the night, and he had come to arrest him (Keliher) for murder. Keliher asked if many Indians were in town, and Yoast reported that there were. Keliher told Yoast that he would ride his horse to Imlay, catch the train into Rapid City, and turn himself in. Yoast, who wasn't sure that he could protect his prisoner if he took him into Conata, agreed.[17]

When the case came to trial, Joe Keliher pleaded not guilty by reason of self defense. It seemed like a hard case to make – Bear had been unarmed. But the defense brought forth several witnesses who claimed that Bear had flashed a shiny object that, in the dark, might have looked like a gun.

The states attorney called Clyde Sharp to the witness stand. The prosecuting attorney asked Clyde to describe what he had seen and heard the night Bear was shot. Clyde told the jury that he was standing beside Bear when Joe Keliher came down the stairs from the dance hall, which was above the general store. According to Sharp, as Keliher walked by he said, "Bear, I am going to shoot you." Bear replied, "Ah, Joe, I don't think you'd do that," and he turned to watch Keliher as the cowboy walked up the street. Suddenly, Keliher turned, drew his pistol, and shot Bear.

Clyde Sharp's testimony seemed to seal Joe Keliher's fate, but it was the defense attorney's turn. The barrister asked Clyde if he knew Joe Keliher's wife. Clyde said that he did, and he knew her quite well. At that, the defense attorney summarily dismissed Clyde from the witness stand. The barrister then went on to prove that Joe Keliher did not have a wife and, according to the county records, he had never been married. According to the defense attorney, Clyde Sharp was a blatant, not-to-be-trusted liar. The defense attorney was right, at least partially. Joe Keliher was not married and he had never been married, even though he and a woman had lived together for years and had a grown daughter. The jury apparently concluded that Clyde Sharp was a liar and none of his testimony could be believed, because they acquitted Joe Keliher.[18] In the Badlands, justice was still in the hands of the cattlemen.

The big cattle companies that came to the Badlands in 1918 with their eyes fixed on rising cattle prices weren't prepared for what the Badlands had in store for them. First, a virulent flu virus struck in 1918. The flu killed a number of whites, but it hit the Indian community particularly hard. In some communities on the Pine Ridge Reservation, Indian people died faster than they could be buried.

The flu disappeared as quickly as it started, and the cattlemen again turned their attention to a steadily rising cattle market. A devastatingly drought struck Texas and the Southwest in 1919, forcing the cattlemen there to disperse their herds to Mexico, eastern Colorado, and Wyoming. When Colorado and Wyoming dried out that summer, many of the southern cattle were bought at temporarily deflated prices and placed in the Badlands.

By fall, cattle prices were at an all-time high. A steer delivered at the stockyards in Chicago brought $100. Unfortunately, the cattlemen found that it was nearly impossible to get their steers to market for lack of rolling stock on the railroads. The U.S. Government had taken over the railroads during the war, and they knew nothing about the business. The cattlemen had to winter thousands of market-ready cattle.

Winter started early that year. Before it was over, the winter of 1919–1920 turned out to be one of the worst the Badlands had seen. Snow started falling in October. On November 10th, while some outfits were attempting to get their cattle to the railroad for shipment, a winter storm struck. By November 12th, the whole area was covered with a foot of snow. The cattle that had been raised on the northern range followed the horses and grazed where they had pawed away the snow, but the southern cattle stood belly deep in snow banks waiting to be fed.[19] Cake, which is bite-sized bits of mixed grains, was shipped in at the exorbitant price of $90 a ton. Most of the cake was made with cotton seed oil, and it froze so hard the cattle could not chew it. Cattle, especially the southern stock, began to die by the hundreds. Then on April 17, 1920, just as winter seemed to be over, a spring rain turned into a three-day blizzard. When it was over most every draw was full of dead cattle.[20]

The devastating winter of 1919–1920 was followed by a drought in the summer of 1920. The dry year forced Arnold to move his remaining sheep (6,000 had died during the winter) to mining claims he leased around Deadwood. But so many of Arnold's sheep ended up on miners' tables that he quit the sheep business.[21]

Coinciding with the dry year, scab (the symptom of intense lice infestations) broke out. The government quarantined the cattle on the Pine Ridge and Rosebud Reservations, and no one could ship a head unless it had been dipped in a lice-killing solution. Huge dipping vats were built. At considerable expense, all the livestock on the two Reservations were rounded up, herded into a holding corral, and pushed down a chute that caused them to plunge into a dipping vat. As soon as the animal's head surfaced, a cowboy used a long, forked stick to momentarily punch it under again. The animals then climbed into a draining pen, from which the excess dip ran back into the vat. Two weeks later, each animal had to be dipped again.

The cost of fencing, putting water on the range, the death losses during the winter of 1919–1920, the difficulty of getting railroad cars to ship cattle, the dry year of 1920, and the anthrax and scab were unforeseen set backs. On top of this, cattle prices broke in half in the fall of 1920. The Newcastle Cattle and Land Company had had enough, and they sold out to the Matador Cattle Company. Other cattlemen hunkered down to wait for the market to bounce back, but it didn't. By the fall of 1921, the commission people did not want a cattleman to come into the stockyards with a trainload of steers. Each outfit therefore dispersed its marketable cattle between Sioux City, Omaha, Chicago, and other places. With everyone following the same tactic, the net effect was that too many cattle came into stockyards. The bottom fell out of the cattle market.[22]

Banks called due their loans on cattle, but the previous disasters had emptied the cattlemen's pockets. The banks, forced to sell their mortgaged cattle on a depressed market, recouped only cents on the dollar. Eighty-five percent of the banks in South Dakota failed. The two banks in Kadoka consolidated in 1924, and then folded in 1925. Gus Craven, who was a large stockholder in both Kadoka banks, lost heavily. When Craven died in 1929, the once rich cattleman was $60,000 dollars in debt.[23] The State Bank of Interior, of which Dude Rounds was president and principal stockholder, failed in 1927. The financial catastrophe in the cattle business was followed by the collapse of the stock market on Wall Street. Then came the "Dirty Thirties" – drought and depression.

In the summer of 1931 disaster struck Interior. About 4:00 one morning, Nels Nelson rolled a barrel that was leaking gas into his hotel. Nelson claimed the gas was accidentally ignited by the wind charger in back of the hotel. Others claimed that Nelson touched a match to it. Whatever the case, the resultant fire burned most of the business district and the school to the ground. Johnson's general store was the only spared building on main street.[24]

Some moisture fell in 1932, but only enough to spawn a typhoid epidemic that killed many people in the Badlands and on the adjacent Indian Reservations. The few crops that grew weren't worth harvesting. A bushel of wheat was worth only 16 cents. Corn brought six cents a bushel. People burned corn that winter to keep warm because it was cheaper than coal. In Conata, E.B. Yoast and Chris Heather, who both had sold farm machinery for 30 percent down and the balance on credit, went broke. Their unpaid for machinery rusted in dirt-blown fields.

The year 1933 was dry again. The grass hardly grew. An old-timer claimed that it was so dry that year that the cows gave powdered milk. A more true tale is of the desperate rancher who rounded up a herd of horses and shipped them by rail to Sioux City. Instead of his expected check, he received a telegram saying that the horses did not sell for enough to cover the freight bill. He telegraphed back, "Have no money. Wire and I will send more horses." They never replied.[25]

The summer of 1934 was even worse. Ranchers had to make feed from the only two plants that turned green: the tops of cottonwood trees and Russian thistles.

Despite having lost his bank, his money, and his cattle, Dude Rounds retained his love of a practical joke. When a naive, young honyocker came into the Interior post office, which Mrs. Rounds ran, Dude asked him if he would be interested in taking down a corral and bringing the lumber into town. The young man was eager to do the job. Then, seemingly as an afterthought, Dude commented, "Oh, there is an old man in these parts who thinks that he owns just about everything between here and Kadoka. He might come by and claim that the corral is his, and try to run you off. Don't let him buffalo you. For all of his gruff talk and surly looks, the old man is a harmless bag of wind. Just keep going about your work and pretend that you can't hear a word he says."

The honyocker arrived at the corral early the next morning. He had a good start toward taking down the corral when an old man rode up on a horse. The young man never even looked up when the man roared, "Just what in the Sam hell do ya think you're doing Sonny?" The old man proceeded to announce for all of the world to hear that the corral was his, and he demanded that the young man stop taking the corral down. The honyocker kept working.

Drawing his pistol, George Porch planted a slug beside the very nail the honyocker was pulling. The young man nearly jumped out of his skin. "Now that your hearing has been restored, Sonny, you tell that god-damn postmaster who put you up this that if he does it again I'll put enough stamps on his behind to mail him to China."[26]

To help the destitute ranchers through the drought and the depression, in 1934 Congress authorized the Emergency Relief Administration to buy a small percentage of each rancher's cattle. Key Wilson was the designated buyer in the Interior area. Frank Troxell was the designated buyer in the Westover area. They paid $18 for a cow and $7 for a calf. Between them, 35,000 head of cattle were brought and branded ERA – standing for Emergency Relief Act.

The ranchers brought in their thinnest, sickest, and wildest critters. Some cattle were so hopelessly emaciated that they were shot and dumped into a big trench rather than shipped to market. Some of the cows crawled through barbed wire fences to get back to their calves that the ranchers had slyly secured in the barn. Many of the ERA cattle were turned over to poverty-stricken Indians and destitute white families who came bearing a government voucher. The cattle that Troxell dispersed to the Indians were driven to Bear-In-The-Lodge Creek, where the Indians camped overnight. They did not designate any night herders. By morning, the cattle were on their way back to their home ranges. When cattle bearing the ERA brand arrived back home, they were immediately butchered before the government sent out a man to reclaim them. Everyone in the Badlands realized that ERA meant "eat right away."[27]

The drought went on unabated in 1935. That summer, grasshoppers covered the ground so thickly that the sun shimmering off their wings made the ground look like water. To get out of the sun, the insects piggybacked three deep on the shady side of barbed wire. When it cooled in the evening, they moved out to eat everything in sight, including the paint off buildings.

No one could make a living off the land, and people left in droves. Weta, Conata and Imlay all but disappeared. Interior and Scenic shriveled up to a few hardy souls. The federal government declared that the Badlands, which it once parceled out as 160-acre homesteads, was "sub-marginal land." The government aggressively acquired much of the Badlands by paying the counties for the tax deeds, foreclosing on the mortgages held by the failed banks, and purchasing the land for two dollars an acre from drought-stricken owners. When the government was finished, it owned most of the Badlands.[28]

Interior, circa. 1920.

The rains finally came in 1937, but the ground was so dry, so bare, and so hard that it was years before the grasslands came back. Cattle prices stayed low. Land remained cheap, and no one anticipated that it would increase in value. Corb Morse, who was then in ill health, lived out his last days in his big house through the benevolence of the bank that held the mortgage. The house's lavish furnishings had been stripped by unpaid creditors. When Corb Morse died in 1940, the biggest, most flamboyant cattleman ever to operate in the Badlands died a pauper.[29] His passing went largely unnoticed, but it signaled that the days of cattle barons, big leases and big celebrations in the Badlands were over.

Epilogue

Today, much of the sub-marginal land that the federal government acquired during the Dirty Thirties is the basis for the 244,000-acre Badlands National Park. The rest of the sub-marginal land is owned by the Bureau of Land Management or Forest Service. The remainder of the Badlands is in the hands of white ranchers and the Lakota Sioux.

As Corb Morse predicted on his death bed, cattle made a come back in the Badlands. But ranching in the Badlands is no longer viewed as a way to make a fortune; rather, it is regarded as a way to earn a modest living. After the Great Depression, Badlands ranchers became some of the first ecologists. They closely monitor their range to prevent overgrazing and so strongly distain the sight of a tire track across their pasture that they run their ranches off horseback. Most of them don't own a plow. These widely scattered ranchers have "made it" by accepting the Badlands on its terms.

Chapter Notes

Chapter 1: Vast, Mysterious and Unknown
1. Cumming, W.D., Skelton, R.A., and Quinn, D.B. (1971). *The Discovery of North America.* American Heritage Press, New York, NY.
2. Breboer, J.B. (1933). *The Explorers of North America: 1492–1806.* MacMillian, New York, NY.
3. Deland, Charles (1915). Verendrye. *South Dakota Historical Collections,* 1: 89–379. Pierre, SD.
4. Schell, H.S. (1975). *History of South Dakota.* University of Nebraska Press, Lincoln, NE.
5. Hyde, George (1937). *Red Cloud's Folk: A History of the Oglala Sioux Indians.* University of Oklahoma Press, Norman, OK.
6. Robinson, D. (1904). *A History of the Dakota or Sioux Indians.* Ross & Haines, Inc., Minneapolis, MN.
7. Hyde, George (1937).
8. Gridley, M.E. (1939). *Indian Legends of America.* Sponsored by Indian Council Fire.
9. Clarence Jurisch interview with author in 1972. Mr. Jurisch presented a collection of Indian beads which he said came from Indian Creek. Jurisch (he was nearly 80 years old at the time) related: "Old-timers told me that when they first came to this country (the Badlands) there were the remnants of Indian scaffolds in the cottonwood trees along Indian Creek.
10. Fools Crow, Frank. Oral history tape. Badlands National Park Archives, Interior, SD.
11. DeVoto, Bernard (1953). *The Journals of Lewis and Clark.* Houghton Mifflin, Boston, MA.
12. Thwaites, R.G., ed. (1904). *Original Journal of the Lewis and Clark Expedition.* Arno Press, New York, NY.
13. Osgood, E.S. (1964). *The Field Notes of Captain William Clark.* Yale University Press. New Haven, CT.
14. Osgood, E.S. (1964).
15. Skarsten, M.O. (1969). *George Drouillard of the Lewis & Clark Expedition and Fur Trader.* Arthur A. Clark, Glendale, CA.
16. Osgood, E.S. (1964).
17. Robinson, D. (1937). The Astorians in South Dakota. *South Dakota Historical Collections,* 10: p.1–97.
18. Osgood, E.S. (1964).
19. Morgan, D.L. (1953). *Jedediah Smith and the Opening of the West.* Bobbs-Merrill, Indianapolis, IN.

20. Camp, C.L., ed. (1960). *James Clyman: Frontiersman.* Champoeg Press, Portland, OR.
21. Camp, C.L., ed. (1960).
22. Schuler, H. (1990). *Fort Pierre Chouteau.* University of South Dakota Press, Vermillion, SD.
23. Parker, D.D. (1951). Early Explorations and Fur Trading in South Dakota. *South Dakota Historical Collections,* 25.
24. Chase I.H. (1967). Forks of the Cheyenne. *Wi-iyohi: Bulletin of the South Dakota Historical Society,* XXI, October.
25. Chase, I.H. and Platt, G.M. (1965). The Missouri River Fur Trade: Thomas Sarpy and the Oglala Post. *South Dakota Review,* 11, pp. 25–39.
26. Anderson, H.H. (1973). Fur Traders as Fathers: The Origins of the Mixed-blood Community Among the Rosebud Sioux. *South Dakota History Quarterly,* 3, 3, pp. 233–270.
27. Robinson, W. (1967). Fur Trade Licensees. *The Wi-iyohi: Bulletin of the South Dakota Historical Society,* 21.
28. Hanson, C.E. (1991). Frederick Laboue and His River. *The Museum of the Fur Trade Quarterly,* 27, 1 & 2, pp. 1–24.
29. DeLand, C.E. (1918). Fort Tecumseh and Fort Pierre Journal and Letter Books. *South Dakota Historical Collections,* 19.
30. Hanson, C.E. and Walters, V.S. (1976). The Early Fur Trade in Northwest Nebraska. *Nebraska History,* 27, 1 & 2, pp. 1–74.
31. Hafen, L. (1965). *Mountain Men & the Fur Trade,* IX. A.H. Clark., Glendale, CA.
32. *The Badlands Historical Basic Data Study.* U.S. Department of Interior, Washington, D.C.

Chapter Two: The Bone Diggers
1. Thwaites, R.G., ed. (1906). *Early Western Travels in North America,* 27. A.H. Clark Company, Cleveland, OH.
2. Nicollete, J.N. (1937) Nicollete's Account: 1839. *South Dakota Historical Collections,* 10.
3. Coues, E., ed. (1897). *Audubon and His Journals,* 2. Charles Scribner's Sons, New York, NY.
4. Sheire, J.W. (1969). *The Badlands Historical Basic Data Study.* U.S. Department of Interior, Washington, D.C.
5. Prout, H.A. (1847). Description of a Fossil Maxillary Bone of a Paleotheirium from Near White River. *American Journal of Science and Arts,* 3, pp. 248–250.
6. Leidy, J. (1847). On a New Genus and Species of Fossil Ruminantia: "Poebrotherium Wilsoni." *Academy of Natural Science Proceedings,* 3, pp. 322–326.

7. Hendrickson, W.B. (1943). David Dale Owen, Pioneer Geologist of the Middle West. *Indiana Historical Collections.*
8. De Girardin, E. (1936). A Trip to the Badlands in 1849. *South Dakota Historical Review.* 1, 2, pp. 51–78.
9. Owen, D.D. (1852). *Report of a Geological Survey of Wisconsin, Iowa, and Minnesota, and Incidentally of a Portion of Nebraska Territory.* Philadelphia, PA.
10. Hendrickson, W.B. (1943).
11. Spencer F. Baird Papers. Smithsonian Institution Archives, Washington, D.C.
12. Culbertson, T.A. (1851). Journal of an Expedition to the "Mauvaise Terres" and the Upper Missouri in 1850. *Smithsonian Institution Fifth Annual Report,* Washington, D.C.
13. McDermott, J.F., ea., (1952). *Thaddeus A. Culbertson's Journal of an Expedition to the Mauvaise Terres and the Upper Missouri in 1850.* Smithsonian Institution, Bureau of American Ethnology, Bulletin 147, U.S. Government Printing Office, Washington, D.C.
14. Meek, F. (1853). Journal of a Trip to Nebraska Territory in 1853. In J.W. Sheire (1969) *The Badlands Historical Basic Data Study.* U.S. Department of Interior, Washington, D.C.
15. McLaird, J.D. and Turchen, L.V. (1974). Exploring the Black Hills, 1855–1875: Reports of the Government Expeditions. *South Dakota History Quarterly,* 4, pp. 161–197.
16. Meek, F. (1853).
17. Meek, F. (1853).
18. Meek, F. (1853).
19. Hayden, F.V. (1956). Explorations in the Dacota Country in the Year 1855. In Lieutenant G.K. Warren's Topographic Engineer of the "Sioux Expedition." Senate Executive Document #76, 35th Congress, Washington, D.C.
20. Hayden, F.V. (1956).
21. Stucker, G.F. (1976). Hayden in the Badlands. *The American West,* 5, 1.
22. Hayden, F.V. (1869). *Geological Report of the Exploration of the Yellowstone and Missouri River.* U.S. Government Printing Office, Washington, D.C.
23. Stucker, G.F. (1976).
24. Stucker, G.F. (1967).
25. Hayden, F.V. (1869).
26. Schuchert, C. and LeVene, C. (1940). *O.C. Marsh: Pioneer in Palentology.* Yale University Press, New Haven, CT.
27. Lull, R.S. (1913). The Yale Collection of Fossil Horses. *Collections of Yale University,* 1.
28. Marsh, O.C. (1892). Recent Polydactyl Horses. *American Journal of Science,* 43, pp. 339–355.

Chapter 3: The Promoter's Trail
1. Thompson, F. (1966). *The Thoen Stone A Sage Of The Black Hills*. Harlo Press, Detroit, MI.
2. Warren, Lt. G.K. (1922). Preliminary Report of the Explorations in Nebraska and Dakota in 1855–'56–'57. *South Dakota Historical Collections,* 11.
3. Parker, W. (1965). *The Black Hills Gold Rush, 1874–1879*. Dissertation, University of Oklahoma, Norman, OK, 1965.
4. Parker, W. (1965). *Gold in the Black Hills*. University of Oklahoma Press, Norman, OK.
5. Parker, W. (1965).
6. Karolevitz, B. (1986). Drink an Irish Toast to Charlie Collins. *South Dakota Magazine,* March, pp. 8–9.
7. Conrad, J. (1972). Charlie Collins: The Sioux City Promotion of the Black Hills. *South Dakota History,* 2 (2): 131–171.
8. Kemp, D. (1992). *The Irish Experience in Dakota Territory*. Rushmore House Publishing, Sioux Falls, SD.
9. Kemp, D. (1992).
10. Tallent, A. (1889). *The Black Hills or Last Hunting Grounds of the Dakotas*. Nixon-Jones Printing Co., St. Louis, MO.
11. Conrad, J. (1972).
12. Andreas, A.T. (1884). *Historical Atlas of the Dakotas*. Andreas, Chicago, IL.
13. Andreas, A.T. (1884).
14. Conrad, J. (1972).
15. Peterson, F. (1904). *Historical Atlas of South Dakota*. S. Wangersheim, Chicago, IL.
16. Krause, H. and Olson, G. (1974). *Prelude to Glory: A Newspaper Accounting of Custer's 1874 Expedition to the Black Hills*. Brevet Press, Sioux Falls, SD.
17. Bingham, J.H., & Peters, N.V. (1947). A Short History of Brule County. *South Dakota History Collections,* 23.
18. Tallent, A. (1899).
19. Conrad, J. (1972).
20. Wells, P. (1948). Ninety-six Years Among the Indians of the Northwest. *North Dakota History,* 25, #2.
21. Conrad, J. (1972).
22. Andreas, A.T. (1884).
23. Conrad, J. (1972).
24. Bingham, J.H. and Peters, N.V. (1947).
25. Conrad, J. (1972).
26. Palais, Hyman (1951). A Study of the Trails to the Black Hills Gold Fields. *South Dakota Historical Collections,* 25.
27. Conrad, J. (1972).

28. McClintock, J.S. (1939) *Pioneer Days in the Black Hills.* Published by Author, Deadwood, SD.
29. *Yankton Daily Press & Dakotan,* March 30, 1877.
30. Osborne, J.O. (1961). A History of the Deadwood Trail. Unpublished Masters thesis, University of South Dakota, Vermillion, SD.
31. Kemp, D. (1992).
32. Andreas, A.T. (1884). *Historical Atlas of the Dakota.* Andreas, Chicago, IL.
33. Van Nuys, L.B. (1961). *The Family Band: From the Missouri River to the Black Hills.* University of Nebraska Press, Lincoln, NE.
34. Peterson, F. (1904).
35. Karolevitz, B. (1986).
36. Peterson, F. (1904).
37. Kimball, F.W. (1924). Reminiscences of an Old Time Engineer. *The Milwaukee Magazine,* May, p. 6.
38. Bingham, J.H. and Peters, N.V. (1947).
39. Kimball, F.W. (1924).
40. Kemp, D. (1992).
41. *Rapid City Journal,* August 20, 1881.
42. Bingham, J.H. and Peters, N.V. (1947).
43. Klock, I. (1979). *All Roads Lead To Deadwood.* North Plains Press, Aberdeen, SD.
44. *Rapid City Journal,* July 28, 1882.
45. Klock, I. (1979).
46. McAllister, L.K. (2957) *Gumbo Trails.* Published by author.
47. *Rapid City Journal,* August 27, 1881.
48. *Rapid City Journal,* August 27, 1881.
49. *Rapid City Journal,* September 3, 1881.
50. *Rapid City Journal,* September 3, 1881.
51. *Rapid City Journal,* September 3, 1881.
52. *Rapid City Journal,* October 1, 1881.
53. *Rapid City Journal,* October 22, 1881.
54. Lawler, M. (1932). May 1880—The Milwaukee Goes Through to the Black Hills. *Milwaukee Magazine,* July, pp. 3-4.
55. *Rapid City Journal,* October 22, 1881.
56. *Rapid City Journal,* September 17, 1881.
57. *Rapid City Journal,* November 5, 1881.
58. *Rapid City Journal,* November 19, 1881.
59. *Rapid City Journal,* January 20, 1881.
60. *Rapid City Journal,* February 3, 1882.
61. Sutley, Z. (1939). *The Last Frontier.* MacMillian Co., New York, NY.
62. *Chamberlain Register,* August 24, 1882.
63. *Rapid City Journal,* November 3, 1882.
64. *Chamberlain Register,* August 24, 1882.

65. *Black Hills Daily Times,* August 15, 1882.
66. *Rapid City Journal,* September 24, 1882.
67. *Chamberlain Register,* November 29, 1883.
68. *Rapid City Journal,* May 20, 1882.
69. *Rapid City Journal,* March 6, 1883.
70. *Chamberlain Register,* November 22, 1883.
71. *Chamberlain Register,* March 5, 1884.
72. *Black Hills Daily Times,* May 24, 1883.
73. Klock, I. (1979).
74. *Chamberlain Register,* January 1, 1883.
75. Van Nuys, L.B., (1961).
76. Kemp, David (1992).
77. Hall, Philip (1992). *To Have This Land.* University of South Dakota Press, Vermillion, SD.
78. Armstrong, M.K. (1901). *The Early Empire Builders of the Great West.* IE.W. Porter, St. Paul, MN.
79. Nelson, Jim (1979). Western Charles Mix County. *Dakota West*, pp 17-20.

Chapter 4: In Quest of Gold

1. Parker, W. (1966). *Gold in the Black Hills.* University of Oklahoma Press. Norman. OK.
2. *Rapid City Journal,* September 7, 1883.
3. Leonel Jensen interview with author in 1983.
4. *Rapid City Journal,* May 9, 1890.
5. Utley, R.M. (1963). *The Last Days of the Sioux Nation.* Yale University Press: New Haven, CT.
6. *Rapid City Journal,* December 4, 1890.
7. *Rapid City Journal,* July 18, 1891.
8. *Rapid City Journal,* September 18, 1891.
9. *Pierre Weekly Free Press,* October 27, 1890.
10. *Rapid City Journal,* October 29, 1890.
11. *Hot Springs Star,* November 7, 1890.
12. *Pierre Weekly Free Press,* March 1, 1891.
13. *Pierre Daily Capitol,* April 26, 1891.
14. *Pierre Daily Capitol,* April 21, 1891.
15. *Pierre Daily Capitol,* April 26, 1891.
16. *Rapid City Journal,* April 16, 1891.
17. *Rapid City Journal,* April 30, 1891.
18. *Sioux City Journal,* April 30, 1891.
19. *Rapid City Journal,* May 19, 1891.
20. *Pierre Daily Capitol,* May 1, 1891.
21. Louis Blummer interview with author in 1973.

Chapter 5: The Last Cowboy and Indian War

1. Utley, R.M. (1963). *The Last Days of the Sioux Nation.* Yale University Press, New Haven, CT.
2. Robinson, D. (1956). *History of the Dakota or Sioux Indians.* Ross & Haines, Minneapolis, MN.
3. Mooney, J. (1965). *The Ghost-Dance Religion and the Sioux Outbreak of 1890.* University of Chicago Press, Chicago, IL.
4. *Rapid City Journal,* September 25, 1890.
5. Smith, R.A. (1975). *The Moon of Popping Trees.* Reader's Digest Press, New York, NY.
6. Utley, R.M. (1963).
7. Hall, Philip (1992). *To Have This Land.* University of South Dakota Press, Vermillion, SD.
8. Utley, R.M. (1963).
9. Buecker, T.R., ed.(2004). "The even tenor of our way is pursued undisturbed": Henry P. Smith's Diary during the Ghost Dance Movement, 1890–1891. *South Dakota History,* 34, pp. 197–236.
10. Hall, B. (1954). *Roundup Years: Old Muddy to the Black Hills.* Reminder Inc., Pierre, SD.
11. *Rapid City Journal,* December 4, 1890.
12. Hall, P.S. (1991).
13. *Rapid City Journal,* November 23, 1890.
14. *Pierre Weekly Free Press,* December 1, 1890.
15. Kelly, W.F. (1971). *Pine Ridge 1890: An Eye Witness Account.* Pierre Bovis, San Francisco, CA.
16. Mooney, J. (1965).
17. South Dakota National Guard Papers, South Dakota Heritage Center, Pierre, SD.
18. *Rapid City Journal,* December 7, 1890.
19. *Rapid City Journal,* December 9, 1890.
20. J.B. McCloud Manuscript, South Dakota Heritage Center, Pierre, SD.
21. *Rapid City Journal,* December 9, 1890.
22. *Buffalo Gap Republican,* December 13, 1890.
23. South Dakota National Guard papers.
24. J.B. McCloud Manuscript.
25. Mellette Papers.
26. South Dakota National Guard Papers.
27. *Rapid City Journal,* December 10, 1890.
28. Report of Colonel E.A. Carr and Monthly Returns of the Regiment. November 1890–January 1891. South Dakota Heritage Center, Pierre, SD.
29. Mellette Papers.
30. J.B. McCloud Manuscript.

250 *Philip S. Hall*

31. Yost, N.S. (1969). *Boss Cowman: Recollections of Ed Lemmon.* University of Nebraska Press, Lincoln, NE.
32. *Buffalo Gap Republican,* December 13, 1890.
33. *Battle River Pilot,* December 19, 1890.
34. *Rapid City Journal,* December 17, 1890.
35. Pete Lemley oral history tape. Badlands Park Cultural Center, Interior, SD.
36. *Rapid City Journal,* December 17, 1890.
37. *Battle River Pilot,* December 17, 1890.
38. *Pierre Weekly Free Press,* December 18, 1890.
39. *Rapid City Journal,* December 18, 1890.
40. Pete Lemley oral history tape.
41. *Deadwood Times,* December 20, 1890.
42. *Rapid City Journal,* December 19, 1890.
43. Report of Colonel E.A. Carr.
44. *Rapid City Journal,* December 19, 1890.
45. J.B. McCloud Manuscript.
46. Pete Lemley oral history tape.
47. *Rapid City Journal,* December 17, 1890.
48. *Rapid City Journal,* December 20, 1890.
49. Utley, R.M. (1963).
50. *Rapid City Journal,* December 23, 1890.
51. Mellette Papers.
52. Utley, R.M. (1963).
53. Smith, R.A. (1975).
54. Report of Colonel E.A. Carr.
55. Smith, R.A. (1971).
56. Report of Colonel E.A. Carr.
57. Remington, F. (1975–date republished). *Pony Tracks.* University of Oklahoma Press. Norman, OK.
58. Utley, R.M. (1963).
59. Remington, F. (1975).
60. *Rapid City Journal,* December 26, 1890.
61. Remington, F. (1975).
62. *Rapid City Journal,* January 4, 1891.
63. Remington, F. (1975).
64. *Rapid City Journal,* May 25, 1890.
65. Smith, R.A. (1975).
66. Mooney, J. (1965).
67. Utley, R.M. (1963).

Chapter 6: The First Family of the Badlands
1. Johnson, J.O. (1980). The Rutabaga Johnson Story. Unpublished manuscript about the Oliver and Mary Johnson family.

2. *Rapid City Journal,* March 6, 1883.
3. A.E. "Doll" Johnson interview with author 1974.
4. Bingham, J.H. and Peters, N.V. (1947). A Short History of Brule County. *South Dakota Historical Collections,* 23, pp. 1–15.
5. Prokop, L., ed. (1965). *Jackson and Washabaugh Counties.* Jackson-Washabaugh Historical Society, Kadoka, SD.
6. Prokop, L., ed. (1965).
7. A.E. "Doll" Johnson interview with author in 1974.
8. Utley, R.M. (1963). *Last Days of the Sioux Nation.* Yale University Press, New Haven, CT.
9. Phillips, G. (1975). *The Post Offices of South Dakota 1861–1930.* J.B. Publishing Company, Crete, NE.
10. Hall, B. (1954). *Roundup Days: Old Muddy to the Black Hills.* Reminder Inc., Pierre, SD.
11. *Rapid City Journal,* June 24, 1891.
12. *Rapid City Journal,* July 22, 1891.
13. *Pierre Daily Capital,* July 6, 1891.
14. A.E. "Doll" Johnson interview with author.
15. Prokop, L., ed. (1965).
16. A.E. "Doll" Johnson interview with author.
17. Letter dated December 20, 1975, from Emma Johnson, Oliver's daughter, to the late Mary Peterson, a cousin living in rural Pukwana, SD.
18. Phillips, G. (1975).
19. Hall, B. (1954).
20. A.E. "Doll" Johnson interview with John Stockert, historian with Badlands National Parks.
21. Johnson, J.O. (1980).

Chapter 7: Missouri John Massengale and the 15 Ranch

1. General History of Macon County, Missouri (1910). Henry Taylor & Company, Chicago, IL.
2. General History of Macon County, (1910).
3. Conversation with Neil Rounds, son of J.C. Rounds, at Old Settlers' Annual Picnic, Interior, SD in 1972.
4. General History of Macon County (1910).
5. www.medicinebow.org/origin04.htm accessed June 22, 2008.
6. Notes on Missouri John Massengale extracted from Carbon Newspaper by Dan Kinnaman, Rawlins, WY historian.
7. Conversation with Dan Kinnamen on June 6, 2008.
8. Kortes, C. (rancher in Carbon County, WY) letter to Byron Bradford (rancher along White River) dated 1988.
9. George Porch's unpublished autobiography as told In 1940 to Nora Steele, publisher of the *Kadoka Index.*

10. www.medicinebow.org/.
11. Burke, J. (undated). Unpublished manuscript of entitled *Early Day Sheep in Wyoming*.
12. Steele, N. (1940). George Porch Stories: A periodic column in the *Kadoka Index*. Copies of the columns now held by Mary Borberly, George Porch's daughter.
13. Rounds, N. (1966). A complete wipe-out. *True West*. December
14. George Porch's unpublished autobiography.
15. Notes on Missouri John Massengale by Kinnaman.
16. George Porch's unpublished autobiography.
17. George Porch's unpublished autobiography.
18. George Porch's unpublished autobiography.
19. *Pierre Daily Capitol,* August 20, 1895.
20. *Pierre Daily Capitol,* September 18, 1895.
21. George Porch's unpublished autobiography.
22. Hall, B. (1954). *Roundup Years: Old Muddy to the Black Hills*. Reminder Inc, Pierre, SD.
23. Wyman, W. (1954). *Nothing But Prairie and Sky*. University of Oklahoma Press, Norman, OK.
24. George Porch's unpublished autobiography.
25. George Porch's unpublished autobiography.
26. Hall, B. (1954).
27. Macon County, Missouri Probate Court Records.
28. Rounds, N. (1966).
29. George Porch's unpublished autobiography.
30. Prokop, L., ed. (1965). *Jackson and Washabaugh Counties*. Jackson-Washabaugh Historical Society.
31. Rounds, N. (1966).
32. George Carlbom interview with the author 1973.
33. George Porch's unpublished autobiography.
34. Prokop, L., ed. (1965). *Jackson and Washabaugh Counties*. Jackson-Washabaugh Historical Society.
35. Hall, B. (1954).
36. John "Lloyd" Thompson interview in 1978.
37. Philip T. Hall recollection of a story told by his father Joe Hall and told on September 20, 1978 to Lloyd Thompson.
38. Prokop, L., ed. (1965). *Jackson and Washabaugh Counties*. Jackson-Washabaugh Historical Society.
39. Prokop, L., ed. (1965). *Jackson and Washabaugh Counties*. Jackson-Washabaugh Historical Society.
40. Steele, N. (1940). George Porch Stories: A periodic column in the *Kadoka Index*. Copies of the columns now held by Mary Borberly, George Porch's daughter.

41. Macon County, Missouri Probate Court Records.
42. Natalie Massengale's letter to author dated November 2, 2002.
43. Hall, B. (1954).
44. Natalie Massengale's letter to author dated November 2, 2002.

Chapter 8: George Porch: A Badlands Character

This chapter is a summary of a 589-page autobiography orally told in about 1943 to Nora Steele, editor and publisher of the *Kadoka Index*. The manuscript is now in the hands of Peggy (Porch) Schoon. She graciously shared it with me.

Chapter 9: Denizens of the Badlands: 1890–1896

1. Phillips, G. (1975). *The Post Offices of South Dakota 1861–1930*. J.B. Publishing Company, Crete, NE.
2. Hall, B. (1954). *Roundup Years: Big Muddy to the Black Hills*. Reminder Inc., Pierre, SD.
3. Hall, B. (1954). *Roundup Years: Old Muddy to the Black Hills*. Reminder Inc., Pierre, SD.
4. Hall, B. (1954).
5. Strain, D. (1978). Jack Whipple: Old Man of the Range. *Dakota West,* 3(4): pp. 12–13.
6. Hall, B. (1954).
7. Hall, B. (1954).
8. Hall, B. (1954).
9. Prokop, L., ed. (1965). *Jackson and Washabaugh Counties.* Jackson-Washabaugh Historical Society.
10. Hall, B. (1954).
11. Prokop, L. ed. (1965).
12. Hall, B. (1954).
13. Ricker Tablets. Nebraska State Historical Society, Lincoln, NE.
14. Prokop, L. ed. (1965).
15. Robinson, J.M. (1974). *West from Fort Pierre: The Wild World of James (Scotty)Philip*. Westernlore Press, Los Angeles, CA.
16. Phillips, G. (1975).
17. South Dakota Census Data for 1900 and 1910.
18. *Rapid City Journal,* October 5, 1958.
19. Hall, B. (1954).
20. Odell, T., ed. (1948). Ninety-six Years Among the Indians of the Northwest. *North Dakota History,* 15.
21. Hall, B. (1954).
22. Prokop, L., ed. (1965).
23. Hall, B. (1954).
24. Hall, B. (1954).

25. Buecker, T.R. (2004). "The even tenor of our way is pursued undisturbed": Henry P. Smith's diary during the Ghost Dance movement, 1890–1891. *South Dakota History,* 34(3).
26. Phillips, G. (1975).
27. Hall, B. (1954).
28. Hall, B. (1954).
29. Original Survey in 1894, Office of Public Lands, Pierre, SD.
30. Hall, B. (1954).
31. Buecker, T.R. (2004). "The even tenor of our way is pursued undisturbed": Henry P. Smith's diary during the Ghost Dance movement, 1890–1891. *South Dakota History,* 34(3).
32. Prokop, L., ed (1965).
33. A.E. "Doll" Johnson interview with author 1974.
34. Andrews, P.M. (1959). Recluse: 1905. *The Wi-iyohi: Bulletin of the South Dakota Historical Society,* 13, No. 6.
35. Caldwell, I. ed. (1983). *Bad River: Ripples, Rages, and Residents.* State Publishing Company; Pierre, SD.
36. Bob Jones (rancher on Bad River) interview with author in 1976.
37. Eloise Trimble Brown (granddaughter of John Farnham) interview with author 1976.
38. Hafen, R.L. and Young, F.M. (1938). *Fort Laramie and the Pageant of the West, 1834–1890.* Arthur H. Clark Co., Glendale, CA.
39. Hallie Trimble Young (granddaughter of John Farnham) interview with author 1976.
40. *Rapid City Journal,* March 4, 1883.
41. Hallie Trimble Young interview.
42. *Rapid City Journal,* December 19, 1890.
43. Report of Colonel E.A. Carr and Monthly Returns of the Regiment. November 1890–January 1891. South Dakota Heritage Center, Microfilm Reel #666.
44. Hallie Trimble Young interview.
45. A.E. "Doll" Johnson interview.
46. Miller. L. Brookens (1992). *Dakota Memories.* Published by Author in San Mateo, California.
47. Hallie Trimble Young interview.
48. Hallie Trimble Young interview.
49. Hall, B. (1954).
50. Prokop, L., ed. (1965).
51. Prokop, L., ed. (1965).
52. Hallie Young interview.
53. Hall, B. (1954).
54. A.E. "Doll" Johnson interview.
55. Hall, B. (1954).

56. Welles, A.G. (1915). Romance Amalgamates Lives of White Adventurer and Sioux. Holiday Greetings from Rapid City, SD).
57. Gilbert, H. (1968). *"Big Bat" Pourier.* The Mills Company, Sheridan, WY.
58. Ricker Tablets: microfilm from Nebraska Historical Society.
59. Yost, N.S. (1969). *Boss Cowboy: Recollections of Ed Lemmon.* University of Nebraska Press, Lincoln, NE.
60. Welles, A.G. (1915).
61. Report of Colonel E.A. Carr.
62. Hall, B. (1954).
63. Hall, B. (1954).
64. Lee, B. and William, R.A. (1964). *The Last Grass Frontier.* Black Hills Publishers, Sturgis, SD.
65. *Rapid City Journal,* October 12, 1891.
66. Hall, B. (1954).
67. Strong, C.W. Oral history tape. Oral History Center, University of South Dakota, Vermillion, SD.
68. Hall, B. (1954).
69. Smalley, J. (1994).
70. Swanson, M. (1977). *Sauerkraut on the Pioneer Trail.* Published by the author.
71. Survey in 1890. Office of Public Lands, Pierre, SD.
72. *Rapid City Journal,* April 28, 1893.
73. Swanson, M. (1977).
74. *Eastern Pennington County Memories.* American Legion Auxiliary, Wall, SD.
75. Philips, G. (1975).
76. Phillips, G. (1975).
77. Early map of the Badlands dated 1910.
78. Prokop, L (1965).
79. Smalley, J. (1994).
80. Clifford Family. Dimming Trails—Fading Memories: Recollections of Mortimer and Julia Clifford. Unpublished family history in Oglala Community College Archives.
81. Whiting, M.E. (1971). The History of Kyle, South Dakota. Unpublished notes in Oglala Community College Archives.
82. McGillicuddy, J.B. (1941). *McGillicuddy: Agent.* Stanford University Press, Palo Alto, CA.
83. Hall, B. (1954).
84. Hall. B. (1954).
85. Big Foot Historical Society (1968). *Reservation Roundup: Stories of Pioneer Days in the Settling of the Pine Ridge Reservation.* Manuscript in Oglala Community College Archives.
86. Hall, B. (1954).
87. Malvin Bale Family History, in possession of Mr. Bale.

88. "Buzz" Benson (Badland rancher and grassroots historian) interview with author in 1993.
89. *Eastern Pennington County Memories* (1966).
90. "Buzz" Benson interview with author.
91. Pete Lemley oral history tape. Badlands Park Archives, Interior, SD.
92. *Eastern Pennington County Memories* (1966).
93. *Rapid City Journal,* Undated article in I.E. Leedy's Collection, Minnelusa Historical Society, Rapid City, SD.
94. Goldie Jurisch (daughter of Herman Kube) interview with author 1974.
95. *Rapid City Journal,* October 20, 1880.
96. Report of Colonel E.A. Carr.
97. *Eastern Pennington County Memories.*
98. *Eastern Pennington County Memories.*
99. Phillips. G. (1975).
100. Nauman, D.S., ed. (1976). Vanishing Trails Expeditions. Vanishing Committee, Wall, SD.

Chapter 10: The Last Years of the Open Range
1. A.E. "Doll" Johnson interview with author 1974.
2. Steele, N. (1920s). George Porch Stories. A series published in the *Kadoka Index.* Now held by Mary Borberly, Porch's daughter.
3. Hall, B. (1954). *Roundup Years: Missouri River to the Black Hills.* Reminder Inc., Pierre, SD.
4. Hall, B. (1954).
5. Casey, R.J. (1940). *The Black Hills and Their Incredible Characters.* Bobbs-Merrill Co., New York, NY.
6. Hall, B. (1954).
7. Hauk, J.K. (1954). The Story of Gus and Jessie McGaa Craven. *South Dakota Historical Collections,* 27, pp. S 15–547.
8. Hauk, J.K. (1954).
9. Ben Craven's talk to the Vanishing Trails Expedition in 1973.
10. Pete Lemley oral history tape. Badlands Park Archives, Interior, SD.
11. Hauk, J.K. (1954).
12. *Rapid City Journal,* June 20, 1897.
13. Carl Leedy Collection. Minnelusa Historical Society, Rapid City, SD.
14. Hall, B. (1954).
15. Steele, N. (1920s).
16. Rounds, N. (1966). A complete wipeout. *True West.*

Chapter 11: Starvation Claims
1. Frank "Fat" Strangle interview with author 1972.
2. *Pierre Daily Capital,* September 11, 1891.

3. The Old Pontoon at Chamberlain. *Milwaukee Railroad Magazine,* March 1919.
4. Andrews, P.M. (1959). Recluse: 1905. *The Wi-iyohi: Bulletin of the South Dakota Historical Society,* 13, No. 6.
5. Lloyd Thompson (son of Charley Thompson) interview with author 1970.
6. Prokop, L., editor (1966). *Jackson and Washabaugh Counties.* Jackson-Washabaugh Historical Society, Kadoka, SD.
7. Prokop, L. ed. (1965).
8. Bill Norman interview with author 1972.
9. George Porch unpublished manuscript now with Stanley Porch.
10. Prokop, L. ed. (1965).
11. Interior Index (1958). Special Golden Anniversary Edition.
12. A.E. "Doll" Johnson interview with author in 1974.
13. Prokop, L. ed. (1965).
14. Mrs. Henry Thompson interview with author in 1972.
15. Jung, H.Y. (date unknown). Conata. Unpublished manuscript given to author by Ann Zeitzig.
16. Jung, H.E. (date unknown). E.B. Yoast Family. Unpublished manuscript given to author by Ann Zeitzig.
17. Best Metal Polish in the World. Holiday Greetings. In C.I. Leedy Collection, Minnelusa Historical Society, Rapid City, SD.
18. Eastern Pennington County Memories (1966). American Legion Auxiliary, Wall, SD.
19. *Rapid City Journal,* July 7, 1908.
20. *Rapid City Journal,* July 9, 1908.
21. *Rapid City Journal,* July 14, 1908.
22. *Rapid City Journal,* November 29, 1908.
23. *Eastern Pennington County Memories* (1966).
24. Jurisch, P.H. (date unknown). A Brief History of Scenic. Unpublished manuscript given to author by Mrs. P.H. Jurisch.
25. Clarence Jurisch interview with author 1972.
26. Eastern Pennington County Memories (1966). American Legion Auxiliary, Wall, SD.
27. Clarence Jurisch interview with author 1972.
28. Lewis, Dale (1984). The Gray Wolf of South Dakota: From the Book by Bud Dalrymple. *Dakota West* 10 (1): pp. 8–11.
29. Dalrymple, B. (1910). *The Gray Wolf of South Dakota.* Altoona Tribune Co., Altoona, PA.
30. Jurisch, P.H. (1982). Sheep Mountain and Mary Hynes. Unpublished manuscript given to author by Peg (Hynes) Jurisch.
31. Schell, H.S. (1975). *History of South Dakota.* University of Nebraska Press, Lincoln, NE.

Chapter 12: Big Leases, Big Celebrations, and Big Busts

1. Big Foot Historical Society (1968). *Reservation Roundup.* Shannon County, SD.
2. Hall, B. (1954). *Roundup Years: Missouri River to the Black Hills.* Reminder Inc., Pierre, SD.
3. Big Foot Historical Society (1968).
4. Tom Arnold interview. Badlands National Park Archives, Interior, SD.
5. Clarence Jurisch interview with author 1972.
6. Hall, B. (1954). *Roundup Years: Old Muddy to the Black Hills.* Reminder Inc. Pierre, SD.
7. Louis Blummer interview with author in 1972.
8. Louie Blummer interview.
9. Clarence Jurisch interview.
10. Louie Blummer interview.
11. Tom Arnold interview.
12. Clarence Jurisch interview.
13. Tom Arnold interview.
14. A.E. "Doll" Johnson interview with Stockert Badlands National Park Archives, Interior, SD.
15. *Roundup and Frontier Days Souvenir Program* August 18, 19, 20. Badlands National Park Archives, Interior, SD.
16. Mrs. Henry "Happy" Thompson interview.
17. Robert Yoast (son of E.B. Yoast) interview with author in 1993.
18. Clyde Sharp interview with author in 1973.
19. Big Foot Historical Society (1968).
20. Clarence Jurisch interview.
21. Tom Arnold interview.
22. Big Foot Historical Society (1968).
23. Hauk, J.K. (1954). The Story of Gus and Jessie McGaa Craven. *South Dakota Historical Collections,* 27, pp. 516-547.
24. A E. "Doll" Johnson interview.
25. Bill Norman interview with author 1973.
26. Steele, N. (1940s). George Porch stories as they appeared in the *Kadoka Index.*
27. Frank Troxell interview with author in 1992.
28. Ingebert Fauske letter (1987). *South Dakota Heritage,* January.
29. *Rapid City Journal,* September 21, 1940.

Bibliography

Books

Andreas, A.T. (1884). *Historical Atlas of the Dakotas.* Andreas, Chicago, IL.

Armstrong, M.K. (1901). *The Early Empire Builders of the Great West.* E.W. Porter, St. Paul, MN.

Audubon, J.J. and Bachman, J. (1974). *The Quadrupeds of North America.* Arno Press, New York, NY.

Big Foot Historical Society (1968). *Reservation Roundup: Stories of Pioneer days in the Settling of the Pine Ridge Reservation.*

Breber, J.B. (1933). *The Explorers of North America: 1492–1806.* MacMillian, New York, NY.

Camp, C.L., ed. (1960). *James Clyman: Frontiersman.* Champoeg Press, Portland, OR.

Casey, R.J. (1940). *The Black Hills and Their Incredible Characters.* Bobbs-Merill Co., New York, NY.

Cones, E., ed. (1897). *Audubon and His Journals.* Vol. 2. Charles Scibner's Sons, New York, NY.

Culbertson, T.A. (18513. Journal of an Expedition to the *Mauvaise Terres* and the Upper Missouri in 1850. *Smithsonian Institution Fifth Annual Report,* Washington, D.C.

Cumming, W.D., Skelton, R.A., and Quinn, D.B. (1971). *The Discovery of North America.* American Heritage Press, New York, NY.

DeVoto, Bernard (1953). *The Journals of Lewis and Clark.* Houghton Mifflin, Boston, MA.

Eastern Pennington County Memories. American Legion Auxiliary, Wall, SD.

Gilbert, H. (1968). *"Big Bat" Pourier.* The Mills Company, Sheridan, WY.

Gridley, M.E. (1939). *Indian Legends of America.* The Indian Council Fire.

Hafen, R.L. and Young, F.M. (1938). *Fort Laramie and the Pageant of the West, 1834–1890.* Arthur H. Clark Co., Glendale CA.

Hall, B. (1954). *Roundup Years: Old Muddy to the Black Hills.* Reminder, Inc., Pierre, SD.

Hall, Philip S. (1992). *To Have This Land.* University of South Dakota Press, Vermillion, SD.

Hayden, F.V. (1869). *Geological Report of the Exploration of the Yellowstone and Missouri Rivers.* U.S. Government Printing Office, Washington, D.C.

Hyde, George (1937). *Red Cloud's Folk: A History of the Oglala Sioux Indians.* University of Oklahoma Press, Norman, OK.

Kelly, W.F. (1971). *Pine Ridge 1890: An Eye Witness Account.* Pierre Bovis, San Francisco, CA.

Klock, I. (1979). *All Roads Lead to Deadwood*. North Plains Press, Aberdeen, SD.

Krause, H. and Olson, G. (1974). *Prelude to Glory: A Newspaper Accounting of Custer's 1874 Expedition to the Black Hills*. Brevet Press, Sioux Falls, SD.

Lee, B. and William, R.A. (1964). *The Last Grass Frontier*. Black Hills Publishers, Sturgis, SD.

McAllister, L.K. (1957). *Gumbo Trails*. Published by author.

McClintock, J.S. (1939). *Pioneer Days in the Black Hills*. Self-published, Deadwood, SD.

McDermott, J.F., ed. (1952). *Thaddeus A. Culbertson's Journal of an Expedition to the Mauvaise Terres and the Upper Missouri in 1850*. Smithsonian Institution, Bureau of American Ethnology, Bulletin 147, U.S. Government Printing Office, Washington, D.C.

McGillicuddy, J.B. (1941). *McGillicuddy: Agent*. Stanford University Press, Palo Alto, CA.

Meek, F. (1953). Journal of a Trip to Nebraska Territory in 1853. In J.W. Sheire, ed. (1969), *The Badlands Historical Basic Data Study*. U.S. Department of Interior, Washington, D.C.

Mooney, J. (1965). *The Ghost-Dance Religion and the Sioux Outbreak of 1890*. University of Chicago Press, Chicago, IL.

Morgan, D.L. (1953). *Jedediah Smith and the Opening of the West*. Bobbs-Merill, Indianapolis, IN.

Osgood, E.S. (1964). *The Field Notes of Captain William Clark*. Yale University Press, New Haven, CT.

Owen, D.D. (1852). *Report of a Geological Survey of Wisconsin, Iowa and Minnesota, and Incidentally of a Portion of Nebraska Territory*. Philadelphia, PA.

Parker, W. (1965). *Gold in the Black Hills*. University of Oklahoma Press, Norman, OK.

Peterson F. (1904). *Historical Atlas of South Dakota*. S. Wangersheim, Chicago, IL.

Phillips, G. (1975).*The Post Offices of South Dakota 1861-1930*. J.B. Publishing Company, Crete, NE.

Prokop, L., ed. (1965). *Jackson and Washabaugh Counties*. Jackson-Washabaugh Historical Society, Kadoka, SD.

Robinson, D. (1904). *A History of the Dakota or Sioux Indians*. Ross & Haines, Inc. Minneapolis, MN.

Robinson, J.M. (1974). *West from Fort Pierre: The Wild World of James (Scotty) Philip*. Westernlore Press, Los Angeles, CA.

Schell, H.S. (1975). *History of South Dakota*. University of Nebraska Press, Lincoln, NE.

Schuchert, C. and Le Vene, C. (1940). *O.C. Marsh: Pioneer in Paleontology.* Yale University Press, New Haven, CT.

Schuler, H. (1990). *Fort Pierre Chouteau.* University of South Dakota Press, Vermillion, SD.

Shiere, J.W. (1969). *The Badlands Historical Basic Data Study.* U.S. Department of Interior, Washington, D.C.

Skarsten, M.O. (1969). *George Drouillard of the Lewis & Clark Expedition and Fur Trader.* Arthur A. Clark, Glendale, CA.

Smith, R.A. (1975). *The Moon of Popping Trees.* Reader's Digest Press, New York, NY.

Sutley, Z. (1939). *The Last Frontier.* MacMillain Co., New York, NY.

Swanson, M. (1977). *Sauerkraut on the Pioneer Trail.* Published by author.

Tallent, A. (1889). *The Black Hills or Last Hunting Grounds of the Dakotas.* Nixon-Jones Printing Co., St. Louis, MO.

Thompson, F. (1966). *The Thoen Stone: A Sage of the Black Hills.* Harlo Press, Detroit, MI.

Thwaites, R.G., ed. (1904). *Original Journal of the Lewis and Clark Expedition.* Arno Press, New York, NY.

Thwaites, R.E., ed. (1906). *Early Western Travels in North America.* Vol. 27. A.H. Clark Company, Cleveland, OH.

United States Department of Interior. *The Badlands Historical Basic Data Study.* Washington, D.C.

Utley, R.M. (1963). *The Last Days of the Sioux Nation.* Yale University Press, New Haven, CT.

Van Nuys, L.B. (1961). *The Family Band: From the Missouri River to the Black Hills.* University of Nebraska Press, Lincoln, NE.

Wyman, W. (1954). *Nothing But Prairie and Sky.* University of Oklahoma Press, Norman, OK.

Yost, N.S. (1969). *Boss Cowboy: Recollections of Ed Lemmon.* University of Nebraska Press, Lincoln, NE.

Articles

Anderson, H.H. (1973). Fur Traders as Fathers: The Origins of the Mixed blood Community Among the Rosebud Sioux. *South Dakota History Quarterly,* 3, No. 3, pp. 233–270.

Andrews, P.M. (1959). Recluse: 1905. *The Wi-iyohi: Bulletin of the South Dakota Historical Society,* 13, 6.

Bingham, J.H., and Peters, N.V. (1947). A Short History of Brule County. *South Dakota History Collections,* 23.

Bradfield, B. (1966). Wolfer Thompson. *The Western Horseman,* February.

Bradfield, B. (1974). The Last Ounce of Strength in a Dying Horse. *Dakota West* 10 (2): pp. 10–11.

Chase, I.H. (1967). Forks of the Cheyenne. *Wi-iyohi: Bulletin of the South Dakota Historical Society,* XXI, October.

Chase, I.H. and Platt, G.M. (1965). The Missouri River Fur Trade: Thomas Sarpy and the Oglala Post. *South Dakota Review,* II, pp. 25–39.

De Girardin, E. (1936). A Trip to the Badlands in 1849. *South Dakota Historical Review,* 1(2): pp. 51–78.

De Land, C.E. (1918). Fort Tecumseh and Fort Pierre Journal and Letter Books. *South Dakota Historical Collections,* 19.

Hanson, C.E. (1991). Frederick Laboue and His River. *The Museum of the Fur Trade Quarterly,* 27, 1 & 2, pp. 1–24.

Hanson, C.E. and Walters, V.S. (1976). The Early Fur Trade in Northwest Nebraska. *Nebraska History,* 27, 1 & 2, pp. 1–24.

Hauk, J.K. (1954). The Story of Gus and Jessie McGaa Craven. *South Dakota Historical Collections,* 27, pp. 516–547.

Hendrickson, W.B. (1943). David Dale Owen, Pioneer Geologist of the Middle West. *Indiana Historical Collections.*

Karolevitz, B. (1986). Drink an Irish Toast to Charlie Collins. *South Dakota Magazine,* March, pp. 8–9.

Kimball, F.W. (1924). Reminiscences of an Old time Engineer. *The Milwaukee Magazine,* May, p. 6.

Lawler M. (1932). May 1880 – The Milwaukee Goes Through to the Black Hills. *The Milwaukee Magazine,* July, pp. 3–4.

Leidy, J. (1847). On a New Genus and Species of Fossil Ruminantia: Poebrotherinfn Wilsoni. *Academy of Natural Science Proceedings,* pp. 322–326.

Lewis, Dale (1984). The Gray Wolf of South Dakota: From the book by Bud Dalrymple. *Dakota West,* 10 (1): p. 8–11.

Lull, R.S. (1913). The Yale Collection of Fossil Horses. *Collections of Yale University,* 1.

Marsh, O.C. (1892). Recent Polydactyl Horses. *American Journal of Science,* 43, pp. 339–355.

McLaird, J.D. and Turchen, L.V. (1974). Exploring the Black Hills, 1855–1875: Reports of the Government Expeditions. *South Dakota History Quarterly,* 4, pp. 161–197.

Nicollete's, J.N. (1937). Nicollete's Account: 1893. *South Dakota Historical Collections,* 10.

Palais, H. (1951). A Study of the Trails to the Black Hills Gold Fields. *South Dakota Historical Collections,* 25.

Parker, D.D. (1951). Early Explorations and Fur Trading in South Dakota. *South Dakota Historical Collections,* 25.

Prout, H.A. (1847). Description of a Fossil Maxillary Bone of a Paleotheirium from Near White River. *American Journal of Science and Arts,* 3, pp. 248–250.

Robinson, D. (1920). The Astorians of South Dakota. *South Dakota Historical Collection,* X: p. 97.
Robinson, W. (1967). Fur Trade Licensees. *The Wi-iyohi: Bulletin of the South Dakota Historical Society,* 21.
Rounds, N. (1966). A Complete Wipe-out. *True West,* December.
Seymour, F.W. (1981). Sitanka, the Full Story of Wounded Knee. Christopher Publishing House, Hanover, NH.
Steele, M. (1920s). George Porch Stories: A Periodic Column. *Kadoka Press.*
Strain, D. (1976). Jack Whipple: Old Man of the Range. *Dakota West.*
Stucker, G.F. (1967). Hayden in the Badlands. *The American West,* 5,1.
Warren, Lt. G.K. (1922). Preliminary Report of the Explorations in Nebraska and Dakota in 1855-'56-'57. *South Dakota Historical Collections,* 11.
Wells, P. (1948). Ninety-six Years Among the Indians of the Northwest. *North Dakota History,* 25, 2.

Government Documents
Hayden, F.V. (1956). Explorations in the Dacota Country in the Year 1855. In Lieutenant G.K. Warren's Topographic Engineer of the "Sioux Expedition." Senate Executive Document #76, 35th Congress, Washington, D.C.
Original Survey Maps, Department of Lands, Pierre, SD.
Report of Colonel E.A. Carr and Monthly Returns of the Regiment. November 1890–January 1891. South Dakota Heritage Center, Pierre, SD.

Newspapers
Battle River Pilot, December 17, 1890.
Belle Fourche Bee, December 30, 1938; November 24, 1939.
The Black Hills Daily Times, August 15, 1882; May 24, 1883.
Buffalo Gap Republican, December 13, 1890.
The Chamberlain Register, August 24, 1882; January 1, 1883; November 28, 1883; November 22, 1883; March 5, 1884; January 10, 1893.
Deadwood Times, December 20, 1890.
Hot Springs Star, November 7, 1890.
Pierre Daily Capital, March 1, 1891; March 24, 1891; April 16, 1891; April 26, 1891; May 1, 1891; July 6, 1891; September 11, 1891.
Pierre Daily Free Press, October 27, 1890; December 12, 1890; December 18, 1890.
Pierre Dakota Journal, September 7, 1883.
Rapid City Journal, January 20, 181; August 20, 1881; August 27, 1881; September 3, 1881; September 17, 1881; October 1, 1881; October 22, 1881; November 5, 1881; November 19, 1881; February 3, 1882; May 20, 1882; July 22, 1882; August 15, 1882; September 24, 1882; November 3, 1882 March 4, 1883; March 6, 1883; May 6, 1883; May 9, 1890; December 4, 1889; July 18, 1890; September 25, 1890; October 27, 1890; October

19, 1890; December 7, 1890; December 9, 1890; December 10, 1890; December 17, 1890; December 18, 1890; December 19, 1890; December 20, 1890; December 23, 1890; January 2, 1891; April 16, 1891; April 30, 1891; April 23, 1891; May 19, 1891; June 24, 1891; July 22, 1891; October 12, 1891; June 20, 1897; July 7, 1908; July 9, 1908; July 14, 1908; November 29, 1908; June 13, 1913; June 2, 1938; April 25, 1939; September 21, 1939; October 13, 1939; February 21, 1976; August 28, 1986.
Yankton Daily Press and Dakotan, March 30, 1887.

Dissertations and Theses
Osborne, J.O. (1961). A History of the Deadwood Trail. Unpublished Masters thesis, University of South Dakota, Vermillion, SD, 1961.
Parker, W. (1965). *The Black Hills Gold Rush, 1874–1879.* Dissertation, University of Oklahoma, Norman, OK, 1965.

Collected Papers
Arthur C. Mellette Papers. South Dakota Heritage Center, Pierre, SD.
C. Irwin Leedy Historical Collections. Minnelusa Historical Museum, Rapid City, SD.
Ricker Tablets. Nebraska State Historical Society, Lincoln, NE.
South Dakota National Guard Papers. South Dakota Heritage Center, Pierre, SD.
Spencer F. Baird Papers. Smithsonian Institution Archives, Washington, D.C.

Oral History Tapes
Fools Crow, Frank. Badlands National Park Archives, Interior, SD.
Lemley, Pete. Badlands National Park Archives, Interior, SD.
Strong, C.W. Oral History Center, University of South Dakota, Vermillion, SD.

Interviews
Arnold, Tom (1972). Badlands National Park Archives, Interior, SD.
Benson, "Buss" (1993). With author.
Blummer, Louie (1973). With author.
Borberly, Mary (1973). With author.
Brown, Eloise Trimble (1976). With author.
Carlbom, George (1973). With author.
Johnson, A.E. "Doll" (1974). With author.
Johnson, A.E. "Doll" (1972). With John Stockert, Badlands National Monument Archives, Interior, SD.
Jones, Bob (1980). With author.
Jurisch, Clarence (1972). With author.
Norman, Bill (1972). With author.
Prokop, Otto (1973). With author.
Sharp, Clyde (1973). With author.

Strangle, Mrs. Frank (1972). With author.
Thompson, Mrs. Henry (1972). With author.
Thompson, Joseph "Lloyd" (1974). With author.
Troxell, Frank (1992). With author.
Yoast, Robert (1993). With author.
Young, Hallie Trimble (1976). With author.

Unpublished Manuscripts
Dakota Memories (1992). The life of Lila Gates-Brookens by Lorene Brookens Miller.
Dimming Trails—Fading Memories: Recollections of Mortimer and Julia Clifford. In the possession of Oglala Community College Archives, Pine Ridge, SD.
Interior Index.
J.B. McCloud Manuscript. South Dakota Heritage Center, Pierre, SD.
Johnson, J.O. (1980). The Rutabaga Johnson Story. Lent to author by Mary Peterson.
Jung, H.E. (date unknown). E.B. Yoast Family. Lent to author by Ann Zeitzig.
Jurisch, P.H. (Date unknown). A Brief History of Scenic. Lent to author by Mrs. Clarence Jurisch.
Marvin Bale Family history. In possession of Mr. Bale.
Nauman, D.S. (1976). Speech to Vanishing Trails Expeditions. Vanishing Trails Committee, Wall, SD.
Porch, George. (Date unknown). Autobiography as told to Nora Steele.
Whiting, M.E. (1971). The History of Kyle, South Dakota. In the possession of Oglala Community College Archives, Pine Ridge, SD.

Letters
C. Kortes to Byron Bradford, 1988.
Emma Johnson to Mary Peterson, December 20, 1975.
Ingebert Fauske (1987). *South Dakota Heritage,* January 1987.

Personal Communications
Charles Hanson, Jr., Director of the Museum of Fur Trade Chadron, NE, to author 1993.

Index

A

Academy of Natural Sciences of Philadelphia: funds third Hayden expedition, 22
Adams, Emil (Major): warns Badlands settlers, 84
Akin, Gene: as a settler leader, 67-68
American Creek: as railroad terminal, 36
American Fur Company: and Lakota trail, 10
Amphibious Creek: (see Lame Johnny Creek)
Anderson, W.W.: 161
Andrews, Prank & Pearl: as new homesteaders, 203-204
Arikara Indians: and Teton Sioux, 4; smallpox epidemic, 4; and William Garreau 7; and fur traders, 7
Armstrong (Lieutenant, U.S. Army): 35
Arnold, Ben: prospects gold 55-56
Arnold, Tom: develops XU Ranch on Pine Ridge Reservation, 228; makes peace with Indians, 228; builds hay slide at Cuny Table, 231; adventure with car at Squaw Humper Table, 232
Asay, Edward, Jr.: Badlands trading post and post office, 86, 161
Asay, James: Pine Ridge Store, 86
Ashley, William: enters fur trade, 7; and Arikara Indians, 7; retreats to Fort Kiowa, 7; returns to St. Louis, 7
Audubon, James: 15

B

Bad River: Oglala Sioux visit, 4; forts established near, 8; sheep grazing, 89
Badlands: part of France's claim, 3; ceded to Spain, 3; missed by early white explorers, 11; Lakota attitude toward, 4; named by Lakota, 4; in Lakota myth, 4-5; "discovery" and exploration by Jedediah Smith party, 7-9; trading routes through, 10-11; neglect of during early 1800s, 11; and fossil seekers, 16-25; gold prospecting in, 52-56; and Ghost Dance uprising, 62-65; Indians seek refuge in, 65; early white settlement, 83-90; settlers' fortify, 85; early mail service, 86; inhabitants in 1895, 153-180; locations, people and brands, 180-184; open range in, 153; cattle roundups described, 195-198; homesteaders, 205-225; tables as sources of fence posts, 229; tables as sources of hay, 230; effects of bank failures, 237; 1932 typhoid epidemic, 237; 1930s drought, 237; decline of the towns, 239; federal government takeover of land, 239
Bartonne, Winnifred: involvement in the Bright murder, 218-221
Battle Creek and Indian disturbances: 65
Bear Creek: as Culbertson's camp site, 18; as a Meek/Hayden collecting site, 20; and second Hayden expedition, 22
Bell, Sam: 67
Belt, Robert: 60
Bennett, Bob: 52
Big Corral Draw: ambush at, 71
Big Foot: leads Minneconjou, 74-79
Black, Barney: 84
Black, John: 84
Black, Phil: Badlands settler, 86; mail carrier, 86; horse breaker, 86
Black Hills: visited by Verendrye expedition, 3; reached by Oglala Sioux, 4; gold fever, 29; end of placer mining in, 51
Black Hills and Fort Pierre Railroad: link to Chamberlain Road, 45
Black Pipe Creek: 10
Black: (see Interior)
Blankerton, James: 31

Blummer, Louie: prospects gold in Badlands, 57; logs at Cedar Butte, 229; invents first hay slide, 230
Bond, E.M.: Missouri River ferry, 34
Box Elder Creek: 65
Bramble, Downer T.: and Chamberlain-Rapid City transport, 42
Breast, Silas: as a bank customer in Kadoka, 208-210
Brennan, John (Rapid City founder): and the Chamberlain Road, 39-40
Brennan, John (reporter for *Sioux City Weekly Times*): and proposed Irish colony, 29
Bright, Frank: (see Dragoo, Marion Francis)
Bright, Mrs. Frank: (see Bartonne, Winnifred)
Brooke, John R. (Gen.): commands cavalry at Pine Ridge, 61; peace mission to Stronghold Table, 73
Brown, I.J.M.: as Corb Morse's foreman, 190
Brown, LeRoy (Capt.): as superintendent at Pine Ridge, 195
Brule City: first development, 31
Brule City-Badlands Trail: route to Black Hills, 32-34
Bull Head (Indian Police Lt.): shoots Sitting Bull, 70
Butte Cache: 10

C

Camp Cheyenne: 74
Campbell, Charles T.: and Yankton-Fort Pierre stage line, 33
Campbell, Colin and Oglala Post: 9
Carr, Eugene (Colonel): deploys Sixth Cavalry, 66; pursues Big Foot, 74
Casey: inhabitants around 1895 and location: 173
Chadron, Francis: 10
Challis, William W.: as early Badlands gold prospector, 52
Chamberlain (Rapid City) Road: concept, 38-39; route exploration, 40; development, 38-42; major use, 41-45; and Indian conflict, 44; abandonment and disappearance, 45; last freight traffic, 45
Chamberlain (town): development, 37; replaces Brule City as county seat, 37; and freighters' entertainment, 43;
Chamberlain Pass: 106
Chartran (fur-trading) Post: 10
Cheyenne (fur-trading) Post: 10
Cheyenne River: William Garreau's trading post on, 7; fur trade outposts along, 9-10; skirmishes along, 67-69
Chicago Milwaukee & St. Paul Railroad: and route to Black Hills, 36; recruits immigrant settlers, 37; carries Indian chiefs to Washington, 41; right-of-way across Indian lands, 41, 145; advertising for homesteaders, 203
Chicago Northwestern Railroad: and city of Pierre, 38
Clark, William: with Meriwether Lewis, 6
Clifford, Hank: guide and interpreter, 23; settler in badlands, 174
Cole, M.D.: kills Indian horse thief, 69; action publicized by press, 70
Cole, Maggie: alerts Army to attack on Phinney ranch, 72
Cole, Warren: 68
Collins, Charley: owner of *Sioux City Weekly Times*, 29; schemes to exploit Black Hills, 29-34; and Irish Colonization Association, 29; and Brule City promotion, 31-34; and transportation to Brule City, 33-34; deserts Brule City, 34; returns to Brule City, 35; appointed Brule County judge, 35; and Chamberlain promotion, 37; recruits settlers in Ireland, 37; later life, 46.
Conata: as railroad reservoir site, 216; town residents, 217; metal polish industry, 218; shooting of Bear at dance, 235
Coonen, M.F.: 30
Corral Draw: 71
Cosgrove, George: as a settler leader, 66
Craven, Cornelius Augustus "Gus": scout for Col. Carr, 75; builds successful

ranch, 195; moves to Indian Creek, 191; as postmaster, 192; has small loss in 1905 blizzard, 192; and bank failures, 237
Craven, Jessie McGaa: as wife of Gus Craven, 192
Creston: store and post office, 179
Crook Commission: 59
Crow Eagle: 64
Culbertson, Alexander: early fossil collector, 14
Culbertson, Thaddeus: fossil hunter, 18; explorations with brother, 18
Cuny Table: 76
Custer, George Armstrong: reports gold in Black Hills, 29-31

D

Dakota Militia: organized, 65; commanded by Merritt Day, 65; retreats from Plenty Star Table, 69; ambush Indians, 71
Daley, Jack: 67
Daley-Torkelson ranch: skirmishes between Indians and settlers at, 67
Dalrymple, Bud: his knowledge of wolves, 223
Darr, John: heads Pine Ridge roundup, 195
Daugherty & Co.: and Black Hills freight, 42
Daugherty, John (Captain): and Chamberlain Road, 42
Davis, Charley: builds flour mill at Chamberlain, 44
Day, Merritt H.: and Brule City development, 30; appointed Brule County register of deeds, 31; and Brule City-Badlands Trail; moves to Swan Lake, 34; failure in politics, 46; as Mellette's aide de camp, 65; arms settlers, 66; cautious Dakota Militia leader, 69
De Girardin, E.: artist, 16
Delano, Columbus: secretary of Interim, 30
Denig, Edwin: 10

Department of Interior: attempt to suppress ghost dancing, 60
Dickinson, H.L.: promotes Chamberlain Road, 41
Dillon, John: and Yankton-Fort Pierre stage line, 34
Dragoo, Marion Francis: his murder at Imlay, 218
Duhamel outfit: 51
Dunn, Mike: 191

E

Edgerton, Charlie: 68
Elk Horn: as John Evans' guide, 16
Ellis, Bob: 15 hand, 98
Emergency Relief Administration: buys ranchers cattle, 238
Erdman, Joe: defends Phinney ranch, 71
Evans, Fred: forms transportation company, 32; competes with Northwestern Transportation Company, 38; develops Chamberlain Road and Milwaukee Railroad route to Rapid City, 41-45; promotes town of Hot Springs, 46
Evans, John: first expedition, 16; second expedition, 19-21

F

Fenians: reject Collins proposed settlement site, 29
Ferguson, Jim: attempt to ambush indians, 68
Fetch, Charles: homesteader, 205
Fiske, Blake: carries mail between Weta and Wanblee, 212
Fort John: (see Fort Laramie)
Fort Kiowa: location, 7; base for Jedediah Smith party, 7
Fort Laramie: supplied by American Fur Company, 10
Fort Meade: 74
Fort Pierre Chouteau: location and fur trade, 8-9; and fossil explorers, 15
Fort Pierre (town of): flood, 38

Fort Pierre-Deadwood Trail: advantages, 38; problems, 38
Fort Pierre-Fort Laramie Trail: origins of, 5; and second Hayden expedition, 31
Fort Tecumseh: location, 8
France: claims to Badlands area, 3, 6
Freemole, Ed: Weta's general store owner and postmaster, 212
Fremont Elkhorn & Missouri Valley Railroad: (see Sioux City & Pacific Railroad)
Fur trade: early efforts of the Missouri Fur Company, 9-10; posts in western South Dakota, 9-10; end of, 11

G

Gallagher, Charlie: Badlands settler, 84
Gallagher, Hugh: agent at Pine Ridge Reservation, 60
Gamble, John R. (U.S. Congressman): and Badlands' mail service, 86
Garreau, William: and Arikara Indians, 7; early trading post, 7; unlikely as "discoverer" of Badlands, 7
Ghost Dance: described, 60; settler fears of, 60; failed early suppression of, 60
Gordon, John: 32
Gossage, Joseph: reports ghost dancing, 60
Grant, Ulysses S. (General & President): and fossil exploration, 22; and Brule City scheme, 33
Great Sioux Reservation: off-limits to whites, 29; illegal white incursions, 32; diminished, 84

H

Hall, James: geologist, 19
Hall, John: Rapid City businessman, 41
Halverson, Hilda (Bright): and the Bright murder, 220
Hancock, Winfield S. (Major General): blocks Collins expedition into Great Sioux Reservation, 30

Harney Hotel: spring roundup organized in, 194
Harnett, Dan: and Brule City development, 29; proposed stage, 33; possible name confusion, 46
Harnett, John: 29
Hart, Frank: as legendary bronc rider, 194; Interior rodeo, 234, uses hay slide for personal transport, 231
Hayden, Ferdinand: first expedition, 19-20; second expedition, 21-22; Civil War duty, 22; academic post, 22; third expedition, 22-23; reports gold in Black Hills, 29
Hayes, Rutherford B. (President): opens Brule County to white settlement, 34
Hebert, Pierre: fur trader, 8
Hegeman, Art: and polish plant in Conata, 217
Hemingway, F.W.: settler in Brule City, 34
Heney, Hugh: and Missouri Fur Company, 6-7
Hengel, A.D. "Tony": his gold find hoax, 53
Herman, D.: laid out Brule City, 29
Hermosa: 65
Hickox, Bill: becomes George Porch's partner, 136; sends preacher on way, 189; introduces irrigated farming, 216
Hinkley, Jack: 74
Hodnett, Dan: and proposed Irish Colony, 29; challenge to Jim Somers, 29; possible name confusion, 46
Hodnett, John P.: and proposed Irish Colony, 29
Hodnett, Tom: and proposed Irish colony, 29
Holland, John: scout for Gov. Mellette, 64
Howard, E.C.: laid out Brule City, 31
Howard, William (Dakota Territory Governor): appoints Brule County commissioners, 31
Hudson, Henry: named 1902 roundup boss, 195
Huggins, Fred: assays Badlands gold, 53; helps form mining company, 53
Hunkpapas: and Sitting Bull's death, 70

Hurley, Charley: 84
Hurley, Henry: 84
Hynes, Mary: as a homesteader on Sheep Mountain, 224

I

Imlay: town described, 218; the Dragoo (Bright) murder, 218; the investigation, 158-160; the trial, 219
Indian Creek: Lakota burial site, 5
Indian police: and Kimball's survey, 36; raid Sitting Bull's camp, 70
Ingram, George: 53
Interior: early growth, 84; origin of name, 89; 1895 inhabitants, 165-166; location, people and brands, 165; bypassed by railroad, 213; town businesses in 1910, 214; fires and firefighting, 215; big 1920 celebration at, 233; failure of State Bank, 237; fire destroys Main Street businesses, 237
Irish Colonization Association: interest in South Dakota settlement, 29; and Charley Collins, 29
Iron Horn: Indian guide, 19
Irrigation Colony: members listed, 216; its short-lived success, 216
Isele, John: gold prospector, 55
Istok-ta: killed at Cole Ranch, 73

J

Jedediah Smith party: travels west from Fort Kiowa, 7; explores Badlands, 8; encounters Brule Sioux camp, 8; reaches Black Hills, 8; employs white guide familiar with Badlands, 8
Jefferson, Ab: grazing disaster, 221; his saloon and hotel in Scenic, 221
Jensen, Leonel: relates cowboy's Badlands gold find, 51
Johnson, Bradford: reports Badlands gold panning, 56
Johnson, Emma & John: 87
Johnson, George & Louis: at Badlands way-station, 83

Johnson, Martin: shepherd, 88; settles near Draper, 162; losses in 1905 blizzard, 199
Johnson, Nels & Margaret: as immigrants, 81; move to Chamberlain, 84
Johnson, Oliver & Mary: their wanderings, 81; Chamberlain area homesteading, 82; family moves to Badlands, 84; found general store, 86; raise sheep, 88; move to Gordon, 89
Johnson, Randine: 87
Johnson, Ruth: 87

K

Kadoka: businesses operating in 1909, 207; failure of banks, 237
Kadoka State Bank: business with Indians, 208
Keliher, Joe: shots Bear, 235
Keliher, Maurice: as a rancher, 228; hay slide at Sheep Mountain, 230
Kicking Bear: and ghost dancing, 60
Kimball, F.W.: surveys Brule City-Black Hills rail route, 35-37
Kyle: 1895 inhabitants, 173; location, people and brands, 173

L

La Verendrye, Louis-Joseph: travels, 3
La Verendrye, Francois: travels, 3
La Violette, Joseph: the guide described, 18
LaChapelle, David: 9
Lakota: dislike of Badlands, 4; name for Badlands, 4; myths of Badlands origins, 4-5; Badlands trails, 5; Badlands uses, 6; burial sites in Badlands, 6; vision quest sites in Badlands, 6; trails used by fur trade, 10; Wovoka's influence on, 60
Laidlaw, William: 9
Lame Johnny Creek: gold find, 51
Lane, John: depot agent, 44
Langdale, Candy: uses hay slide for personal transport, 231

Index 271

Langlois, Toussant: first Badlands gold prospector, 51
Lawler, John ("Chief Bushy Eyes"): and Indian chiefs go to Washington, 41
Lear, Pete: gold prospector, 52
Leedy, H.M.: and Brule City promotion, 30; appointed Brule County commissioner, 31
Leedy, Henry: and Chamberlain Road, 39
Leidy, Joseph: describes camel fossil, 15
Lemley, Pete: 71
Lemmon, Ed: 69
Lewis, Meriwether: explores Louisiana Purchase area, 6
Lewis, R.F.: builds hay slide at Philip Randolph Table, 230
Lewis and Clark expedition: in South Dakota, 6
Lindsey, Bill: 69
Link: 1895 inhabitants, 179
Little Buffalo Creek: corral, 106
Little Wound: 65
Lodge: as trading post, 161; 1895 inhabitants, 161
Louisiana Territory: French claim, 3; ceded to Spain, 3; returned to France, 6; bought by United States, 6
Louisiana Purchase: (see Louisiana Territory)
Loveland, Ed: 40
Lynn, Frank: 187

M

Madsen, Kruse: and frontier justice, 106
Marsh, O.C.: professor at Yale, 23; fossil-collecting zeal, 23; expedition, 23-24; work on evolution of the horse, 25
Massengale, Missouri John: origins, 93; Wyoming, 95-97; founds 15 ranch in Badlands, 99; races horses, 101; sells ranch, 106; dies, 121
Maximilian of Weld: 15
McChesney, Charles: as agent at Rosebud, 195
McCloud, Joe: wanted, 68
McGaa, Al & George: cedar loggers at Sheep Mountain, 229

McGillycuddy, V.T.: Mellette's representative, 64; investigates shooting at Cole ranch, 73
McGregor, Mac: 68
McHenry, James: and Brule City saw mill, 30
McLaughlin, James: agent at Standing Rock Reservation, 60
McManus, J.: and Brule City, 30
Medicine Root: 1895 location and people, 127
Meek, Fielding: expedition, 19-21
Mellette, Arthur (South Dakota Governor): responds to Indian unrest, 63-66; arms settlers, 65; restrains Militia, 73
Merchants' Transportation & Freighting Co.: and Chamberlain Road development, 38, 40; move to Chamberlain, 42
Miller, Riley: 68, 72
Mills, Anise: as early Weta resident, 212
Milwaukee Railroad: (see Chicago Milwaukee & St. Paul Railroad) towns, business, and homesteaders along route to Rapid City, 206-225; transports passengers to Interior's 1920 celebration, 233
Minneconjou people: ghost dancers, 74
Missouri River steamboats: 34
Moore, Van: gold prospector, 55
Morse, Corb: buys 15 Ranch, 106; succeeds financially, 190; wiped out by 1905 blizzard, 199; dies a pauper, 240

N

Neiss, John: supervises 1905 Rosebud roundup, 195
Newsome, Bill: cattle rustling, 103-106
Nicollet, Joseph: 15
Niobrara Transportation Co.: route to Rapid City, 46
Northwestern Express, Stage & Transportation Co.: competition with Fred Evans' company, 38; challenged by Fred Evans, 45

O

Oglala Indians: first visit Black Hills, 4
Oglala Post: founding, 9
Open Buckle Ranch: founded by Gus Craven and Mike Dunn, 191
Owen, David Dale: sends Evans to find fossils, 16

P

Parody, George: gold prospector, 55
Pass Creek: Ghost Dancer's encampment, 64
Peabody Museum: construction, 23; fossil collection, 25
Pearson, J.B.: gold dust, 34
Pennington, John L. (Dakota Territory Governor): 34
Perry, David (Major): 69
Pettigrew, Richard F. (U.S. Senator): patronage appointments of Indian agents, 60
Philip, Scotty: spies on ghost dancers, 64
Phillips, Thomas (Sr. & Jr.): 52; and Hengel's gold hoax, 53
Phinney ranch: looted by Indians, 65; defended by Dakota Militia, 71
Pine Ridge Reservation: as Big Foot's destination, 75; land leasing on, 227; 1918 flu epidemic at, 236
Pino (Balboa Pynaux): and Meek/Hayden expedition, 19; origins, 25
Porch, George: at 15 Ranch, 97; judge at horse race, 101; sends preacher on way, 189; in the 1905 blizzard, 199; has near-fatal leg injury, 211
Potato Creek (village): 1895 inhabitants, location, people and brands, 167
Price, H.: 42
Prout, Hiram A.: early article on Badlands fossils, 15
Purcell, Ed: prospector in Badlands, 52

Q

Quinn Draw: near Scenic, 221

R

Randall, Ernest: and the Dragoo murder, 218
Red Cloud Agency: and Marsh expedition, 23
Red Cloud, Chief: and Marsh expedition, 24
Red Shirt: 1895 inhabitants, location, people and brands, 176
Rencontre, Alex: 35
Reynolds, Charlie: 31
Rounds, Julius Caesar "Dude": selects Badland ranch site, 97; at 15 Ranch, 99; rewarded by Massengale, 107; organizes 1920 celebration at Interior, 233; and failure of State Bank, 237; his practical joking, 238
Roy, Bill: gold prospector, 52
Royer, Daniel P.: appointed as Indian agent at Pine Ridge, 61; flees reservation, 61
Ruger, Thomas H. (Brig. General): orders protection of settlers, 67
Rustaad, Ludvig: (see Nels Johnson)
Rustaad, Margarita: (see Margaret Johnson)

S

Sage Creek: and Lakota trail, 5; as Evans camp site, 16; as Culbertson camp site, 18; gold found on, 52; and later gold prospecting along, 53
Sarpy, Thomas: 9
Scenic: the town's beginnings, 221; gambling, 222; businesses, 222; churches founded, 223
Seven Mile Hill: 203
Sheep Mountain: vision quest site, 6
Short Bull: and ghost dancing, 64
Shumard, Benjamin: expedition, 19
Siberts, Bruce: his cattle rustled and horse stolen, 106
Sieck, Jerry: Brule City settler, 34
Sioux City & Pacific Railroad: competes with Chamberlain Road, 46

Sitting Bull: death of, 70; effect of death on Indians discussed, 70
Six, Jimmy: Interior resident, 87
Smith, Jedediah: (see Jedediah Smith party)
Somers, Jim: and Irish Colonization Association, 29; and Brule City site, 30; appointed Brule County sheriff, 31; his character, 47
Sorrel Tom: Massengale's race horse, 101
Soule, Miss: Weta's heroic teacher, 213
Spain: ceded Louisiana Territory, 3; returns land to France, 6
Spaulding, David W.: and Collins' Brule City scheme, 29; appointed Brule County treasurer, 31; and Chamberlain Road, 41
Spaulding, Mrs. D.E.: Brule City teacher, 33
Spotted Tail: and transport routes across Lakota land, 37; goes to Washington, 41; interprets railroad right-of-way along Chamberlain Road, 44
Sprague, Parley: among Dakota Militia, 68; uses Indian tactic to ambush Indians, 72
Sprague, H.J.: 68
Spring Creek: 66
Standing Bull party: "discoverers" of Black Hills, 4
Standing Rock Reservation: 60
Stanton, Frank: ranch as patrol base, 71; service to Dakota Militia, 71;
Steele, H.M.: ranch on Battle Creek, 65
Stearns (town): 1895 inhabitants, location, people and brands, 155
Stout, H.H.: settled in Brule City, 34
Stronghold Table: Indian war preparations described, 59
Sumner (Lt. Col.): pursues Big Foot, 74
Sun Dance: at Rosebud, 37
Sutley, Jack: explores Chamberlain Road route, 41; restrains freighters, 43
Sweeny, Tom: his big bet, 194

T

Tarbox, George: set a trap for Indians, 68
Teton River: (see Bad River)
Teton Sioux: condition in 1700s, 3; lifestyle, 3-4; and Arikara Indians, 4; cross Missouri, 4; reach Black Hills, 4; dominate northern Plains, 4; original boundaries of area, 4, 57; shrinkage of their lands, 59; famine and disease, 59; at Pyramid Lake conference, 59; Ghost Dance ceremonies of, 50
Thode, Hans: 100
Thompson, Americus: as guide, 39; supports Badlands freight trail, 44; deserts Army, 75
Thompson, Charley: 15 Ranch, 112; Recluse, 163; welcomes Frank and Pearl Andrews, 204; as acting postmaster, 205
Torkelson, Nelse: 67
Touch-the-Cloud's village: 74
Trimble, Guy: 84
Trimmer, George: 29
Tupper, T.C. (Major): posted at Box Elder Creek, 67; aids soldiers ambushed at Spring Creek, 71
Turner, Frank: shots Lynn, 187
Two Bits: LaPlant & Jones's race horse, 101
Two Strikes: Indian leader at Wounded Knee Creek, 64

U

U.S. Geological and Geographic Survey of the Territories: established, 23; Ferdinand Hayden as head, 23

V

Valle, Jean: and Missouri Fur Company, 6-7; travels, 6
Van Wyck, Charles: and Chamberlain Road mail route cancellation, 45
Valentine, Johnny: Interior blacksmith, 87

Verendrye expedition: route in South Dakota, 3

W

Wakantanka: in Badlands myth, 4
Wanblee: as Indian village, area ranches in 1895, location, people and brands, 160
Wandall, Joe: gold prospector, 52
Wandall Mining District: gold area in Sage Creek Basin, 53
Warren ranch: defense of, 67
Wells, Almond (Captain): 77
Wells, Eugene (Captain): 69
Wells, Philip Fairbault: illegal gold seekers' scout, 32
Wells, William "Wallace": Army scout, 72; inspects work on Chamberlain Road, 42
Weta: as first Badlands town, 212; as railroad reservoir and service site, 212; school started, 213; town businesses, 213
Whipple, Jack: and frontier justice, 106; 1902 Roundup, 197

White Clay Creek: (see White River)
White River: Lakota landmark, 4; and Jedediah Smith party, 7; posts on, 9; shallowness of, 10; mouth as settlement site, 29; iron mining along, 52; suspension ferry, 88
White River Badlands: (see Badlands)
Whitfield (post office): 1895 inhabitants, location, people and brands, 156
Whitfield, Robert: and frontier justice, 105; employs Porch, 136; court, school teacher, 139; ranch, 157
Witcher, Eph: 32
Witcher, H.N.: 32
Wood, Chauncey L.: and Chamberlain Road, 39
Wounded Knee Creek: Lakota landmark, 5; massacre at, 77
Wovoka: and the Teton Sioux Ghost Dance, 60

Z

Z Bell ranch: gathering at, 68